PADDY ON THE HARDWOOD

Paddy on the Hardwood

A Journey in Irish Hoops

Rus Bradburd

UNIVERSITY OF NEW MEXICO PRESS ALBUQUERQUE

Design and composition by Melissa Tandysh

LIBRARY OF CONGRESS CATALOGING-IN-PUBLICATION DATA

Bradburd, Rus, 1959–
Paddy on the hardwood : a journey in Irish hoops /
Rus Bradburd.
     p. cm.
ISBN-13: 978-0-8263-4027-6 (pbk. : alk. paper)
ISBN-10: 0-8263-4027-X (pbk. : alk. paper)
1. Bradburd, Rus, 1959–
2. Basketball coaches—Ireland—Biography.
3. Tralee Tigers (Basketball team)—History.
I. Title.
  GV884.B68A3 2006
  796.323092—dc22

                            2006005464

PHOTOGRAPHS BY MICHAEL JAMES

FRONTISPIECE: Man with basketball and violin case
by Dennis Daily, road by Michael James

CONTENTS

PROLOGUE

An easy job. That's what I was looking for.

So in August of 2002, I took work in the Republic of Ireland coaching a professional basketball team.

How I wound up there—after fourteen years of coaching major-college basketball in the States—and what unfolded in the town of Tralee is less a story than a tale. In fact, it's less a tale than a ballad; a ballad without discernible meter, which might make it what the Irish call a "slow air."

Ideally, this slow air would be sung for you, in a respectfully quiet pub with thick stone walls and an open turf fire. The blunt wooden tables would be covered with pints of Guinness, their white heads blossoming like fresh-cut flowers. By the end of my song you'd know all about my time in Ireland. The glasses of stout would be dry, save for streaks of foam clinging to the sides.

Sadly, I can hardly sing, even after drinking. And living in Ireland wasn't really slow moving like an air. Perhaps I should shoulder my fiddle instead and play a tune that would tell my tale. I'm a far better fiddler since my time in Tralee. You would come to understand my year through a wordless fiddle tune, a wandering jig with a bouncy 6/8 rhythm. It would be in both a major and minor key, draped in the simultaneous sorrow and joy essential to Irish traditional music. Quirky and mysterious, the tune might lodge in a dark corner of your head long after our evening—and my story—was over.

Then the pub owner would bolt the front door and take down a bottle of Irish whiskey. We'd all lean forward on our stubby stools, elbows on the tables, and try to recall or invent the tune's name. The odd appellations of fiddle tunes are a constant source of mystery, and therefore entertainment, to musicians in Ireland. Someone might suggest for mine the title "How Far From the Course You've Strayed, My Lad." A bearded man would stand, wobble in his shoes, pound the table, and declare it "Irishmen Can't Jump." That would break something open in the psyche of the loyal pub dwellers, and suggestions for the tune's name would flow freely, each subsequently shouted down or drowned in laughter: "What Makes A Man Happy?", "The Winding Road to Oblivion." Soon enough, we'd all forget about the tune for the time being, and the remaining townsmen would sit perched and connected, shoulder to shoulder and knee to knee, having heartfelt talks about everything on God's green Irish earth, until the bottle of whiskey was empty.

Instead of a song to sing or to fiddle, what I have is a journal of my year coaching professional basketball in Ireland. Each section is the title of a traditional Irish tune. Maybe my story will linger in your ear and resonate long after the last note is played, the way it has in mine. You'll have to supply your own drink.

PART ONE

HERE WE GO

"This man is the new coach of the Tralee Tigers, like," Junior Collins announced inside the phone shop. I forced a smile for Junior's benefit.

I'd known Junior, the Tralee Tigers' team manager, for less than a minute when he decided that the first thing I needed in Ireland was a cell phone. A "mobile," he called it. For a guy in his forties, Junior had an unusually large gut that threatened to burst his black Tralee Tigers jacket, a garment that cried out for laundering. His hair was a mess, although it was only an inch and a half long, as if he'd slept on it funny. He added the word *like* to nearly everything he said, a not uncommon Irish tic.

The fellow behind the phone shop counter had a pierced lip. A chunky girl with a navel that shouldn't have been exposed leaned against the wall behind him. They looked blandly at me—the new coach—then back at Junior.

"He's just off the plane from America, like," said Junior, nodding at me.

More silence. Finally the pierced fellow said, "What's the *Tigers?*"

The belly button girl looked at us hopefully. "A football team. Right?"

"Basketball," Junior said. A small line of customers was forming behind us.

"You're not so smart," the pierced one said to the girl. Then back to us: "I didn't know Tralee had a basketball team."

Right off the plane, and already I was letting the team down in some unexplainable manner—if only I were a better coach, these two wouldn't be ignorant of the Tralee Tigers, and in fact would be season ticket–holding fans. It was my first indication that coaching basketball in Ireland carried the same cachet as teaching the tin whistle in downtown Detroit.

"*Professional* basketball," Junior insisted a bit aggressively. I thought he might offer to fight the pierced guy. "With an American coach and everything." Junior placed his hand on my back for support and added, "All he needs is a mobile and a good night's rest."

Ireland was hopelessly hooked on cell phones, worse than in the States, Junior admitted when we left. He called cell phones "a disease," although he smiled when he said it. On this late August morning, we'd passed through a dozen small towns and villages on the eighty miles from Shannon Airport to Tralee. Men huddled on street corners, each looking at his cell phone, plugging in important numbers, or maybe checking messages. In one village, three teenage girls strode in unison alongside a crumbling stone wall, each talking on her own phone. Getting me a mobile had to be done before I unpacked or saw where I'd be living for the next seven months.

Anyway, I had my first mobile. Junior even showed me how to set it so it would wiggle instead of ring. "Now it's time we got you a *fry*, like," he said.

Junior and I left my suitcases, computer, and fiddle in the trunk and went for breakfast, where we met up with John Folan. Junior said Folan would be the Tigers' assistant coach again.

The Full Irish Breakfast, a fry, was awaiting us: two eggs (fried), rashers (ham, fried), sausages (fried), chips (french fries, fried), black and white pudding (blood sausages, fried). And toast (toasted).

You would have thought we were mobile phone salesmen instead of basketball folks. After we had talked about phones for five minutes, Folan said, "There's more phone shops in Tralee than fish and chip shops."

To which Junior answered, "Although there are still plenty more pubs than phone shops. There are forty-five pubs in Tralee, like. Forty-five!" The fact that there were just twenty thousand people living in Tralee made this even more remarkable. We had a new topic.

Folan, without using a pencil, noted that this meant one pub for every 444 people. I thought it was a good sign. My assistant coach had a head for statistics. That could come in handy on the bench in a tight game.

When my new colleagues paused to chew their breakfasts, I brought up basketball and the state of the current Tralee Tigers team, going over our roster on a napkin. They argued about nearly every player, but they did agree on this: Tralee had a good team in place, with the potential to win a lot of games.

Folan said he had to get to his real job—managing a pub. I didn't know then that I'd see John Folan less than once a week that season. I assumed we'd be working closely all year; instead it would be my manager, Junior Collins, whom I would see every day.

Before Folan left, he said that Tralee having a successful season didn't necessarily guarantee financial success or even stability for the club. That seemed strange logic to me. "The last time the Tralee Tigers won the championship," he said, "was 1996."

"And?" I said.

"Tralee didn't even have a team the following year, so. The club shut down." Folan hoisted on his raincoat, leaving me to Junior.

There have been professional basketball leagues across Europe for decades. The general rule is that each team is allowed two Americans. Most salaries are tax-free, and the players get their accommodation and perhaps some meals. All of the upper-echelon countries provide a car. But the pay scales differ greatly across the world.

Italy, Spain, and Greece pay their Americans the equivalent of several hundred thousand dollars a year. Many of their Americans have NBA experience—sometimes years, sometimes weeks.

Just below that top level are countries like Japan, Australia, France, and Germany, where the imported Yanks might make six figures in a season.

Then there are mid-level nations like Switzerland, Finland, and England, where a former U.S. college star would command $30,000 or $40,000. Before Irish basketball began losing its sponsors in the 1990s, Ireland was on the verge of joining the mid-level countries.

The lower mid-level are places like Sweden, Norway, or Luxembourg, where an American might make anywhere between $15,000 and $20,000 a year.

Last in the hierarchy is Ireland, where the imports pull in $7,000 for the season, plus accommodation. Why would an American play in Ireland for so little? Likely it would be the best he could do if he wanted to continue playing ball after college. A good season in Ireland might lead to a bit more money in the mid-level countries.

The imported Americans were one of the few things any coach had control over. We were more or less stuck with our Irish players, who were too provincial—parochial, the Irish said—to switch towns or teams. Anyway,

Ireland was a place for an aspiring player to make a name for himself on his way up the ladder. Or where a guy who used to be a good player could make a nest at the bottom of the road downhill.

That still may leave unanswered this question: Why would a moderately successful American college coach pack up his fiddle and laptop for Ireland to coach a team at Europe's lowest level?

Junior Collins had been raised in New York City until he was sixteen, when his Irish-born parents moved the family back to the countryside ten miles outside Tralee. His first love was American football, and he hadn't paid attention to basketball until he got involved managing the Tigers. He didn't have a New York accent anymore, but he retained what might have been a Big Apple bluster.

Junior said that both he and Folan worked as volunteers. In fact, everyone who worked for the Tigers did it for free. Except me. "Folan trained as a butcher, like, but moved to the area a few years back to help the Tigers and settled into his pub work."

Junior looked hard at my breakfast plate, which still had plenty of pork left. By some sort of telepathic agreement, we both understood that Junior would finish my meal. I silently slid the plate across to him.

I asked Junior about his own profession. He obviously loved the Tigers and was so busy that he didn't have time to launder his jacket or slacks. Being team manager, he said, meant many things: reserving gym times, setting the game schedule, communicating with the Irish Super League office, arranging for the team bus, getting work permits for the Americans, carting players around—and now carting the coach around, the Tigers' first imported one. Junior did all that as an unpaid worker.

"A few years ago my wife and I decided to switch, see? She went to work at a department store, and I take care of the kids and cook." He had five kids total, but only three living at home these days. Junior was married to the previous coach's sister. Junior said his wife Jaci was not mad at *me* for her brother getting sacked.

Junior cleared his throat, hacking as though he were about to spit. Then he began shuffling the sugar packets on the table. He had a scruffy but saintlike street urchin quality—dirty hands, but perhaps he'd been out working in the yard since sunrise, before my flight arrived. Although he seemed a likable guy, he was maybe not someone you'd wish for as a roommate. He'd be fun at a party, but you wouldn't expect him to pitch in and do the dishes or the wash. At our table he was tapping his hands in what could have been some ancient Gaelic Morse code. I sensed that he had something important to say.

"You know when your teams in the States won those conference championships, like?"

I nodded. I'd been fortunate at both the University of Texas–El Paso and New Mexico State.

"The entire team got championship rings, right?" he said.

"That's right."

"Did the players have to buy their own rings? Or did the schools buy them for the players?" He was leaning across the table, and we were almost nose to nose.

I was fading. My eyes were drooping from flight fatigue and the massive breakfast, the Full Irish fry. I momentarily saw two Juniors in front of me.

"The University bought them. Why?" Did he want a New Mexico State ring as a souvenir? I'd packed some NMSU shirts and caps in my luggage for my new team, but certainly not rings.

"We'd like to get them for the lads this year," Junior said.

"This year?" I said. "You mean last year?" The Tigers had done reasonably well the previous season, but I didn't get it.

"No, in six months," Junior said. "We're going to win this whole thing, like."

I told him I appreciated his optimism.

Junior had no paying job but a fierce loyalty to his Tigers, along with visions of greatness. He struck me as a guy desperate to belong, to believe in some cause, maybe any cause. I used to be the same way, except I was much younger when I put my naive faith in basketball. I looked at Junior's ringless fingers. His hands seemed to have gotten dirtier just sitting there. He was hefty, scruffy, the common man, clinging to an illusory cause; he saw me as his champion in this mythic land, ready to do battle. He reminded me of—well, someone.

I had put in fourteen good seasons in college hoops: eight at UTEP and six at New Mexico State. As an assistant coach I'd been to eight NCAA tournaments. For a while I believed that I would be tabbed a head college coach, christened by my mentors, Don Haskins and Lou Henson, in the same way that Don Quixote was dubbed a knight at the start of his adventures, then scooped up by some mid-level college.

It never happened. I ran out of gas. I can admit that here, but if I had mentioned it to my brethren in the college coaching fraternity, it would have branded me as an oddball, as my interest in literature and fiddling did. Not that the workload was like being a Chicago cop, or a Detroit autoworker. But coaching was a grind, with hardly a free weekend. I spent those coaching years calling teenage recruits on the phone, or watching an endlessly rewinding game tape. Or I was stuck in bleachers in places like Dodge City, Kansas, and Morris, Illinois. A college assistant spends 90 percent of his time recruiting, scouting, monitoring academics, scheduling, and planning. If you have the energy after that, you can help coach your team.

I didn't love basketball anymore, as hokey as that sounds. The job had become too entwined with my self-worth, although I realize that's not unique to coaching.

Never even good enough to make my high school team, I was a point guard in college, but a Division III walk-on, the lowest in the hoopster food chain. I was so bad in fact that I got cut from the team before my senior year. Just earning a uniform on a college team took relentless work, especially on dribbling skills, which was how I made a place for myself. Being a major-college assistant at two prominent programs was good for my frail small-college benchwarming self-esteem.

But as a coach I saw the hypocrisy of major college sports up close. I made more money as an assistant coach at NMSU than any professor in the English Department. The football and basketball coaches at nearly every major university are the school's (and often the entire state's) highest-paid employees. It seemed ridiculous to me, although—and here was the rub—it took me six years of making great money at NMSU, then socking it away in investment accounts, to do something about it. I'd outgrown basketball and didn't want the game to control my life anymore. I had two new romances: literature and music. I wanted to try my hand at writing fiction.

I feared I couldn't get the NMSU head job if coaching legend Lou Henson retired. And who would want to follow his success and popularity? I was overpaid at NMSU, my first really good-paying job, and when I quit I was actually making more from the stock market than from coaching. Why hustle a sixty-hour week when I could live off my investments?

I sheepishly told Lou Henson one morning that I'd decided to resign and pursue an MFA in Creative Writing. Coach Henson was sympathetic. He had a son, a successful junior college coach and aspiring writer, who had died in a car accident in the early 1990s. Lacey Henson, Lou's granddaughter, Lou Jr.'s girl, was a talented young writer who would soon pursue a graduate MFA degree.

Coach Henson arranged to have NMSU pay for my graduate school—not much of a parachute for a big-name head coach, but unheard of for an assistant.

I applied for all kinds of writing fellowships after graduating and was summarily rejected. But being in Ireland would give me time to write, I reasoned. The demands on my time would be manageable. I'd win a lot of games without getting emotionally involved. The point of the job was to give me time to finish my collection of short fiction set in the murky but exciting world of college basketball. Coaching in Tralee would be just like a fellowship, a break-even proposition that would allow me time to really write. All of which is another way of saying that coaching was the one thing I could do to make money, in this case without doing much work at all.

When I arrived in Ireland, I had nine stories, almost enough for a book, and they all needed polishing.

Also this: I'd met a woman named Connie at a dinner party where we played charades, of all things. She was a new professor at NMSU, a poet. She told me that she was interested in learning to play the Mexican accordion. A writer interested in music, from the Canadian border, a native French speaker with long black hair? Things moved quickly—too quickly for me, considering my disastrous dating history. So this trip would also serve as a seven-month trial to sort out my feelings toward Connie.

I had to do something to make a living, something part-time that would allow me to maintain a psychological distance from the job. And I wanted to finish my book and play some music, to enjoy myself in a country that appreciated the fiddle, and, most importantly, where basketball couldn't overwhelm my life. Now you tell me: what better place than Ireland?

The Dark Island

My first afternoon in Tralee, weary of unpacking boxes, I took a ten-minute walk to the Sports Complex, the gym where my new team would play their games.

The Tralee Tigers proudly boasted the highest attendance in Ireland's Super League. That was good enough for me, so I never bothered to ask during my phone interview exactly where the Tigers played. Junior Collins had explained to me after breakfast that we didn't really have our *own* gym to practice in.

"What do you mean we don't have our own gym?" I said.

Junior said we trained at a local high school. "It's clean, well lighted, and has glass backboards," Junior stressed. We rented the place for thirty euros an hour, which at the time was about the same as U.S. dollars. I was relieved we didn't play the games there when he said our practice facility could seat only two hundred.

"But the thing is," Junior added before he dropped me off, "we don't really have our own gym to play the *games* in, either. We rent the Sports Complex for that, like. Near the train station."

The Sports Complex was Tralee's community center, which I found by following street-signs that said, *Swimming Pool* ➔. Sure enough, the brochure in the lobby bragged about the state-of-the-art swimming pool. It also mentioned the modern weight room and cardiovascular fitness machines, six handball courts, and a multipurpose hall for "all indoor sports activities." Nobody asked for an ID, so I marched past the front desk and stepped into a corner of the gym, into the midst of an indoor soccer game, to see for myself where the Tigers played.

The floor—the gym floor—was a dingy ceramic tile. Pull-out bleachers stood on only one side. The lighting was prehistoric. It was so dark, I thought we'd have to ask the fans to bring candles. Much of the reason it seemed so dark was that the walls were painted forest green, a mysterious choice. They must have felt the earth tones would go well with the mustard-brown floor. I instinctively folded my arms across my chest. It was shivering cold, although still summer. Maybe candles could help raise the temperature as well.

One hoop, which wobbled precariously on a wooden backboard, tilted to the side and was low. Really low. I was tempted, even at age forty-three, to run out and try to grab it when the soccer game shifted to the other end. The lines on the tiled floor were complex, hundreds of them, in five different colors, denoting all different types of sports. I made an appraisal of the lines: volleyball, team handball, or soccer maybe. Badminton or tennis. I had to walk around the edge of the floor to decipher which color lines were for our basketball court—the thin red ones. A soccer ball whizzed past my ear, slammed into the folded bleachers, and was chased by two wheezing men about my age.

I opted for the safety of the lobby. Behind the front desk, two women were chatting over a cup of tea. For a long minute I waited to get their attention, then pretended to read some of the announcements on the bulletin board until they noticed me, Tralee's new basketball coach. Conscious of my American visitor status, I didn't want to be too pushy and interrupt the ladies while they were exchanging recipes. They were discussing something called porter cake that included sixteen ounces of beer as one of its main ingredients.

Since it was only August 20, I reasoned, maybe I could work with the Sports Complex's director to get the gym in shape before the Irish Super League basketball season began in early October. A cardinal rule of coaching in college in the United States is to ask for anything you need your first week on the job. The ladies finally took notice of me and told me that a man named Liam Something could see me in five minutes.

Rather than sit, I paced, but not from nervousness. I feared that if I sat, the jet lag would catch up to me and I'd fall asleep. Getting a wooden gym floor and glass backboards before the season began was too critical to succumb to sleep. Anyway, I had time to check out the rest of the complex. The pool did look terrific. A decent weight room stood behind the gym. But the locker room smelled like a urinal. I say locker room, but there were no lockers, just hooks. And no chalkboards.

Back in the lobby, I waited for Liam to help me work through the list of demands I'd composed on 3×5 cards. In the spirit of diplomacy, I crossed off *demands* and wrote *requests*.

Liam showed me into his office and offered me a cup of tea. He looked like a former athlete of some sort, but he quickly pointed out that he'd never played basketball. Or even been to a game—a match, he called it. "Would you believe," he said, "that I was a swimmer?"

I told him I sure would.

He asked me how he could be of service.

First, I said, we needed a wooden floor. Although we might have to wait until perhaps Christmas to get a purchase order, let folks put in bids. Maybe we'd have a week off at Christmas to give the workers time to install it. Then we had to have glass backboards. The locker rooms would need a complete overhaul. Liam would have to take up all those ridiculous lines, then widen the ones for the basketball court.

He listened to my requests without interrupting me a single time. "Did Junior Collins send you in to ask for all this?"

No, I said. I had thought of it myself.

He brightened. "It's a good list you've got. You'll be a fine coach."

I said thank you.

"I'm afraid we won't make much progress on the floor. Funding being what it is, you've got to be realistic."

I swallowed hard, as if forcing a chunk of tile down my throat.

"Now the backboards," Liam continued. "Wood is what we've got there already, you see."

I told him I hadn't seen a wooden backboard in the States since the 1970s.

"It's a shame, isn't it?" Liam said. "It's the funding again. Although we did recently get a grant from the government so we can modernize the pool." He was glowing now, as if he'd just climbed out from a morning swim.

"The pool is the most modern thing here," I said.

"We're certainly proud of it," he said. He described the high-tech pool that they were planning on putting in instead, then poured me another cup of tea. The funding levels would also keep the locker room as it was. The "stripes" on the floor, he explained, were necessary for the other sports that shared the hall. "We're a multipurpose facility," he said. Then he clapped both palms on the thighs of his neatly pressed pants and asked if he'd covered everything on my list.

I rose. But then I remembered: the forest-green walls. Surely we could paint the walls a lighter color, to brighten up the court. That would be the least expensive demand—er, request—on my list. I said that I could even get my Tralee Tigers to do the painting, on a free weekend.

"Sure," Liam said, "but we can't do it. It's dark green so the lads can see the shuttlecock."

"See the what?"

"It's the badminton players, you know. Our dark walls ensure they can pick up the flight of the shuttlecock quickly. Badminton is one of the town's most popular participant sports. It's even bigger than indoor soccer."

Liam offered me a third cup of tea, but I declined. When I was almost out the door, he thanked me for stopping by and welcomed me to Ireland.

On the walk back from the Sports Complex, I bypassed my new apartment in the heart of Tralee. The town was bustling with shoppers; a long line of taxicabs waited outside a row of department stores. The International *Rose of Tralee* Festival, a huge beauty contest, was in full swing. Tralee felt more like New York City than the capital of County Kerry in rural southwest Ireland. Just as Junior had promised, a pub was posted every twenty yards, sometimes every ten. The town was not at all touristy even with seemingly all twenty thousand residents on the street for the festival. Tralee was the smallest town in Ireland to have an entry in the Super League, but I envisioned a community that would rally around its club.

Oddly, some of the women had terrific tans. Were they beauty contestants? There were bakeries, a fresh fish market, cafes. Sandwich shops. Hardware stores. More pubs. Not one franchise, or at least not one American franchise. There was a tobacco shop named "The Casket." Four bookstores. Winding streets, a lovely town park awash with roses. More pubs still. I forgot about the dark green gym, or perhaps I was overcome with sleep deprivation. Everything I could possibly want was within a hundred yards of my apartment. Tralee seemed to be a wonderful market town, without the sprawl of western American cities. I knew I could be happy here for at least the year. I was happy already.

And then, a giant cathedral, St. John's. I was marveling at the towering steeple when an old woman came out, sweeping up outside the church using an old-style broom: some straw tied to a crooked stick. She looked like she'd stepped out of the nineteenth century, with rags wrapped around her head and thick ankles. Her skin was callused from work, but she had bright, moist eyes. Embodied in this woman was the Ireland I'd anticipated. I asked her if she had any idea what time it was—I'd forgotten to reset my watch when I landed. I halfway expected her to look up at the angle of the sun, or patiently wait for the bells overhead to chime.

She whipped out a cell phone and told me.

Bill Dooley had tipped me off about the Tralee Tigers coaching opening a year earlier, in 2001. Dooley had been the University of Richmond coach before leaving the States to become the Irish National Coach. The national team had prospered since he took over. The Irish were on the verge of qualifying for the Olympics for the first time; the Irish press was hailing Dooley as a hero, and the international basketball community was calling him a brilliant tactician.

Dooley and I had met while I was at the end of a two-week vacation in Ireland. I told Dooley—I was having such a fantastic time on holiday—that I'd love to live there. In just ten months I'd be finished with my graduate degree at NMSU.

I'd been visiting Ireland's sacred sites, touring castles and the James Joyce museum. I saw much of County Kerry peddling on a rented bicycle through the narrow country roads, my fiddle stupidly wedged sideways behind my seat as cars passed me with inches to spare. My nights were spent in spirited pubs. If traditional music was being played I awkwardly tried to follow along quietly on my fiddle, or just stared, mesmerized by the tunes.

I'd heard Irish music growing up on Chicago's north side, but on that vacation the tunes grabbed me hard, as though they were transforming me, or calling out to some unknown corner of my soul. Or maybe I'd had too much Guinness. But each evening became a quest to find the best traditional music.

The country had everything I was passionate about since walking away from college basketball—music and literature first, but also engaging politics, gorgeous hikes, and absorbing characters. It seemed like heaven. Leaving Ireland at the conclusion of that vacation, I found myself weeping on the airplane as though I was leaving my ancestral homeland. Which I was not.

Dooley, I could sense, thought I was nuts. I'm sure it was confirmed for him when I asked, "Are there any coaching jobs?"

"You want to *coach* here?" he asked. "Or just find any job," as though that were a more reasonable suggestion. Being the national coach of any country was prestigious, but he made it clear that coaching a club team in Ireland was not.

"Coach," I said.

"Only a few of the teams in the country even pay a livable wage," Dooley said. "The other coaches work practically as volunteers." He insisted that Ireland would be a dead end for me, but he'd let me know if he heard of any jobs. His tone was that of a father trying to talk a misguided son out of something he really wanted, like a big tattoo or a Harley-Davidson.

I said, "Ireland might be dead end for basketball, but you can't convince me that I wouldn't enjoy a season here."

Bill Dooley smiled and nodded at me.

The following year I completed a Master of Fine Arts degree in fiction writing at New Mexico State. I'd all but forgotten about coaching in Ireland when Dooley surprised me just before I graduated in May of 2002 with a call about Tralee. A man named William Main was their club president, and he'd be calling me. The Tralee Tigers had one of the few paying jobs, and they were interested in bringing over an American coach.

"Actually," Dooley said, "they're called the *Frosties* Tigers. Frosties are what the Irish call Kellogg's Frosted Flakes. The breakfast cereal, with Tony the Tiger." Dooley said Tralee had a good team assembled, though they were notorious for underachieving, then self-destructing. Then he added a comment that worried me. I wasn't sure whether it was meant to be ominous or optimistic. "I want to make sure you understand, before this William Main calls you," Dooley said. "This isn't what you're used to in Division I college ball. This is another world. Forget everything you think you've learned about basketball."

The Good-Natured Man

When William Main finally phoned—rang, they say—we talked for thirty minutes. Years before becoming the Tralee Tigers' president, William had been a priest, and he was now giving meditation workshops around Ireland. A pacifist at heart, he said he hated confrontation. He wanted to know where in Ireland I had visited the previous summer. Had I made it to Tralee? I had not, and William Main had never been to New Mexico. He said he loved ethnic food and wanted to know all about New Mexican cuisine. It was as though I was sharing a cup of tea with this gentleman, having a happy chat. How did New Mexican food differ from Mexican food? Which was hotter? He had a weakness for Asian food, any kind of Asian. You name it: Chinese, Thai, Malaysian. His father lived in France, he said, and the food there was superb. William lived an hour south of Tralee, near the fabled Ring of Kerry. His family had a small hotel and restaurant there. He was exceedingly polite, like an ambassador or a senator, or, I suppose, an ex-priest. We exchanged numbers and addresses.

He never mentioned the word basketball or job.

During our next conversation I asked William Main if the Frosties Tigers indeed had a job open and what the job paid. I asked enough questions that perhaps William thought I wasn't excited about Tralee. (Indeed, maybe I was having doubts and sounded skeptical. A coaching pal had laughed loudly and made a comment about coaching leprechauns when I told him I was contemplating a job in Ireland.) William reminded me that the Tigers had perhaps the best sponsor in all of Irish basketball: Kellogg's. I was direct this time at the conclusion of the call. "I want to come to Ireland and coach your team," I said.

Later that week, William phoned again. This time he said, "The Tigers do indeed have a position, and it would pay fifteen hundred euros a month, plus an apartment. Would that be enough?"

I asked William what would be included. College coaches like to think in terms of perks. Courtesy car, summer camp money, country club memberships. William said there would be no car, or any other perks. I'd be on foot all year. There'd be no health insurance either. But the free apartment included utilities. I'd merely have to eat, and he assured me that the town was small; I could get around.

Then William Main voiced his big concern: whether I could discipline the Frosties Tigers. Seems they'd had problems with guys not showing up on time, or not showing up at all, as well as players trying to coach the team themselves. "We want every player to give one hundred and ten percent," he said.

I began calling Bill Dooley each week to get an informed but neutral viewpoint on the Frosties Tigers situation. Dooley, as part of his National Coach duties, showed up to Super League games in order to scout potential Irish players who might someday be good enough to play for his National Team. And I trusted Dooley; he was the only one I knew who understood both the world I was coming from and the one I had chosen.

A big part of the Frosties Tigers' problem, it seemed—literally and figuratively—was Ricardo Leonard. He should have been a built-in advantage. Ricardo Leonard was an African-American who had dominated the country a few years ago, then married an Irish woman in Tralee. Teams in the Irish Super League were allowed two imported Americans. But Ricardo no longer counted as one of the Tigers' two imported Americans; he was, by rights of his marriage, an Irish citizen. In effect, the Tigers could have *three* Americans.

Unfortunately, Ricardo had consumed more than his share of Frosties. He stood 6'8" but was well over three hundred pounds. I found photographs of him on the Internet and he looked terrible.

"It's major trouble finding him shorts that fit," Junior Collins told me.

Ricardo should have counted as two Americans himself. He was the highest-paid player in Ireland, at about fourteen hundred euros a month. He was also known as the team bully, and used his value as the precious third American to squeeze the club, making demands and threats. Still, even carrying the extra eighty pounds Ricardo was better than most of the Irish players.

"Do you suppose, Rus, that you can sort out Ricardo?" William Main asked. "You know, get him in line?"

Ricardo wouldn't practice hard, or show up on time, or even finish an entire practice. The younger players, the Irish kids they hoped would help build the future teams, were afraid of him. Ricardo yelled at them, tried to coach the team himself, and was chronically injured because of his poor conditioning.

"The first thing I would do," Bill Dooley said, "if I were the Tralee coach, would be to fire Ricardo Leonard. You won't have any fun coaching him." Fire Ricardo? He was going to be my big advantage, my third American. Dooley's advice seemed pretty harsh, but when a successful college coach who knew the Irish scene as well as anyone suggested that, I paid attention.

Most important, William Main was tired of the confrontations that having Ricardo around required. The club, William assured me, would back me on disciplinary actions I needed to take.

"Give me Ricardo's phone number," I said.

Ricardo Leonard had grown up in inner-city Washington DC and played at Old Dominion University in Virginia. He'd had a fine college career, leading his league in scoring and steals as a senior. Still, he was the classic underachiever. Conditioning had been a problem for some time, but as a young man he was able to play himself into shape as the season progressed.

In the last couple of years his lifestyle—lying around, doing nothing all summer but gaining weight—had caught up to him. Instead of rounding into condition by November, he got himself hurt and further behind. Ricardo averaged 35 points a game in Ireland early in his career. But he was now in his thirties and coming to a premature end of his playing days. At three-hundred-something pounds, his best games were a never-ending buffet line behind him.

William Main gave me the phone numbers of the other players on the Tigers, as well as the number of my future manager, Junior Collins. Everyone had a new morsel to add to the Ricardo Leonard plate: He'd averaged 14 points per game the year before, but at what cost? Every young player in County Kerry snickered at him because he couldn't run. His teammates blasted his performance on the court. The referees despised him. He was mouthy at halftime. I didn't want to lose our unique third American, but I wanted, more than anything, to enjoy the season. If that meant losing a few games with some hustling younger kids, so be it.

Common wisdom was that Ricardo could have earned six figures in France or Italy if he weren't overweight and lazy. I needed to "get him sorted out," but I knew that if I came over in August and he was still fat, it might be Christmas before he could play through a whole game. He could get hurt trying to play hard, although such effort seemed unlikely. It was early May; it would be nearly four months before I'd arrive in Ireland to coach the Tigers. Nevertheless, I felt that Ricardo's situation needed to be dealt with.

I made a calculated move, my first as Frosties Tigers coach: I called him from the States. In what I'd like to think of as an uncharacteristic move, I decided to rattle Ricardo's silverware.

"Ricardo, you've never met me," I said the instant he answered, "but I'm the new coach of the Tralee Tigers. I just wanted to tell you that I don't like fat players or lazy people, and you need to lose seventy pounds. If you're not down to two hundred fifty by August fifteenth, we're going to have a problem."

It was quiet. I thought maybe he'd hung up on me. He hadn't, so I continued. I was pretty hard on him, telling him I wouldn't tolerate laziness. Then he went into a scattered speech about how he had gotten a bad rap, pontificating uninterrupted for twenty minutes about what a coachable guy and good listener he was.

The next day Ricardo met with William Main and announced he was quitting the Frosties Tigers. He'd never been so insulted in all his days, he said. Where did they get this new coach?

William Main called me immediately. "Perhaps you were a wee bit too hard on Ricardo," he suggested. "We don't want to lose him to another club, especially Killarney." Twenty miles away from Tralee, Killarney was a big rival.

I could hear the panic—for the first time—in William Main's voice. My phone call to Ricardo may have seemed over the top, but it was planned. I wanted to get him thinking that he had to shape up. It would be easy to lighten up on him later. Everything pointed to Ricardo Leonard being a ball and chain, dragging down the drowning Tigers.

In any case, Ricardo told William Main he was going to look for another team. I decided to sit still and see what unfolded.

My next decision as the Frosties Tigers coach also took place before I arrived: Would I live in Tralee, or a nearby town?

I was concerned I'd see too much of the players if I stayed in town. I'd never been to Tralee, or the stunning Dingle Peninsula, which was close by. So I asked for some phone numbers of folks associated with the Tigers and called from the States.

"I've taught school in Tralee all my adult life," one woman told me, "and I wouldn't live in Tralee for all the riches in the world. They're too Irish there. Go live in Dingle."

Too Irish? I wanted Irish. Everyone I talked to had a differing opinion and would insult—or slag on—the other towns. They couldn't mention another town or village without bashing it.

I took an apartment above the Women's Resource Center in the heart of Tralee. Their offices occupied the first two floors and I had the top. They were only open from 10 A.M. until 3 P.M., so the place was pretty quiet. My first day, as I staggered up the stairs, loaded to my ears with baggage, the director warned me: "Don't tell anyone in Tralee who you've seen here. Ever."

I swore I wouldn't.

After that, things were much more relaxed. We'd joke and chat briefly as I was going in and out during the day. The women would bring me cookies and I screwed in light bulbs for them. Like real neighbors. They insisted they couldn't hear me sawing away on my fiddle every morning.

The Mist-Covered Mountain

My third day in Ireland I went to the sporting goods store where Ricardo Leonard worked. As I had guessed, his threat to sign with another team had been a bluff. Ricardo would have had to uproot his family, and the other teams had to know his reputation.

In last season's team picture he was embarrassingly fat. So I was surprised to see him. He looked—well, not slim, exactly, but slimmer. He was still huge, but he'd obviously taken off a lot of weight since our phone conversation a few months earlier.

Before meeting Ricardo, I had taken a lap around the massive store, but uncovered absolutely no basketball equipment, save for some cheap rubber balls, and just two styles of basketball shoes. Sticks and balls for sports that I didn't yet recognize took up the most space.

Ricardo was helping a family select shoes for their young daughter. He smiled easily and often. I felt awful. Here was a man working another job, still playing ball, supporting his wife and kid. And I'd deliberately insulted him in our first conversation.

We had a good talk that afternoon, then met for dinner later with his wife and boy at the Stoker's Pub. He seemed like a decent enough fellow, a good father and husband, and the kind of guy I could coach. I decided to put my first opinions of him behind me, and hoped he'd return the favor.

The weather was superb my first week in the country. Hardly a cloud, mid-seventies.

My average day went like this: wake up at sunrise and hack away at my fiddle for thirty minutes. Plenty of fresh fruit for breakfast. Read some Irish fiction, then a cup of tea, and I was ready to take a crack at one of my own stories. After lunch, with the story fermenting in my head, I'd go for a long walk through and around the town park. All autumn, a gorgeous section the size of half a football field was a riot of color, boasting every species of rose imaginable. I'd go five or six laps around and I'd contemplate my story in progress, what needed to change, what was missing—a scene, or an action by a character. Upon my return, I'd wave to the Women's Resource Center ladies and call Connie in New Mexico, where she would be waking up.

I remember thinking those first weeks: I've never been happier. Since practice hadn't begun, I wasn't doing any real work. In a week I'd be putting in two hours of coaching every day and digging into my fiction. I sensed that great Irish music was out there waiting for me, and I only had to sift through the many pubs to find it.

"The good weather won't last," William Main warned me over tea and scones one morning. "It never does, you needn't worry about that." William was decidedly cheery and upbeat, even when predicting nasty weather. He had decided to take an apartment in Tralee. That way he wouldn't have to drive the hour to his home, and he'd be that much closer to the excitement of Frosties Tigers basketball. He would keep the place for the season, and wound up spending over half his nights in Tralee. Plenty tall enough for basketball, about 6'3", and near my age, William was slightly knock-kneed and admitted to a lack of coordination.

William shared some of the hard truths about my new job with the Tigers: we didn't have an office. Or a secretary. Or a printer, or a photocopy machine. We didn't have a fax machine, or stamps, or up-to-date stationery. But, William said, the other basketball clubs probably didn't either.

In fact, my salary when I stopped coaching at NMSU—over $70,000—was more than the Tigers' entire yearly budget.

Practice, we decided, would commence on August 25. Over the summer most of the Frosties Tigers had been playing pickup games.

"There's quite a buzz around Tralee," William told me that morning. "The players are ready to give one hundred and ten percent. The team has never been so excited, and that's why they've had the new training regime since May."

"What regime is that?" I wondered.

"Playing twice a week. The lads have become so dedicated." He smiled broadly. "I have to say, it's because of you, Rus. They're so thrilled to have an American coach."

I gulped some tea, and smiled back at him. If twice-a-week training was an improvement, it might be a more difficult season than I anticipated.

Junior Collins was the only person in Ireland who invited me into his home during my first few months. Ireland's social scene happened in the pubs, which served as large living rooms. Junior didn't drink; he'd never gotten the taste for it, he said.

He lived in the countryside, so I looked forward to visiting a home nestled in the rolling hills of Kerry with an authentic Irish family. I anticipated sitting around a peat fire, eating lamb stew, maybe learning about Ireland's storytelling tradition, singing the ballads from the Irish rebellion of 1916. Maybe they'd teach me a few words of Irish. Perhaps there'd be some stone circles or sacred sites nearby.

When we arrived, all three of Junior's boys were huddled around the TV set, watching American professional wrestling, cranked up loud. Really loud.

"Who do you like better," one shouted at my face, "the Rock or Stone-Cold Steve Austin?"

After a few pro wrestling bouts, Junior Collins and I moved to his kitchen table. We needed to make out the practice schedule. Although we didn't have an actual game schedule, the season was only six weeks away. The Tigers would play every Saturday night.

"Five days a week practice seems like a good start," I said. The Frosties Tigers played most Saturdays, and I'd give them every Sunday off.

"Don't you think that's too much, like?" Junior said.

Junior's ten-year-old son Tomas, a handsome, freckled kid, was sitting with us. He pointed at me every few minutes and said, "You're from America!"

No, I told Junior, I didn't think five days was excessive at all.

Then Junior let me in on some of the facts that William Main had left out: we could train merely *three* days a week, maximum. Two hours on Tuesday and Thursday, and then one hour in our glamorous Sports Complex, Friday night at 10 p.m., because of all the soccer and volleyball and badminton. That meant five hours a week total. "Remember," Junior assured me, "Irish teams only train twice a week. And it costs our club thirty euros an hour for gym rentals."

This was one of the tenets of Irish basketball that Bill Dooley first warned me about. "It's impossible to find gym time in a country where it rains nonstop," he'd said. Ireland had enjoyed its first true economic prosperity in the past fifteen years, but the country lagged behind on athletic facilities. Although the pubs were first class, nobody seemed overly concerned about fitness facilities in general, and basketball in particular. In his book *Big Game, Small World*, Alexander Wolff described the state of basketball on the Emerald Isle as "an epic quest for shelter."

The next afternoon I met with our team captain, John Teahan. He had been voted Irish Player of the Year by the coaches and media the previous season. Teahan had a thick accent he'd acquired growing up in the hills out-side Castleisland, and he was soft-spoken—a difficult combination. We'd talked on the phone from the States on a few occasions before I arrived and I could hardly understand a word. "John, listen," I said once, trying to get him to speak clearer, "we've got a bad connection. Can you talk a little slower?"

"It's this phone," he seemed to say. "I'll just switch."

He changed receivers, but I was back where I started.

Bill Dooley said that Teahan was a tough competitor, and for Ireland's National Coach to endorse him meant a great deal. Teahan was 6'1" and a sturdy two hundred pounds. Although he was wait-for-Christmas slow, he was an accurate shooter out to sixteen feet. He had the square jaw of a heavyweight boxer, and would often look hard at you for a few uncomfort-able moments before he spoke.

"Teahan is a wagon," one of the players told me.

A *wagon*, I asked?

"Tough. Rugged."

Teahan had scored 48 points in a single game the previous season. He was a model for the young Irish kids: a shorter guy with plenty of determi-nation. The same age as Ricardo, Teahan had been in the Irish Super League for fourteen years. He had done his time as a teenage benchwarmer, which, he was quick to point out, Irish kids today wouldn't do as happily. Teahan seemed to be sort of the yin to Ricardo's yang—a guy who was now playing his best ball, well into his thirties.

Teahan worked on an ambulance, as what we'd call an EMT in the States, and he seemed just the kind of guy you'd want trying to save your life. He lived an hour from Tralee, and according to William Main, refused to take a cent from the club despite driving eighty miles roundtrip for prac-tice—training, they called it.

He was also a bit of a worrier, so competitive that it carried over into his personal life, and I suspected the Frosties Tigers were all he thought about. After I arrived in Ireland he called every few days with something he'd been worrying about. Were the Americans going to be good enough? Should we be playing in a preseason tournament? Did we have gym times reserved over the Christmas holidays?

"Can you give the players a bit of discipline?" he asked me that first day we met. "Everyone is late to practice."

Late to practice? I told Teahan they wouldn't dare come late with me coaching.

Teahan was not the only one who was concerned. It seemed a different player called each day to express concerns about something. Ricardo Leonard was the worst. And he could really talk. The Irish guys had a gossip mentality that resembled the advice I was given when trying to decide where to live. The players would—gently, I'll admit—slag on each other, then admit their own faults, "to be fair." Then slag a little more.

I figured Teahan would be the team's cornerstone, and likely one of my favorites, despite him saying one odd thing that made me question his judgment: "I love the Sports Complex."

LAST NIGHT'S FUN

The last weekend in August, I went to the *Fleadh Cheoil* in nearby Listowel. It means "Music Festival" in Irish. (The Irish don't use the term *Gaelic* for their language.) It may have meant "Music Festival," but I would have guessed it meant "Drunken Masses." The crowd got drunker as the day went on. People kept bumping into me as I tried to wriggle through the streets. They don't say, "Excuse me" in Ireland. They say, "Sorry."

Sean Ryan came out from Dublin and drove me to the festival. Sean had played basketball for Notre Dame ten years earlier. He'd moved from Chicago to Dublin for computer work, but primarily because he was a world-class piper and flutist. He was also the guy who introduced me to Coach Bill Dooley. As we walked from pub to pub to hunt for an appropriate music session, Sean would whisper the names of the tunes being played, and we'd nod our heads or bounce in time to the lively music.

The tune titles were catchy and curious. "Last Night's Fun." "Around the World for Sport." "The Mist-Covered Mountain." The tune names seemed to suggest something deep and rich about Irish life.

In the States, a coach wouldn't broadcast this information, but I will now: I'd been playing the fiddle for the past ten years. The only hobby that was not looked at suspiciously by American coaches was golf. I'd never met another college coach who played music. And very few who didn't golf.

I'd been playing primarily "old-time" mountain music, the predecessor of American bluegrass, concentrating largely on the music of West Virginia.

I even kept a West Virginia map on my wall at home, marking with colored tacks where the great old fiddlers were from.

I kept a card in my pocket to jot down tips on the Tralee traditional music scene, and any leads on a possible teacher. I was fairly accomplished playing old-time, but self-taught, and a rank beginner in Irish music. I only really knew a half-dozen Irish tunes—none of which I heard at the *Fleadh Cheoil.* Even if they had played them, the pace likely would have been too fast for me.

The Irish music scene wasn't huge even in Ireland, and Sean Ryan seemed to know lots of the top players. Each time we'd bump into someone he knew, he'd put this question to them: "Do you know anyone in Tralee that would give Rus fiddle lessons?"

There was a name that kept resurfacing: Paddy Jones. But the comments were, well, interesting.

One man suggested, "You could try Paddy Jones if you don't mind sounding like you came out of the nineteenth century." He said "nineteenth century" the way you might say outdoor plumbing.

Another guy said, "I wouldn't bother with Paddy Jones. He'll spend half the lesson talking about the meaning of life, and how Irish music relates."

Still another said, "Paddy's a brilliant fiddler, but he's nearly a hermit. He spends his entire life fiddling."

And finally this: "He'll have you reading philosophy as part of your lesson. And what does Irish mysticism have to do with fiddling, so? Anyway, he's far too demanding. Who needs help finding their spiritual path?"

Well, I did, so that last comment did it for me. I felt like an Old West gunslinger, ready to test himself. I had to find Paddy Jones.

Our first basketball practice was August 25. Training, I mean.

I'll admit I was a bit put off when I found that Teahan was correct. Nearly every player came strolling in at exactly 8:02 P.M., even the Americans, who would depend all year on an Irish teammate giving them a lift. John Teahan came in ten minutes late. So we began with a harsh meeting, where I insisted that I wanted them dressed, laced up, and stretched out *before* our starting time. One of our better Irish players, a big kid named Micheal (say "Me-HAUL") Quirke, couldn't make it. He was training with his Gaelic football team for another month.

The highlight of that practice was Ricardo Leonard: he worked his ass off. Or a small part of it; it was still pretty substantial. But he didn't say a word and hustled like he was trying to impress everyone. And he did. Not only could he score inside, he could really pass the ball for a big man. He was intelligent, and I decided then to build the offense around him.

Our two American imports were young, each a mere twenty-two years old. I selected them at that age on purpose, because Teahan and Ricardo were both over thirty. I figured we needed youthful energy, as well as two guys who would appreciate the meager thousand euros a month.

One American was Eric Siebrands, from Minnesota State. His coach, Dan McCarrell, had been my college coach. An athletic 6'8", Siebrands could shoot three-pointers, which neither Teahan nor Ricardo could do. He was a white guy, slim, red-haired, and even looked Irish. That worried all the Irish players. They'd seen enough white guys who couldn't play—they were all over Ireland. I was hoping Siebrands would be a good counterbalance to Ricardo. Figuratively, I mean.

The other American was Sherman Rochell, a 6'5" do-it-all kind of player—quick, lefty, and versatile. He gushed with encouragement for the Irish guys. Rochell was second-team All Sun Belt Conference at the University of Denver, which had been in New Mexico State's league when I worked there.

Rochell brought a video camera to document his travels. The first day he was pointing it out the car window at the sheep and green fields. I didn't want to embarrass him and say we'd see sheep every few minutes for the next seven months.

I did tell both Americans that they'd have to produce quickly. This was professional basketball, even at a thousand euros a month, and we needed results. I didn't know then how little time the two actually had.

As a college assistant I'd spent hours each day poring over recruiting possibilities. But with my new job, Bill Dooley had convinced me that we had a good team of Irish guys in place, so I believed that as long as our two imports were solid and could blend in, they'd be able to help us win. It had taken me less than a day of phone work to find Eric Siebrands and Sherman Rochell. I wasn't willing to get wrapped up, time-wise, in recruiting players like I had as a college coach.

The thing was, our starting five were pretty good, even by American standards. We'd be a decent American college team. We were still waiting on our point guard, a guy named Barnaby Craddock, who hadn't yet arrived from his home in Canada.

Unfortunately, our substitutes would make a weak high school team in the States. The younger Irish players were more than a little lost. They didn't know helpside from seaside and they had lots of bad habits I would have to wring out of them. I was already concerned about playing some of them, especially if I had to play more than one at a time. Injuries to our starters could leave us in serious trouble. But we had to keep the subs satisfied so they'd continue to attend practice. If they got discouraged and quit, it would be difficult even to train with fewer than ten players.

Irish basketball would never improve if the Irish kids didn't play some. That was a big point that William Main stressed—he wanted badly for the Irish kids to develop and contribute.

Ireland formed its amateur national basketball league in 1969. The sport has always been a poor man's game, so Ireland and basketball seemed a natural fit. Parts of Ireland were deluged with seventy inches of rain per year, and that would also make an indoor sport popular, the reasoning went. Still, basketball is a city game, and Ireland's population has never been very urban.

Ten years after the league's formation, in 1979, the Irish team in Killarney followed the trend started on the European continent: they recruited two American players and *paid* them. Killarney easily won the championship and the other Irish teams followed suit. Eventually every team picked up two Yanks.

Professional basketball, however modest, was born.

At that time, Ireland's two most popular sports—Gaelic Football and Hurling—were so purely amateur that neither sport would accept a corporate sponsor. So basketball did, in order to pay their new American imports.

What followed was the golden era of Irish basketball. Riding on the wake of the new popularity of America's NBA (and players like Magic Johnson and Larry Bird), the Irish basketball teams went aggressively after corporate sponsors. Salaries during the 1980s for U.S. imports were often the equivalent of $2,000 a month. Games were played in front of sellout crowds all over Ireland. In Cork, despite an unemployment rate of nearly 40 percent, hoops tickets became a hot item. Many club officials were unemployed, which allowed them time to really promote basketball. Jobless fans would wait in line for a chance to get off the rainy streets. One American of that era, Mario Elie, later went on to play with the NBA's championship team, the Houston Rockets. But he had gotten his start on the Emerald Isle.

In Tralee, basketball became the number two sport, behind Gaelic Football. Even though Tralee was a small town, local basketball leagues, men's and women's, sprouted up whenever there was an open gym. A "hall," rather. Tralee townsfolk wedged in to cheer their neighbors. Overflow crowds, even for these recreational leagues, were the norm. Occasionally Tralee would have a team entered in the top national league, what became known in the 1990s as the IBA Super League.

But Gaelic Football and Hurling—the only pure Irish sports—soon realized their error. They could still go after sponsorships, they reasoned, and maintain their amateur status by funneling the money back into youth teams, training facilities, uniforms, and travel. Basketball teams slowly lost their top sponsors, and the Super League, its spending power diminished, declined in prestige.

It was time for a change, so the IBA tried to curtail club spending. In the early 1990s, it decided to limit clubs to only one paid American. But fans had come to appreciate the American flair for the game, and resented this move. Attendance plummeted and the entire league nearly folded.

Despite the Michael Jordan era in the 1990s and cable television, which lifted basketball to new popularity all over the globe, basketball in Ireland continued to struggle. Ireland was the only country in Europe that wasn't able to take advantage of the new surge, even as the Irish economy improved dramatically. The strongest teams, like Cork's two traditional powers, the Blue Demons and Neptune, were able to survive, but other teams occasionally folded or restarted from year to year.

The Irish custom of slagging on each other got out of hand after just three practices. And who was the culprit? My captain and leader, John Teahan. His worrying was spilling over into the locker room. Evidently after practice he had announced to a handful of young guys that Eric Siebrands was not good enough for our elite Irish standards. "He should be replaced," Teahan said. After one week.

Teahan had been in William Main's ear as well, telling him that we should have brought back the American who had played with the Tigers the previous season. I was starting to see why last year's coach was fired. Whenever a team captain goes around bitching, it's cancerous. I suspected immediately that Teahan had been the leader in the "sack-the-coach" movement. He was learning a completely new system, had missed the second practice because of work, and still he had time to evaluate our American players and start a mutiny. Amazing.

In the meantime, Ricardo Leonard had lost fifty pounds, went by to check on the two Americans every day, and brought nice new water bottles for the entire squad. I was starting to think Ricardo might not be the problem at all.

The Cripple With the Crutches

The fourth night at practice Ricardo Leonard went down in a heap. He didn't yelp or grimace, he just grabbed at the back of his ankle. I thought maybe he'd slipped, although it sounded like thunder when he hit the floor. The players looked like pygmies standing over a dead elephant before five of them hoisted Ricardo to his feet. Ricardo had worked himself into almost adequate shape but now he seemed seriously injured. Were our hopes for winning the league being carried out with him?

Later, the hospital confirmed my worst fear: ruptured Achilles. Trainers say when an Achilles goes you can actually hear it pop. Of course, you'd have had a hard time hearing a marching band over the sound of Ricardo hitting the floor. Junior and I visited the hospital after practice that night. Ricardo's wife and son were there, red-eyed from the anguish. He'd worked hard to drop all that weight, and now this. It would be a long time before Ricardo could play again.

With Gaelic Football still in season, we only had nine players left for practice. Bill Dooley had warned me that this was the state of Irish basketball. Nearly everyone on my team, except the paid Americans, had missed a practice after two weeks. We'd trained just four times, but jobs or family commitments got in the way. With the loss of Ricardo, we might never have ten guys, which meant we couldn't really practice. We could get good and stingy on our defense, but it would be impossible to get our offense going by playing four on four.

I was already a bit frustrated with the Irish players. They were good guys, and they hustled. But they were lost. They hadn't grown up playing basketball, and their bad habits were ingrained. I had to stop play constantly because they kept throwing one-handed passes, a big no-no that any American eighth-grader would understand. Many of them held the ball far too low, nearly on their hip, when they shot. And they'd foolishly dribble right into trouble without a second thought.

Without Ricardo, our built-in advantage in Tralee, things were suddenly looking bleak. We'd gone from being the squad with the best personnel to, well, I didn't know where we'd be without Ricardo.

'Tis Little for Glory I Care

The next morning I couldn't sit still at my computer. The short story I was plodding through seemed frivolous—I kept seeing the struggling Frosties Tigers, who looked like grim pallbearers, lugging Ricardo Leonard out of the gym.

So I decided to give myself a pep talk about why I was even in Ireland. Of course I would have liked to win a bunch of games. It was my first head-coaching experience since I had coached high school in Chicago in 1982. I had come to Ireland to write, after quitting coaching in 2000 to get my Master's. It was a three-year program, but I'd been sneaking in one class—free for NMSU employees—every semester while coaching the Aggies. Then I "retired" at age forty to complete my MFA.

Would that explain why a major-college coach would walk away from a lucrative job, only to resurface in Ireland? No? OK, let me keep trying.

Even as a Physical Education major in college, I was reading a lot on my own—Kerouac, Steinbeck, Hemingway. One year after graduating, when I couldn't get full-time teaching work, a job as a security guard at a Chicago high school was my only opportunity. I devoured sixty books that year and got paid for it, six bucks an hour.

Then, a miracle: UTEP hired me as an assistant in the fall of 1983. There are only three hundred Division I basketball programs, so those jobs are highly coveted. I worked at UTEP for eight seasons, including seven NCAA tournament appearances, and five WAC titles. I was fortunate enough to discover and recruit Tim Hardaway, who was later a fixture on the NBA All-Star team. That led to other fine players, including Antoine Gillespie, who broke Hardaway's career scoring record. In some ways Gillespie was a more prestigious signing than Tim Hardaway, since he was an unknown who had broken Hardaway's scoring marks. (Strangely, "Gillespie" is a common Irish name, but Antoine was African-American.)

The UTEP job ended badly in 1991. That same year my fiancée, an opera singer I'd been dating for five years, dumped me two days before the wedding. It was a bad year all the way around. Maybe that's why when I first met Connie in New Mexico, despite our obvious chemistry, my impulse was to run in the other direction.

But UTEP was well behind me, and I hardly thought about my firing anymore. I had no way of knowing that my feelings toward UTEP would be dredged up midway through my Irish basketball season.

After accepting a spot at New Mexico State in 1994, I met the novelist Robert Boswell. He approached me at a campus art opening and asked how the Aggies were going to be. It was surprising that anyone, let alone an esteemed writer, would be familiar with a new assistant coach. Boswell recognized my face from the small mention I was given in the newspaper.

"Boz" sat in row four at NMSU games, straight across from our bench. Beginning my first season in New Mexico, I'd give Boz the signal when the game was over, the thumb-as-bottle—I'm coming over for a beer. We'd sit at his kitchen table, rehash the game, and I'd try and change the subject to books and writers. Talking about basketball was not my thing, especially after a game; it seemed like more work. But Boswell was one of the few non-coaches who didn't ask dumb questions. He didn't have a fan's point of view, and not a coach's, but perceptive insight.

Nonetheless, our typical conversation would be a game of verbal ping-pong:

"Why did you guys go zone in the second half?" Boswell might ask. "They shoot too well for that, don't they?"

"Foul trouble," I'd say. "Hey, I finished that Richard Ford collection you loaned me."

"Great book. What did you think of Rodney? He hasn't played the point before, huh?"

"Last year, some. Hey, have you read this Canadian writer, Alistair MacLeod?"

"Speaking of Canadians, isn't Nevada's center—"

And so on. Until one of us would gain control, or his wife, Antonya Nelson, would come in. She is a writer who knows zilch about hoops, so we could double-team Boswell, and like a good trap, force him to go where we wanted.

Let me be clear: it was not that I had *no* free time as a college coach. The problem was that when I had time, I was exhausted or wrapped up in the team's struggles and couldn't switch focus quickly. After earning my MFA, I could have applied for any number of assistant jobs, or, with my new degree, made a run at some head jobs in Division III or Division II. But I feared they would be just as consuming emotionally. I'd fallen in love with the sport as a teen, and spent thousands of hours in the gym trying to prove it, first as a player, then as a coach. Maybe, I thought, it was time for me to adopt another lifestyle.

So that's why I was in Ireland. I'd hoped I'd find a way to divorce myself from basketball, in terms of its taking up so much energy.

Before leaving Connie to go to Ireland, I told her one of my theories about sports. "With coaches, there's not going to *be* a happy ending," I said. "The odds are stacked against you—eventually a coach gets fired. Only a small percentage have a long career, and even fewer enjoy a happy ending."

Connie looked at me like I was a bad freshman essay and it was hard to know where to begin. She finally said, "Why are you climbing back on, if you know it's a going to be a bad ending?"

"That's exactly why," I said. "Because I know the ending is going to disappoint me, so who cares? I won't *worry* about the Tralee Tigers, because I know we're going to win at least enough to keep me from being miserable. I'll write, and when I need a break from the writing I'll fiddle."

Connie said, "So you're getting involved in this project with the assumption of a train-wreck ending."

I knew what she was getting at.

She continued anyway. "You start every relationship assuming it will end badly?"

"Those weren't my exact—"

"You only consider a relationship if you can remain unattached, right?"

I tried to explain the Zen Buddhist nonattachment stuff, and how it had worked for Phil Jackson's coaching in the NBA. Surely she'd heard of Phil Jackson. He had written three books.

Literature and music—my new loves—seemed like a wiser investment than basketball. They'd last a lifetime, and nobody ever had a discouraging day reading good books or sawing out fiddle tunes. So I'd sort out how I felt about my *old* love, hoops, and then come to a mature and amicable agreement, and get on with my new life. Maybe I'd walk away from basketball for good.

Connie sighed. "I don't get it," she said.

Junior Collins came by early one September morning. It was an intrusion. I was in the middle of working on a short story. Still, Junior tromped in and spread himself across one of the kitchen chairs. I had no choice but to put my writing away. He had a way of demanding every bit of my attention. Maybe that was because of his size.

I carried my laptop to the other room—I'd actually been writing about him—and left Junior with the warming teakettle and an unopened roll of cookies. *Biscuits*, the Irish said. I made certain to click *save* before shutting things down, then gently placed the computer on a bookshelf. When I came back—and I'm certain it was less than twenty seconds later—the biscuits had been opened, but Junior had none on his saucer. And he wasn't chewing.

Junior looked over at my old notebook, where I'd scribbled a few offensive sets that I'd been toying with since Ricardo's injury. "You have to dust off the old armor and playbook and get ready for battle, like," Junior said.

Dust off the armor? Battle? What's with this guy? The chair creaked below Junior. I poured him a cup of tea. Junior said something about how we still might be able to win the Irish Super League title, even without Ricardo Leonard. What a dreamer this guy was. Was he living in a total fantasy world, or what?

Then it occurred to me. *Sancho Panza.* I very nearly said the name out loud. Perhaps Junior was the Irish basketball version of Sancho Panza. He didn't have a donkey to ride, but his car sort of smelled like an old Irish dairy farm. Still, Sancho Panza was more of a realist. At least I think he was, in the beginning of the classic Cervantes novel. Maybe I was supposed to be Junior's Don Quixote.

Sporting Paddy

Even after ten years, I kept my fiddling life private. Fiddling started as a self-taught hobby, something to do other than watching David Letterman late at night. The music developed into a passion. In Ireland I could proudly tote my fiddle case, so I began doing just that in mid-September.

I tracked down Paddy Jones through the Kerry School of Music, where he taught just once a week, and I enlisted for a semester. I'd be his first student every Tuesday; he and I cramped into a tiny second-floor room with cheap chairs and a hissing radiator. They would be the first regular private lessons I had ever had.

Paddy Jones was stout and barrel-chested with a shock of wheat-colored hair. Although he was nearly sixty years old, his robust energy made him seem younger. He was the last living student of the legendary Kerry fiddler Padraic O'Keeffe, who had a sweeping influence on music throughout Ireland, but especially in County Kerry. As a boy, Paddy had learned dozens of tunes from O'Keeffe. When he was a young man desperate for work, Paddy Jones moved to England and toiled as a bus driver. O'Keeffe died in 1963, but Paddy was determined to keep his music alive when he came home to Ireland in the 1970s.

Before I played a note with Paddy that day, he reached into his satchel. "This is the Bible," he said.

And I thought, oh, geez, here it comes already. But it wasn't a real bible. It was a CD by Denis Murphy and his sister Julia Clifford called *The Star Above the Garter*.

"This music—ahhhh, it's pure magic," Paddy sighed. "Keep this close to you at all times. Listen to it whenever you can," he said with his cloudy Kerry accent.

Denis Murphy and his sister Julia had learned tunes from Padraic O'Keeffe as well, and the record was a cult classic among County Kerry musicians.

O'Keeffe had been quite a hell-raiser and disdained work. Paddy Jones, despite being an O'Keeffe disciple, didn't mind work one bit. Fingering work, scale work, bowing work. Homework. Hard work. Any old kind of work. A drill sergeant with a fiddle, he loaded me up with fundamental exercises.

He stopped me constantly that first day. "Slow down," he said. "You're too impatient. It's too much too soon for you." Whenever it was time for him to play and for me to listen, he would simply say "So!"—and off he'd go. His head flopped back and forth with the music, his chair rocking as he swayed from side to side.

Despite his enthusiasm, he was tsk-tsking me plenty that day. He found flaws in everything I did, starting with the way I held the fiddle, too low for his tastes. My grip on the bow was too far from the frog. My tone was ragged, not clear enough.

Near the conclusion of that first lesson, Paddy demonstrated one of the cornerstones of Irish fiddling—the roll. Rather than play one single note, an Irish fiddler might play that note, then the note above it, then the original note, then the note below, then the original note again. So, in essence, *five* notes in the space of one. All in a single bow-stroke. It gave the tune an ornate and graceful lilt. My response: this Irish fiddling was going to be more difficult than I imagined.

"Use longer bow-strokes, too," Paddy said. He'd ask me to play something for him, then he'd cut me off, smile, and say, "Try to make it sound like this." And he'd saw away.

When our time was up that first lesson, Paddy took a deep breath and sat back.

"You seem like a fine fellow," he said.

I thanked him.

"But this is going to take some time. You've got heaps of bad habits. But I can tell you're trying your best. There are many problems, Rus, that I see need to be slowly worked out. It's not your fault—you weren't raised in the tradition."

Our point guard finally arrived, three weeks after everyone else. His name was Barnaby Craddock, a Canadian with a British passport. He claimed that William Main told him it was all right to arrive the first week of September, and not wanting to have a conflict with my president, I had to let it pass. Barnaby was fairly quick, shot well, and he was regarded as one of the better guards in Ireland, maybe the best "Bosman."

Each Super League team is allowed one Bosman player, meaning a player with a European passport who wasn't born in Ireland. The term comes from a pro soccer player who went to court to force a country in the European Union to allow him to play as a citizen of *any* country in Europe. Bosman was a common term in European basketball, sort of the Curt Flood of European sports.

A Bosman playing in Ireland wasn't usually as good as the Americans, but because good Bosmans were difficult to find, they were valuable. Most good Bosmans commanded big salaries somewhere in continental Europe.

Barnaby spent most of his time in our first meeting complaining about how his apartment didn't have a toaster like last season or cable TV. He was actually paid a little more than the Americans—as much as Ricardo Leonard. Barnaby had gotten to be great friends with last year's coach; they would play golf and go for pints of beer. I'd been warned by John Teahan not to become friends with paid players, but I didn't need the warning. Seeing these guys three or four times a week would be plenty.

In mid-September we went to Killarney for a "friendly game," an unofficial scrimmage where they wouldn't turn on the scoreboard. Their Irish guys were older. Their players seemed like, well, men. I guess professional leagues were supposed to have men. Wide, tattooed, with full beards. Four of my seven Irish-born Tigers were nineteen, and their inexperience showed. Killarney, which often finished near the bottom of the league, had hardly practiced, and we'd had eight training sessions.

Without Ricardo Leonard we looked very weak up front. Our American forward, Sherman Rochell, was quick and bouncy, but the red-headed Eric Siebrands was a different story. Due to an injury, Killarney had had only one import, which would normally be a distinct disadvantage. But their lone American conducted an offensive clinic with Siebrands guarding him—or trying to guard him—and scored every way imaginable. Soon after that, Siebrands told one of our Irish players to try and guard Killarney's American.

William Main was there, and he mentioned that Eric Siebrands looked poor. For the club president to recognize it was a bad sign. Siebrands's thin frame and finesse style were exposed, but without Ricardo it was not entirely his fault. Offensively he was okay, but he got gassed quickly and played soft.

"Soft as church music," Junior said.

William Main, John Folan, and Junior took me out for a pint afterward. I knew what was on their mind: find a replacement for Siebrands, and quickly. We didn't have time for him to develop as we might have in college; he was going to have to produce in a hurry. I felt bad for him because he was a likable kid. It was the merciless business side of basketball. And we hadn't even had a real game yet.

I convinced the others to give Eric another few days. They convinced me to start looking around and making calls just in case. I was back to being a recruiter already. I had to buy my own pint of Guinness for the first time amongst our committee. Worse, nobody else had one.

My mini-cassette player was part of my lessons with Paddy Jones. I'd tape his tune of the week, then go home and listen to it repeatedly while I was eating. I noticed the next morning, on the tape of my first lesson, that I was talking as much as Paddy. What a fool I was. I resolved then and there to be quiet and let him lead.

Despite my fiddle frustrations, I was hoping to start playing soon in the pub sessions—loose gatherings of local musicians, most often flute, accordion, tin whistle, guitar, and fiddle players. I'd found the music the summer I was on holiday the previous year, but I couldn't seem to locate it in Tralee.

Much of the time that first month I'd wind up at the wrong pub—no Irish music. Still, I'd stay, and maybe have a chat with whoever was close by. I noticed this: if I mentioned to someone that I was the coach of the Irish Super League's Frosties Tigers, I got a blank look and a vague nod. But if I said I played the fiddle, I got a slap on the shoulder, a handshake, and best-of-luck wishes. Sometimes a pint of Guinness. Of course, it was exactly the opposite in the States. Even at musical gatherings back home someone wanted to pull on my coat about basketball.

In Ireland, nobody seemed to care.

With my years of contacts and friends in the basketball business, I had been certain I would quickly land the Tigers two good imported players before arriving in Ireland. I was wrong. I'd been too quick to sign Eric Siebrands and Sherman Rochell.

I went over to the players' house to tell Siebrands that he was done with the Tigers; we were sending him home. His freckled face turned pale, but other than that he took the news pretty well. Twenty-three years earlier, his college coach—our coach—had cut me from the team, just before my senior year. And now I was cutting *his* player.

John Folan had already called some other assistant coaches, and two teams from Dublin were interested in Siebrands. He'd get to see some more of Ireland by bus, and another club might pick him up. Ricardo's injury was common knowledge, and I supposed they thought Siebrands might not be too skinny for them. So he left Tralee hanging onto that hope. The two Dublin teams turned him down after seeing him in action.

Siebrands handled getting cut better than I had. I nearly dropped out of college, and I was a wreck for two years. To say I was dedicated would be like saying the Irish appreciate beer. But if there was a worse player than I was in North Park College history, it's hard to imagine. I had a grand total of 13 career points. Still, I was an absolute fanatic about practicing, and making my college team was a holy quest. I would like to think that this history had made me sensitive about squashing a player's hopes for a career.

All alone in Ireland, I could look back on my so-called career in sports and see a pattern. High school playing career: frustration and heartbreak. College playing career: frustration and heartbreak. College coaching career at UTEP: frustration and heartbreak. At New Mexico State I'd been smarter: of course there were frustrations, but I quit to pursue the writing career before the heartbreak part.

So why would I think that basketball in Ireland would end any differently?

Oh, Irishmen Never Forget

The other issue introduced at that basketball meeting was this: Tralee's youngsters should have been flocking to the Tigers' youth teams, since they could then, theoretically, aspire to play at the top level some day. Every Irish Super League team was supposed to have a load of youth teams. But Tralee's Irish kids saw the Americans and Ricardo and Barnaby out on our tiled court, and thought, "What's the point? I'll never get to play." In that regard, having Ricardo had been a disadvantage for the Tigers, since he took an Irish player's spot. So while it was good to have his imposing frame rooted in the middle, he'd inadvertently driven away some young Irish players from developing in our youth division.

In the 1990s a handful of disgruntled Tralee players formed their own basketball club and called it St. Brendan's. Soon after, the Frosties Tigers' best young players defected—even though St. Brendan's had youth teams only, no Super League entry. But St. Brendan's coaches had convinced the kids that they'd give them more attention.

Very Irish, the Tigers' committee explained: get disgruntled, have a disagreement, split, and start your own organization. Ireland's political history has been plagued with such divisions. Although nobody was going to get killed over this schism, it was bad for basketball in Tralee.

The problem was that you were not allowed to play for St. Brendan's lower-level teams and suit up as a Frosties Tiger. Ideally, a lad could play for, say, our under-nineteen team for forty minutes a game, and play eight or ten minutes a game in the Super League, getting valuable seasoning with the Tigers. Unfortunately, you could cross over in age groups or levels, but not between clubs. It was like in the States. A guy might play junior varsity at Central High School and still play varsity as well. But he couldn't play jayvee for Central and also play varsity for arch rival Washington High.

What the Frosties Tigers were left with was basically very sorry youth teams, and thus a bleak future. We had a couple of Super League Irishmen on the Tigers who wouldn't be good enough to be starters for their theoretically lower-level St. Brendan's county league team. Junior said some of the St. Brendan's guys would love to play for the Tigers, but social pressure kept them from joining us.

"There's a young fellow named Kieran Donaghy," Junior said, "who could be our best Irish player some day." But St. Brendan's perceived us as the money-grubbing, American-dominated, professional Frosties Tigers.

Another Irish quirk: provincialism has a more powerful pull than individual achievement. Can you imagine an American kid who would choose to play small-college ball instead of at a Division I university? It wouldn't happen. The only near-example that I could think of was when Bill Bradley decided to attend Princeton over dozens of offers to more prestigious basketball programs. And when was that? 1961?

In the month I'd been in Tralee, I'd had four kids ask me why we couldn't join forces, have one club. The town wasn't big enough for two teams. And it was the usual story—kids got hurt because of adult egos. The Frosties Tigers didn't want to turn our youth teams over completely to St. Brendan's, who didn't want to give in by affiliating with the likes of us. The result would be, I was told by parties on both sides, that soon the Irish Super League would see that basketball was dying in Kerry and would pull the franchise from Tralee, which was the smallest town to host a team. We were sort of like the Green Bay Packers in the NFL. And we might thrive like the Packers if we could unite the town.

I talked Junior and William Main into meeting with the St. Brendan's folks and offering to consolidate the clubs. Briefly. The Frosties Tigers— Junior, William Main, and I—sat down with seven representatives of the St. Brendan's basketball club. We proposed our merger. I offered them full control of all the youth programs, but they'd have to leave us with total autonomy of the Super League entry, the Tigers. We met at a local hotel, and I could feel the tension between St. Brendan's working-class folks and our elite William Main. Although nobody would describe Junior as elite, they didn't seem to like him either. After an hour we came to an agreement, sort of. We'd all take a few weeks to think about things.

Of course, it was easy for me, as the new face, to say, "Why can't we all just get along?" I'd heard Americans say that about the situation in Northern

Ireland, where Catholics and Protestants had been embittered for centuries; I'd said it myself. But outsiders couldn't possibly understand years of bad feelings. It may take a new face with a fresh view to come in and say, "Let's get together and make some compromises."

That was the kind of thinking that has gotten so many leaders in Irish history killed.

TEAHAN'S FAVORITE

Ireland was political, divided, and bitter after years of infighting. Alliances shifted, egos got in the way of the common good, and people got hurt. You didn't know who to trust. I'm talking about my basketball team, but the history of the country indicated this might be business as usual.

We all agreed that Eric Siebrands was too weak without Ricardo in the middle. We had to cut him and bring in another American. Then John Teahan took his captain duties too far by trying to convince William Main to bring back last year's American. I considered Teahan's move to be an act of insubordination.

Actually it was more complicated than that.

Last year's best American in Tralee was a guy named Jermaine Turner. By his own admission he'd never played on a winning team in his life until the Frosties Tigers. He was a sensational athlete, but a bit wild. I wanted to bring in my *own* Americans. They needed to be loyal to me.

Eric Siebrands's lack of muscle caused Teahan to lose confidence in my judgment. So Teahan called me after midnight one October evening. I put him off, and he rang me back early the next day to say Jermaine Turner, Jermaine Turner, Jermaine Turner. I got highly irritated; it was not his place to tell me which players to hire. On top of that, he slagged on Eric to the young players at a time when I was trying to get the Tigers to think as a team. Teahan and I had words. Or, I had words and he stewed. Then he called William Main and demanded a meeting with the committee. Had Teahan handled things differently maybe I would have too. Like if he'd whispered, "Here's Jermaine's phone number and a video tape from last year. Jermaine might be a guy we'd be interested in if our Americans don't work out."

That evening Junior Collins called me. "I'm afraid that John Teahan will quit the team if we don't bring back Jermaine Turner, like."

Fishing for help, I rang assistant coach John Folan, who doubled as a committee member. He said that if we brought Jermaine Turner back, Barnaby, our Canadian point guard, would quit immediately. Jermaine and Barnaby had roomed together the year before, and they hated each other. Whoever we brought in would have to share a three-bedroom townhouse with Barnaby the Canadian and import Sherman Rochell. Anyway, Folan insisted that Barnaby would be impossible to replace if he quit. It was a mess.

Not that Teahan would be easy to replace either. Barnaby and Teahan were *both* irreplaceable, and that was where it got sticky. Coaching in the United States, you'd have a bench full of players, and more leverage because of it. If a guy makes you unhappy, you plop him on the seat next to you. But we only had nine guys until Gaelic Football was over. Four guys on the bench might seem like enough, but it would be a problem for two reasons: we couldn't have a normal practice without being able to compete five-against-five. Also, any additional injuries could mean a disaster. Having fewer than nine could mean a collapse.

Was I being paranoid? Maybe I needed to be paranoid. I had the feeling that Teahan's dislike of the old coach's coaching is what *made* the old coach the old coach.

I suggested to William Main that I come to this meeting a half-hour after everyone else, to give John Teahan a chance to air his complaints with less pressure.

When William came out to the hotel lobby, he looked grim. "Things went from bad to worse," he said. "Teahan is *demanding* we bring back Jermaine Turner." These damn confrontations, his face seemed to say.

They were gathered in a tight circle and everyone stared at the ground. I made a little speech about the coach being in control of all basketball decisions. Teahan wouldn't look at me; when he finally did, it was as though he wanted to strangle me. He was upset after our phone call. And he was worried, he said, that the Frosties Tigers might not win a game all season. He wanted Jermaine Turner back.

Then, in the middle of the meeting, a committee member named Donal, whom I had only just met, suddenly resigned. He stood up and walked out, saying he didn't want to be a part of a team that had a disrespectful player. Nobody said, "Wait, Donal!" In fact, nobody blinked.

I asked Teahan if he was going to give Eric Siebrands the news that he was fired.

"Is that my job?" he asked.

"That's my point," I said. "If you're going to hire them, then you have to fire them, too."

Teahan didn't like that too well. He also didn't like it when I asked him if Jermaine Turner was better than the other six players we were considering. I could see him sinking into a bitterness that I feared might take me all year to get past. Teahan wouldn't shake my hand when I offered it to him.

We had gotten nowhere. From bad to worse, then nowhere.

Junior Collins could see it as well. "Let's get out of here and let these two talk, like," he said, and Junior, William, and Folan suddenly left. John Teahan and I were alone.

The mood shifted. Teahan was embarrassed, but not as much as I was. I'd been too harsh on the phone, and apologized for it. He said he only wanted to win and was sorry he was being a headache. I said his stubbornness was what made him a good player. Finally, I offered to call Jermaine Turner. Teahan said no, it would just get Jermaine's hopes up.

"How about this?" I suggested. "We bring in a replacement for Eric Siebrands. If you're not happy with him after two weeks, I'll fly Jermaine Turner out myself, and we'll play with him."

Teahan seemed fine with that. We were both exhausted from the tension, and he had an hour drive ahead of him. At least I got a strong handshake when he left.

The pressure was intensifying and we hadn't played a game. I had thought Ricardo Leonard would be my big problem. But he shocked me by rolling up his sleeves, dropping his knife and fork, and going to work. Then he broke our hearts by getting hurt. Now we had gone from being one of the league favorites to an average club.

Oddly, I was certain before my arrival that Teahan and I could become close. He was a tough veteran at the end of his career who claimed he'd never had a good coach. Now I might have destroyed his trust in me, alienated him—unless the Frosties Tigers were to win a bunch of games.

Ruffle the Hag in the Corner

If you've ever wished to get chosen for a pickup basketball game—and maybe you were short and slow like I was—you can begin to grasp what it is like for an American waiting to be absorbed into a traditional Irish music session. You're on the outside of the circle, hoping to get in.

My first few weeks in Tralee I wandered the wet streets every evening looking for traditional music. It was more difficult to uncover than you might guess. Junior Collins was right—nearly fifty pubs were open for business seven days a week in Tralee. But many had no music of any sort. Some had TVs blaring. Some had pounding disco, others heavy metal, and quite a few had Karaoke. A couple pubs (was I getting warmer?) had ballad singers wailing about finally booting the Brits out of Ireland. I learned that most traditional musicians consider ballads trite, but that didn't stop the locals from shouting along.

I'd ask a bartender or waitress if they knew where a good music session was. But I soon realized it was bad form to walk into a pub and bark out a question. So I'd settle in for a pint of Guinness, and halfway through my first one, I'd ask. This quickly led to me stumbling from pub to pub. And then I couldn't recall either the directions or what pub I'd been into. Tralee's streets were not on built on a grid, and it was easy to get confused. One evening I wandered into a pub called Sean Og's, only to realize that I'd been inside earlier, but had come through another door.

Finally I got a good lead, a tiny place called Betty's Pub that had an open fireplace and catered to an older crowd. On one wall hung a poster dedicated to the great writers in Irish history—I took that to be a good omen. In the hall on the way to the bathroom (toilet, the Irish always say) was an overhang of an old thatched roof, the kind that used to top nearly every Irish home. I never deduced why the edge of an old thatched roof protruded from an indoor hallway. And I never asked—I had a thousand-year-old fiddle tradition to worry about.

The musicians huddled in one U-shaped corner of Betty's Pub. At most of the sessions, one musician was in charge and got paid a hundred euros to play host. That meant leading things and calling local players to join in. The sessions were more or less open to everyone, but I was trying not to be too pushy and wanted to get comfortable first. Also, I was so new to Irish music, I didn't want to make a fool of myself.

Two fiddle players were playing lively reels, and that made me fear a rookie wasn't needed. I scrunched in as close as I could; I didn't have my fiddle and it was noisy with chatter. Other than the few loyal drinkers circled around the musicians, most of the pub considered them background music.

The tunes came fast, one after another. Reels, jigs, and hornpipes. Slides and polkas. Sometimes the musicians would smile at me after a tune and hoist a pint up in salute—appreciation for the appreciator. I still knew only a dozen Irish tunes. Maybe once every few hours one of them might get played, and I'd halfway wish I'd brought my fiddle.

One of the musicians—a rugged giant of a man, at least 6'5"—switched instruments every few tunes. Guitar. Mandolin. Fiddle. Then the Irish version of the banjo, the tenor banjo, which has four strings and is played with a pick. It was an astonishing display of versatility. Near the end of the evening, he pulled out an old *five*-string banjo.

This will be interesting, I thought. Irish music on an old-time instrument.

But he didn't play Irish tunes. He played one of my favorite old-time tunes, a West Virginia number called "West Fork Gals." I immediately recognized a tune from my numerous vacations in West Virginia. The man played the banjo in the clawhammer style—the oldest way to play, no pick, using his thumb, and dragging the back of his hand against the strings. (The banjo was originally a slave instrument. Over time the banjo, and the African rhythms, were integrated into American music, along with Irish, Scottish, and English dance tunes.)

I memorized the striking face of the banjo/fiddle/mandolin/guitar player.

Midway through our next practice I called things to a halt and gathered everyone in a circle at half court. We'd been doing a basic four-on-four shell drill to teach defensive positioning. The Irish Tigers were getting a decent grasp, with our imports providing verbal guidance. But as soon as I complicated things—having a cutter slash through—nearly every Irish player was on the wrong side of his man. I wanted them on the *ball* side. We'd be giving up layups all night if we couldn't get this fixed.

"Listen guys," I said. "It's not that we're not working hard. But we're so full of bad habits. We're too sloppy and careless. It's not anyone's fault,"

I added. "You weren't raised in a basketball tradition, and so the things that every American player knows instinctively you still have to master."

The Tigers took this criticism well—the American standard was what they all aspired to—and I let them shoot some free throws before returning to the defensive fundamentals again.

But watching them take turns at the foul line I had a revelation: I sounded just like my new fiddle teacher, Paddy Jones.

On September 18, Barnaby the Canadian went golfing. That may not sound odd to you, but I'd never coached a guy who golfed before, not during the season. My heart had sunk when Eric Siebrands came through baggage claim carrying golf clubs, and again when Barnaby told me he was an avid golfer. Maybe it was an unfair prejudice on my part. I certainly had outside interests, but I didn't want my players to have hobbies.

Or maybe the golfing bothered me because Barnaby called up the old coach to borrow his car to do it. What a good fellow the old coach must have been: he didn't tell Barnaby to get lost. Could I be jealous of the old coach?

Anyway, Barnaby stopped to gas up and put regular fuel in the diesel tank. He wound up staying at the service station for three hours while they siphoned off the tank, therefore showing up late for practice. No word on whether the car's engine was permanently damaged.

All In Good Time

The next day, looking out my window onto Ashe Street, I saw the giant man from Betty's Pub who could play anything with strings walking into a photocopy shop. I tore downstairs and waited like a stalker for him to come out. He must have needed a bunch of copies; it seemed to take him a half-hour. When he reappeared I made my move.

"Hey," I called to him as he was unlocking his car. "Sir! I admire your clawhammer banjo playing."

He was jiggling his key in the lock and didn't stop. Perhaps he thought I was dangerous. Were banjo fans stalkers?

I continued. "What other styles of music do you play?"

I was a bit off. He wasn't a giant at all, though he was taller than I was, maybe 6'1". But he was sturdy, and looked as if he could have ripped the car door open without a key. Still, he kept at the lock, trying to get away. When

I said, "Appalachian mountain music?" he stopped and dropped his arms as if I'd caught him.

His name was Ciaran Dalton. He'd noticed me standing close to the musicians at Betty's every week and wanted to know how I got so interested in the music. I told him that I played old-time fiddle but wanted to learn Irish music. Ciaran invited me to play at his Sunday session, paused, then insisted we go right that minute for a cup of tea.

We talked about Irish and American old-time music over a pot of tea and scones. Ciaran was extremely opinionated, but knew more about traditional music—Irish and American—than anyone I'd ever met. He was the postman in the neighboring town of Ardfert and had taken an avid interest in the music, folklore, and local history.

Two pots of tea later, I asked Ciaran about Tralee's place in Irish history. I'd learned that the whole of County Kerry had strong ties to Ireland's rebellions and had fiercely resisted British domination. In Ireland *Republican* meant someone who wants to drive the British out of Northern Ireland, to form, at long last, a united Ireland. Kerry, a sparsely populated rural county, had never been completely controlled by the British. There were no big urban centers for the oppressors to conquer. In any case, when the history of the Tralee area came up, Ciaran—after stressing that he deplored violence of any kind—gave me directions to Tralee's library, where I could get a town map and also learn about Tralee's past for myself. Before he left he also gave me his phone number and a list of weekly music sessions in the Tralee area. Suddenly I had a full music schedule.

The biggest statue in Tralee, thirty feet tall, was what locals called The Pikeman. It was a rural Kerryman brandishing a crude farmer's weapon that looked like a hooked spear. A pike, I suppose. It commemorated the 1798 rebellion and featured quotes from Republican martyrs.

My apartment was on Ashe Street. Thomas Ashe was involved in the Easter Rising rebellion of 1916. (The Easter Rising triggered the war for independence with England.) Ashe was from near Tralee but lived in Dublin at the time. While in prison, he was also the first hunger striker to die for the Republican cause. He had been seeking status as a political prisoner.

Tralee native Charles Kerins killed a policeman for the Republican cause in the 1940s, and was executed for it, the last man hanged by the Irish

Republic at Mountjoy prison. Kerins's story was a little more controversial because the man he shot was an Irishman, and many people believed that Ireland had a legitimate government in place. Still, each spring Tralee's Republicans honored Kerins's memory with a ceremony at his commemorative statue that stood fifty yards from Betty's Pub.

Padraic Pearse, a poet who was one of the martyred heroes of the 1916 Easter Rising, was honored with his own statue in Tralee's town park.

Austin Stack, another leader in the rebellion of 1916, was from Tralee. One of Tralee's Gaelic Football clubs was named after Austin Stack, as was County Kerry's impressive GAA park, where the biggest matches were played. Another club was named after Charlie Kerins.

A small monument at a traffic circle commemorated the life of Kevin Barry. He had been executed around the time of the rebellion, at the age of eighteen, and was the youngest patriot ever hanged at Mountjoy. (Who came up with the name for that jail?) There was a famous ballad that honored Kevin Barry, about how he held his head up high even though they were carting him off to be executed. Kevin Barry might be a good role model for a coach.

Twenty minutes away was the bay at Banna Strand, where the British caught Roger Casement in a German boat with a load of guns intended for the Easter Rising rebellion. Casement was executed. A statue of him stood ten miles away in Ballyheigue. And the bus station in Tralee, just a five-minute walk from my apartment, was called Casement Station. Casement wasn't raised in Ireland but took up an Irish cause, like me.

Outside town, on the road to Killarney, was a huge monument commemorating the Ballyseedy massacre, where the Free State army tied a dozen rebels into a tight circle and threw a bomb into the center; all but one were killed.

Martin Ferris lived in nearby Ardfert. He had spent ten years in prison during the 1980s for gunrunning for the Irish Republican Army, who (to oversimplify things) have opposed British occupation in Northern Ireland since the 1920s. After Ferris was released, the county elected him as its TD, the American equivalent of U.S. Congressman, a position he still holds today.

County Kerry had a proud history, although it made me nervous that most of its leaders had been executed.

The Cat in the Corner

We thought we'd go after another big guy to replace Ricardo. But Irish Super League rules dictated that since it was after the October 1 deadline, any new addition had to have been living in Ireland for the previous six months. I sensed that Europeans who could really play would not be floating around Ireland in the autumn. But Junior Collins got word of a Croatian living up north in Donegal.

I finally got him on the phone—Miroslav something, something Miroslav; I was not certain which.

"I am six foot seven point guard," he said. "Shoot good the three."

Fine. Shoot good the three. The Frosties Tigers could use that. So I invited him to take the train to Tralee and said we'd reimburse him when he got here. He came the next day.

Junior and I went to pick Miroslav up at Casement Station. I wasn't sure if the tall guy on the platform was Miroslav, since he was smoking like a fiend.

It was Miroslav.

He said he hadn't played basketball for six months, although he'd been playing some Gaelic Football, of all things. He was a veteran of the war in Yugoslavia, an unusual veteran—he'd fought on both sides. His mother was Serbian, his father Croatian. Fighting in the war, he said, gave him two bad habits: smoking two packs a day and downing a dozen cups of coffee. For someone who spoke such fractured English, he sure loved to talk. He had some great stories, if I understood them correctly. As it turned out, his brother was also living in Donegal. "If I come, he also come too. And your cloob must find brother a job."

Our what? Ahhhh. Our club, the Frosties Tigers.

We lost another scrimmage to Killarney in Tralee a few nights later, despite our veteran of the Serbian and Croatian armed services. The friendly game would not count on our record, but still the outcome made me anxious. Sherman Rochell was awful, and actually missed the rim on two driving layups. The next day he was hanging his head as though his dog had been hit by a truck. I wondered if he knew his job could be on the line.

Miroslav looked awkward. Had he said it was six months since he'd played? Maybe he said six years. His strength appeared to be arguing with the lone referee.

Junior Collins approached me after the scrimmage with an idea. Someone from Tralee had to wear the Tony the Tiger suit at every match, Junior said. "How about Miroslav for our mascot, Tony the Tiger? He has the outgoing personality, like."

I told Junior I'd think about it. We practiced again the next night, and Miroslav was a bit better. But when we sat down to discuss the chance of him joining us, he wanted us to drive up north, then move him *and* his brother to Tralee and provide them both with a place to live. We sent him home the next day, which was sad because he needed the job.

And I nixed Junior's mascot idea. We couldn't have somebody who might smoke cigarettes in the Tony Tiger suit. It would be a fire hazard, plus the local kids might see him setting a bad example.

On September 20, I decided to fire Sherman Rochell. Not that I was alone in my sentiments. We needed two post players. He took the news a bit harder than Eric Siebrands—he got deathly quiet.

John Folan's assistant coach connections helped get Rochell a week-long tryout with Limerick. They still needed an American. But he declined; he wanted to go home. That surprised me. I figured as long as he was here in Ireland he might as well give Limerick a try. He had to travel through Limerick to get back to the airport anyway.

You didn't need to be an expert to see that things were off to a bad start. My built-in advantage had busted his Achilles tendon, and my American imports were gone before they'd gotten over their jetlag.

I was supposed to be working on my story collection during my free time, but with the firing of our Yanks, I was on the phone constantly. I was back to the hassle of being a recruiter, except now I was being paid minimum wage. When I tried to write, I had trouble focusing. The Frosties Tigers problems were swallowing me and I was getting a familiar ache in my gut.

Also, the mobile phone was making me sick. Really sick. I got nauseated and had a headache after two minutes on the thing. (I put it in a drawer then gave it away in January.) I was told that phone nausea was a common Irish complaint. Then I did some research, and learned that according to British doctors, cell phones could be linked to brain cancer. Yet a mobile phone was the first thing they'd given me when I arrived. They might as well have given me a carton of cigarettes. Maybe my nausea was psychological. And maybe some of this was my own aversion to technology. Had old-time fiddling done that to me? The first time Junior Collins came to my apartment he was miffed. "Where's your television, like?" he wondered. I hadn't had one for years. Purchasing a laptop was a big technological concession for me. Other Americans might not have noticed Ireland's proliferation of cell phones. It's possible it stood out to me due to the ancient history that lurked behind everything.

Legend has it that St. Patrick drove the snakes out of Ireland. If he ever returns, maybe he can drive out the mobile phones.

The New Road

After Ciaran Dalton blessed me with the Irish music schedule, nearly every evening was taken up with traditional tunes. At first I'd only listen—there were terrific players and it was a little daunting. Some of the Betty's Pub musicians played the other sessions, and soon they recognized me lurking on the edge of the music. They'd introduce me to the others, and naturally, that would lead to an invitation: "Bring your fiddle next time." I didn't right away, as I was still a bit intimidated.

I'd started to become familiar with the Irish sense of humor and indirectness. After a catchy set of tunes, I'd asked the nearest fiddler, a man named Kerry Barrett, the names of the ones they'd just played. He said, "Well, the first tune is called "The Maid Behind the Bar." And the second tune isn't." When I asked Ciaran Dalton if I could get to his Saturday session by taking the Listowel road, he thought for a second, then offered this: "You could take the Listowel road, but you'd be going the wrong way."

I learned later that slowly easing my way into the music scene was a major plus. It seemed that the common American brashness was a turn-off to the Irish, especially the musicians. I lacked confidence, but that endeared me quickly to the Irish players.

Once I did start bringing my fiddle to every session, someone would say, "Rus, go on and start up a tune." Or, "Let's hear an American tune." And I'd sheepishly decline. And they'd say, "Aww, go on, go on. You will. You will. Do." And I'd decline again. I only wanted to learn *their* tunes. It turned out that in Irish music session culture, this was exactly the correct etiquette.

The Kerry Star

The last weekend in September the All-Ireland Gaelic Football Championship was played. Each of Ireland's thirty-two counties, including Northern Ireland, has a team. That season it all boiled down to our Kerry team, a perennial power, against underdog Armagh from the North. Kerry had won more than thirty All-Ireland titles in the last hundred years. No other county had been close to being as dominant. Armagh had never won the All-Ireland, and they were dismissed as having no chance before the game began. At least that was the prevailing opinion in Tralee, the capital of Kerry.

Tralee was a ghost town a half-hour before game time. I tried a couple of restaurants for lunch, but they were shut down. Green and gold flags were flying everywhere. Finally I gave up on eating a real meal and settled for peanuts and Guinness at the Greyhound Pub. People cheered every play lustily, as if the fate of free Ireland hung in the balance.

It looked like the boys from Kerry had the match under control, but at the very end County Armagh took the lead and kept it, stunning Kerry—and everyone in the pub, as well.

And there I was, surrounded by sports fans. Yet nobody said, "How are the Tigers shaping up, Coach?"

The Boys of the Town

I wasn't supposed to bitch at the Irish guys. They played for free, and would remind me of that fact occasionally. This frustrated me at first. We only trained three days a week, for a total of five hours, yet we had fewer than ten guys at nearly every practice. We were competing in Ireland's equivalent of the NBA, but our practice schedule didn't approach the rigors of high school ball in the States.

The two American replacements got to Ireland three days later. I hoped this would be our last roster change; it was getting harder to keep their names straight. I had tried to implement the man-to-man defensive system that I'd learned from Don Haskins at UTEP. We would stress, first, our getting back on defense and not surrendering fast-break baskets. Staying in a stance and helping each other on defense was critical. On offense I put in a double post set I'd learned from Lou Henson. Barnaby Craddock would ignite our offense, depending on which side of the court he entered the ball.

The season started in three weeks. Here was the scouting report for the Frosties Tigers, including our two new imports:

Chris Thompson   6'7"   Northwestern   23 years old
                                          State (Lousiana)

Led NSU to its first-ever NCAA tournament. His coach was the respected but little-known Mike McConathy, who said Thompson had rabid intensity, could guard anybody, was a good passer and a tenacious board-man. The downside to Thompson's toughness was that he could come across as mentally unbalanced. He was so hyped up that at times it was scary. At his college coach's suggestion, we decided to fine him fifty euros for any techni-cal foul. Thompson's stats at NSU were about the same as Sherman Rochell's at the University of Denver. But Thompson led his team to the NCAA tour-nament, and Rochell's team did poorly. Also, Coach McConathy let Chris Thompson baby-sit his kids last year when his eligibility expired and he was finishing school. That was a good sign. No coach would let a bad egg around his children.

Chris Davis   6'7"   Pensacola JC/   29 years old
                                      Auburn U/Lynn U (Florida)

Another Chris. For the Irish guys that meant two tall, black, American Chrisses. Davis had been considered one of the best junior college players in the country eight years earlier. At Auburn he played well before academic problems dragged him down. He was cat-quick when he wanted to be. He had good stats for Killester of Dublin the previous season, but they didn't bring him back. That scared me. Rumor had him being more interested in the nightlife than the games. But the Frosties Tigers had to take a chance on an experienced player. Davis had been making a living each summer by raising and selling dogs, he told me. That sounded nice—an animal lover. I found out later that he raised pit bulls. Davis loved to cook, which would make him popular with his new roommates. His JC coach, Bob Marlin, was now the coach at Sam Houston State. I phoned Marlin the night before Davis was to arrive, hoping for reassurances. "Chris is a fine player when he gets in shape," Marlin said. "Don't let the dreadlocks bother you."

Dreadlocks? Nobody said anything to me about dreadlocks.

Davis had a vast array of low-post moves and had tremendous balance. He could make shots with either hand at all kinds of angles, his dreadlocks swirling. But he was laid-back. And he was very interested in when our "off days" would be. He was a little loose and carefree for my tastes. Davis arrived in Tralee with a woman from Dublin under his arm, although he kept reassuring me she wasn't his girlfriend. When she went to the toilet, I reminded him that he was in Ireland to play ball, and that we weren't going to be subsidizing a Dublin vacation. Dublin was nearly five hours from Tralee on the train. Davis was at a crossroads in his career and should have been making bigger money somewhere else in Europe with his talent. I told him as much—he'd either go up or down from Tralee.

Those were my two Americans. The rest of the Frosties Tigers:

| **Micheal Quirke** | 6'6" | Bouncer/College student/ | 22 years old |
| | | Gaelic Footballer | |

Quirke was finishing his degree at Institute of Technology of Tralee. At 230 pounds, he was puffy with baby fat. Of course he was downright svelte compared to a certain injured Tiger. Quirke was one of the better Gaelic Footballers in Tralee; not yet good enough to be on the prestigious County Kerry team, but close. Despite football training curtailing his attendance at Tigers' training, he dragged himself to basketball and joined us for the last hour. He was a fine shooter, a bit slow, but a deft passer because of Gaelic Football, where field vision is a must. He was likely a starter for the Tigers as soon as football ended. If his football club advanced in the county playoffs, I wouldn't have him until December, meaning he'd miss a half-dozen games.

| **John Teahan** (captain) | 6'1" | Ambulance EMT | 32 years old |

Teahan came to only half the practices because of work and family commitments. He was married with two young kids, a boy and a girl. When he showed up, practices improved. He was rugged and aggressive but as slow as Irish history. Also he was extremely stubborn, at least off the court. I wasn't sure if that helped his game or not. Still, he could score. Teahan was respected throughout Ireland for his battling style. The only Irish player who didn't live in Tralee, it took him an hour to drive to practice.

Kevin O'Donoghue   5'6"   Grocery Store Manager   23 years old

Kevin had the most difficult Kerry accent on the team. When he introduced himself I thought he said he was somebody's little brother. A common mistake, probably, because he looked like a little kid. His job at Garvey's SuperValu was nine-to-five. His attendance at practice was good, and he was an adequate backup point guard. A smart player, he made a minimum of mistakes. Kevin was one of my favorites, I'll admit, mostly because he was so dependable. He'd stick his tiny frame in there and scrap. Also, he cared about the history of Ireland and Tralee. We'd be in trouble if he had to play a lot, but Kevin was a great guy to have as our ninth or tenth man.

Aidan O'Shea   5'6"   Unemployed   22 years old

A lefty, Aidan was awful at first. He had a bunch of tattoos (one of Bob Marley, or perhaps Chris Davis), and a gut. He told me he hadn't played basketball in six months, a common ailment in the Irish Super League. Then he got in better shape, learned the offense, and improved. Then he got diagnosed with diabetes and was out for a month.

Alan Keane   5'11"   Health Club   24 years old
                              Instructor

Alan was easily my best three-point shooter. Fairly athletic, Alan was in terrific shape because he swam for an hour every day. He swam because he had shin splints, which was why he hadn't played basketball for a few years. Alan was a bit injury prone; he'd already had a sore throat the first week. And he missed practice sometimes because he worked at the Sports Complex, where we played our games, teaching swimming and weight training. Still, his shooting would be important, and I was counting on him to be a key reserve and possibly start some games. Unlike most good shooters, who bristle with confidence, he seemed introverted and sensitive.

David "Super Dave" Cronin   5'11"   Stockboy   20 years old

David had glasses as thick as scones, and the minute he started sweating, his glasses fogged up and he couldn't see. Until they fell off, which happened a lot, because he didn't have a strap on the back of them. He was about fifteen pounds overweight. His gym shoes should have been in a museum. They looked like Irish historical artifacts. "Super Dave," as the Americans affectionately tabbed him, kept those shoes barely tied, because he only had one shoelace, which he'd divided between the two shoes. The name "Super Dave" was in homage to the guy who'd appear on *The Late Show with David Letterman* to do fake stunts where he'd crash at the end. The TV would switch to a video of Super Dave, ready to jump over ten semi-trucks on a motorcycle. Then the bike would smash right into the first truck. Both Super Daves were clumsy, heroically unheroic. Our Super Dave never missed a practice.

Liam Culloty   5'11"   Student-UCC (Cork)   18 years old

Liam could shoot three-pointers if left open. But he needed lots of time, because he shot from his hip. He could help us in spots because he was a smart passer. But by September 15, he was off to college in Cork, two hours away, and couldn't practice. Liam reminded me before he left for college that he would still be available to play in the games. I was hoping I wouldn't have to use a guy who couldn't attend practice. Liam knew his limitations. His father was a basketball coach, one of the few I'd met, and Dad seemed appreciative of the attention I was giving his son.

Barnaby Craddock   6'1"   Canadian/Golfer/Bosman   31 years old

---

Perhaps because he'd missed the first two weeks of practice, he was already a bit of a mystery to me. Was I unfairly jealous of Barnaby being pals with the ex-coach? Barnaby had been a terrific player, but he seemed dissatisfied from the minute I'd met him. He was a sharpshooter that we needed to play the point guard spot. He had the skills to be a good point guard, but seemed to be a whiner. Could it be that a few years in the Irish Super League would spoil a guy? Before Ireland, Barnaby played in Norway, where basketball ranked well below fishing in national sports prestige. And before that he toiled for Canada's Lethbridge College, another basketball hotbed. So it was hard to figure why his head was inflated.

But I was stuck with him, at least for the year: Super League rules dictated that after October 1, you couldn't change Bosman players. I had less than a week to make a change, and figured we'd better try and ride it out. I never learned if his golf game was any good.

Roscoe Patterson	6'4"	Nike Store Clerk	39 years old

Roscoe had been a Super League star in the 1990s and was an American who lived in Tralee. He could practice, but wasn't allowed to play in games unless one of our two Yankees got hurt—sort of a one-man taxi squad. He was smart and crafty, and having him at practice was a big boost. He had been in the States until October, so he missed our first twelve practices. Roscoe was impeccably dressed at all times, but his style was sort of teen-hip-hop sports: maybe a loud orange Tennessee jersey with matching orange shoelaces and cap. His outfits matched his personality. He had a bright and wide smile, laughed easily, and he was a talker on the floor, in a good way.

Ricardo Leonard	6'8" 270 and rising	Sporting Goods Clerk	32 years old

Likely out for the year with an Achilles injury.

And our dynamic coaching staff:

John Folan	5'5"	Assistant Coach/ Pub Manager	32 years old

John would be at practice when he was not managing the pub in Dingle or getting married or on his honeymoon. His fiancée/wife Tara was our statistician. John's busy pub schedule meant that he would only be at a third of the practices, so I'd often only see him once a week.

Rus Bradburd	5'11"	Head Coach/ Fiddler/Writer	43 years old

I suppose if I was honest, my coaching bio might read like this: *A once-promising college coaching career fizzled at UTEP, then was put on hold at New Mexico State in order for Bradburd to, bizarrely, get a degree in writing. Perhaps the only basketball coach in the world to play the fiddle. Sorting out his true feelings toward basketball could help the new mentor of the Frosties Tigers be more effective. Does he want to be a writer or a basketball coach? And can his relationship with Connie last?*

My player's bio would have read like this: *Neurotic practicing has given him marvelous ball-handling skills, but his heavy-legged yet lean-framed, nonathletic body means he'll never be a player. Still, his maniacal obsession resulted in him being impressive at dribbling drills. A small-college benchwarmer, he was a decent shooter if nobody was near him. Likely could not have been a starter even in the Irish Super League.*

COME ALL YE GOOD FELLOWS

I continued to try to merge the Frosties Tigers with St. Brendan's club. Surprisingly, after two meetings, it looked like it might work. Years of bickering, jealousy, and divided loyalties would be put behind us. This time I met with the St. Brendan's folks alone. The word had filtered back to them that the new American coach was offering to do dribbling clinics at schools around Tralee for free. I wasn't an altruist; rather, the gesture would boost interest and attendance, improving the Tigers' financial situation. The St. Brendan's folks were impressed that I wasn't out to gouge Irish kids for their last euro.

I could tell that the St. Brendan's folks were put off by William Main and Junior Collins. They looked at William as a guy who talked through his checkbook. Fair enough. He was a successful businessman. He was not from Tralee, and he represented all they thought was wrong with our top-heavy structure that ignored the local young kids. Too bad, because William, if anything bad could be said about him, was merely too nice a guy. When he was not telling me our season would be lost if the Frosties Tigers did not win the first game at Belfast, William repeatedly told me how important it was to get our youth programs rolling.

Junior Collins was a different story. He was a little too rough around the edges, even for their working-class committee. At the previous St. Brendan's powwow, Junior spent much of the time looking over his own shoulder at the soccer on television. Or else he was holding his face in his hands and shaking his head. That was no way to come to an agreement for a merger. He seemed to be the target of much of the animosity from St. Brendan's and admitted to bitter arguments with their people in the past.

Junior told me, "I nearly came to blows with one of them a few years ago, like."

"What was that about?"

"Because he told me I didn't know the difference between a basketball and a turnip."

I knew Junior knew the difference, so I didn't ask for proof.

Was it Junior's outspokenness or his appearance that bugged St. Brendan's? He wore *exactly* the same clothes every day: black polyester pants, with either paint or milkshake stains on them, and a black Frosties Tigers jacket. He shaved once a week. His hands were always soiled, and his hair was a mess. Yet Junior was point man on a lot of our business deals. That was largely because he was in Tralee all summer, which William Main and John Folan were not. It was Junior asking for donations for our poster. He was the first person the American players met when they got off the plane. And it was Junior going to the bank to set up our account. And knocking on doors, fund-raising.

Junior hated every other team in the Super League, but not as much as he hated St. Brendan's.

Here's a riddle I wouldn't tell Junior:

Q. What do you get when you cross an Irishman with a turnip?
A. A turnip with a grudge.

When William did come to town, we were quite a group. Me, the American coach they were genuinely proud of. William, the tall and priestly businessman. And Junior Collins. Junior was a volunteer, as were William and John Folan, so I couldn't complain. How could I complain about volunteer help, from committee members to Irish players?

The next time, I met with the St. Brendan's committee alone. Nobody offered me a pint of Guinness or a cup of tea. I could feel the hostility radiating, and I had just met these people. But I was able to get them to cool down by promising that the American players and I would volunteer our help every Sunday, the only day their youth teams practiced. They said they'd need a few days and they'd give me their final decision. It sounded good but they'd have to discuss it when I wasn't around.

Bung Your Eye

In Ardfert, a village ten minutes from Tralee, there was a lively Thursday music session. A dozen musicians—banjo, fiddles, whistle, accordion, mandolin, guitar—welcomed me with a seat right in the middle of the group, where I tried to keep up with the bouncy reels until my third Guinness. At that point I just smiled and tapped my toe to the music. I was improving, and could play more Irish tunes, but I knew my limits and didn't want to annoy the others.

I'd rented a bicycle and ridden through Ardfert the previous week. The ruins of a twelfth-century cathedral, one of the best preserved in Ireland, stood fifty yards from the pub. The patrons of the pub were shoulder to shoulder, and they were enthusiastic about traditional music. Black slate covered the floor, and the corners of the pub were filled with eighty-year-old men in the tweed caps that were still worn in the rural parts of old Ireland. It was a session where musicians drank free; the table in the middle of the circle teetered with full pints of Guinness, patiently waiting behind half-full pints.

Near evening's end, I mentioned to the fiddler next to me that I'd started taking lessons from Paddy Jones, thinking maybe he might know Paddy.

"What right," he yelled over the chatter between tunes, "does Paddy Jones have to teach *ye* the fiddle? What the hell right?" His face turned a bright pink, as if I'd insulted him.

Suddenly I was on the brink of a brawl. Gee, I didn't know, I said, I suppose Paddy Jones has to earn a living, and it depends—

"Is he qualified to teach you? What are his qualifications?" he said. And so on. He looked like he might grab my fiddle and smash it on the table. But it was just the usual slagging. Maybe this fellow was joking. He certainly couldn't have believed that I was too advanced for a lesson, or that Paddy Jones was giving me lessons against my will. He did have one good piece of Zen-like advice that the Frosties Tigers could have used:

"Just play hard, play the hell out of that thing. You'll be all right."

On October 2, St. Brendan's rejected our offer to merge. This meant the Frosties Tigers were stuck practicing with fewer than ten players all year. The long-term future of the Frosties Tigers was in serious jeopardy. The Tigers didn't have enough good young players to leave much of a team when Teahan and Ricardo retired.

St. Brendan's didn't trust our stability, which might have been smart on their part. I later discovered that we owed money to Presentation School, where we rented the gym for last year's practices, and a couple other small accounts around Tralee still needed to be settled. Also, the Tigers had a track record of funneling money and effort into the Super League and ignoring the young kids.

One victim was an eighteen-year-old by the name of Sean Carroll. Like Liam Culloty, he was off at school in Cork, but he was going to play with us on the weekends. Now he had to choose: Super League Tigers, or county league St. Brendan's? To most American kids it would be a no-brainer: play at the highest level, especially if you were not going to be a benchwarmer. And Sean could have wound up our sixth man, with Alan Keane's shins the way they were. Junior reminded me that the kid named Kieran Donaghy was in the same boat, "Although there's no fear of Kieran Donaghy going off to college," he said.

But both were being tugged at by old loyalties. The woes and burdens of being Irish.

The Garden of Daisies

We were to play our first game in Belfast October 5th, less than a week away. At a rare Sunday practice, my country-clubbing Canadian waltzed in forty minutes late, golf bag in tow.

This had huge ramifications because Barnaby, along with my Americans, was getting paid. If I let this go, what would happen when Davis, my Rasta power forward, came in late? Would we let that go, too? How could I keep the Irish players punctual if the paid players were late?

I didn't say much, letting him into the drills after he'd warmed up a minute. I was trying not to react in anger. When we finished practice I told him he'd have to run a few "17s"—a grueling running drill. And, true to form, Barnaby had a better idea:

"Why not," he suggested, "have me do a drill that would incorporate shooting *and* dribbling, all the while—"

I cut him off. No, I said. Run.

I decided to fine him, which I hadn't had to do until then. Three euros a minute. So, one hundred and twenty euros. He'd understand the big fine better than the half-dozen talks we'd had about getting his head in the right place. Besides golfing and complaining, he spent most of his time badgering William Main for perks.

This was a guy who, by the way, told me he'd like to be an American college coach when he was done playing, although he still had a year's worth of schooling to finish his Physical Education degree. Thirty-one years old, couldn't complete a Phys Ed degree, a big ego, and a committed golfer. The American universities would be clamoring for him to coach the minute he retired from playing.

On a dreary morning in early October, one of the ladies from the Women's Resource Center knocked on my door and said that Junior Collins was looking for me. I had been in the shower and hadn't heard the bell.

Junior was waiting outside. He said, "William Main wants to meet with us for lunch. It's urgent, like."

At the pub, William and Junior suddenly grew somber.

"We've decided that Chris Thompson isn't good enough for Ireland. We should fire him immediately," William said. Now keep in mind William had attended, in his lifetime, about fifty basketball games. Neither William nor Junior had ever played or coached. William usually prefaced his comments with, "Now I don't know anything about basketball, but—" And Junior was the one who the guy from St. Brendan's challenged on the basketball/ turnip issue.

"Thompson has only been here ten days," I said.

"We don't think Chris Thompson can shoot it well enough, like," Junior said.

"Although we don't doubt he's giving one hundred and ten percent," William added.

It didn't take me long to suspect that my captain, John Teahan, was behind this. William claiming it was his idea alone made it seem all the more obvious.

When I asked William whom he proposed we hire, he didn't miss a beat: Jermaine Turner. I imagined John Teahan sitting behind William and whispering in his ear.

I hoped I was wrong because I'd started to appreciate Teahan. He was a fighter. Still, Teahan had spearheaded the "dump the Americans" campaign last time.

"Listen," I said. "William, you promised me control of the basketball decisions of the Frosties Tigers. And I consider Chris Thompson's ability a basketball issue."

William nodded and smiled, but he seemed near tears. I was trying to be nonconfrontational, but I had to stand my ground.

"If the committee wants to fly Thompson home, that's fine, but fly me home as well," I said. They needed to decide if they were going to back me or not. I couldn't run a team where the players outranked the coach.

Altogether, it was a very discouraging day with my basketball judgment being called into question. The panic was on because we might have to start 5'6" Kevin O'Donoghue, who could be mistaken for the ball boy, or Alan Keane.

Later that day, William called me and told me he'd met with our esteemed committee. Guess what?

"We've decided to back you, Rus, one hundred and ten percent."

The entire committee would have been perplexed by the turnip question. But I thanked him for the vote of confidence anyway.

The Crooked Road

Belfast was a seven-hour ride from Tralee. Junior Collins suggested we drive the seven hours on the Saturday of the game, then stay over in a hotel *after* the game. "That way," he said, "the lads won't be worried that they have a long bus ride back to Tralee after the game, like."

That was the dumbest thing I'd ever heard. Why wouldn't we go up to Belfast the night before, and lounge around the hotel on game day? Instead Junior wanted to cram everyone into a bus for seven hours, then play the game. How could any player think about the bus trip back during the game? Finally I convinced Junior of the logic of my plan.

Then the bad news hit. Alan Keane, our swimming and fitness instructor, rang me. "I can't go to Belfast with the Tigers," he said. "I've signed up for a seven-week course, teaching English as a second language, and it kicks off this weekend."

Alan Keane was now a starter, our best shooter, but he couldn't go to our road games for the next two months. It was awful timing too, four days before our first game.

Here was another quandary that the Irish National Coach, Bill Dooley, tried to warn me about: a coach couldn't operate in Ireland with his American compass. Seven Frosties Tigers remained. Two of them were 5'6". In the States I would have dumped Alan Keane. But if I did that in Tralee, we'd be stuck with *six* players until Micheal Quirke finished Gaelic football, which continued to drag on at the local level. I was missing Ricardo (Achilles), Aidan O'Shea (diabetes), and Quirke (football). Roscoe was only practicing to help us out. Teahan had work and family issues. Liam Culloty was off at college in Cork during the week.

Alan Keane was the worst with excuses: swollen glands, couldn't get off work at the Sports Complex, bad ankle, bad shins. Keane was frail, but you wouldn't think so from looking at his weightlifter's build. He'd never played much in the Super League. Now that he'd earned a starting assignment he shied away.

This job was supposed to be like a vacation. Now the worst thing that can happen to a coach was happening to me: I was starting to dislike all my players.

The St. Brendan's folks told me the kids in Tralee didn't flock to the Tigers because they didn't want to sit on the bench behind the paid Americans. Yet Sean Carroll told me he'd decided to play for St. Brendan's. The rumor was that Kieran Donaghy was going to as well. And Alan Keane wouldn't step forward. Anyone who did would be a full-time player in the top league in Ireland.

Unfortunately, the guy stepping forward was 5'6".

The Piper's Despair

Barnaby came over that Wednesday to complain about the 120 euro fine. He declined a cup of tea, and instead took out a piece of paper with his figures. "By my calculations," he said, "the club is fining me thirty-three percent of my weekly salary, yet I only missed a fraction of my workweek." He was looking past me when he said it, as if there were someone behind me.

We practiced only three days a week, I told him, looking over my shoulder to try and figure out what he was staring at.

But Barnaby claimed his work hours included weightlifting and the vast amount of stretching he did at home. He was counting stretching as work? That was an interesting concept. He figured the fine should only be sixteen euros, based on the percentage of time he missed.

It occurred to me at that moment what he was leering at: my shiny new toaster, which had come with my furnished apartment. We had the same landlord, and I was sure he'd complain to William Main if he thought his toaster was not up to snuff.

I didn't want to get mucked up in Barnaby's contractual situation, but I needed him emotionally focused. I was disliking him more than was healthy for a coach.

I sat at the window, looking down at the wet streets, with Barnaby walking away and the locals scurrying about. I took out my computer to try to come up with a less-sentimental ending to the short story I was working on. Minutes later the doorbell rang again.

This time it was Chris Thompson. He had heard, from Barnaby, that some people on our committee wanted to fire him and bring back Jermaine Turner. Only three of us were at that meeting—myself, William Main, and Junior Collins. And that was something no coach would want: one of your best players feeling unwanted.

Junior must have mentioned something to his wife, who was the old coach's sister. And the old coach told Barnaby, over golf. Or toast.

I tried to calm Thompson. He was excitable by nature, and he knew it. I assured him that he was not on the chopping block, not before we'd even played a single game.

The instant I restarted my computer, the doorbell was buzzing. This time it was William Main, with his ever-present briefcase. Three kitchen-table meetings in one day. It suddenly seemed I might never again have the peace and solitude to write or fiddle.

"I had a lovely Chinese meal at the Rose Garden," William said. Then, after a pause, almost as an afterthought, he added, "Barnaby is insisting on a meeting with the committee. He claims the fine you hit him with was unfair. Also you don't give him enough notice as to when he's required to lift weights." William again looked as though he might start weeping. I tried to calm him, and he reminded me how he hated confrontation of any kind. William said he feared Barnaby would quit if he didn't get his way on this matter. Often a coach has to build up a player emotionally, tell him he can play, that he can do the job. But I seemed to spend more time doing it with William than with any of the Frosties Tigers.

"You *have* to back me on this fine," I told him. "Remember how your first question to me was could I discipline the Tigers?"

He did. And I told him that it would ruin my authority to be overruled on this. Barnaby was a problem that I had not yet figured out, I admitted.

"Do you think Barnaby is giving one hundred and ten percent?" he asked.

"William," I said, "*approaching* one hundred percent is all we can ask." Then I asked him if the committee was involved in the decision to fire the old coach.

No, he said, he made that decision himself. He snapped his briefcase shut and headed for the door.

Maybe I'd be going home sooner than I thought. I'd been in Ireland six weeks.

Later that evening, Barnaby met with William and backed down from his demands. A few days passed. I went for some long walks to Tralee Bay, and decided I'd come down on Barnaby too hard. So I decided to drop the fine to a euro per minute, making it an even forty. Then I went and told Barnaby. He was grateful. I couldn't afford to lose him, and he said he didn't really want to walk away.

Daddy on the Turnpike

The day before we left to play Belfast's Star of the Sea team, the police in Northern Ireland raided a Sinn Fein office and arrested four people. Sinn Fein is the political wing of the Irish Republican Army. The arrests put the latest never-ending talks in limbo, and there were already rumors of violent reprisals on both sides.

This made a few of my Irish Tigers nervous, since Kerry was known in the north as a Republican stronghold. Especially fidgety was Kevin O'Donoghue, who had the best sense of history on the squad. The Frosties Tigers had been targeted in minor incidents before—some rock-throwing at the bus by Protestant Belfast kids. But the Belfast team played out in the suburbs now, so I wasn't too worried.

I became worried, however, when I was the only one waiting for the bus at the allotted time. Fifteen minutes later, we had an impromptu team meeting. I told the newly arrived Frosties Tigers I didn't just want them to be on time for practices. They had to be ready to travel at the appointed time. Then, as if to prove me a fool, the bus driver was thirty minutes late for our trek across Ireland. We stood around in the drizzle, the players using their mobile phones to track down William and finally the bus driver, who was waiting in the wrong place. We were scheduled to stay at a hotel after getting most of the way to Belfast, so we wouldn't be on the bus for long on game day.

As soon as the bus got out of Tralee, the players continued what I learned was a Tigers tradition: trying to stump Junior Collins with movie trivia. The whole team ganged up on Junior, but he knew it all. Actors, directors, film titles. Junior had brought his son Tomas, who munched on candy and stared out the window, not as impressed with Junior's cinematic expertise as I was.

Five hours later, the hotel had no record of the Frosties Tigers' reservations. I paced in the lobby as the players snoozed in lounge chairs for an hour until the rooms were ready.

The next afternoon, on the two-lane highway to Belfast, our bus driver cried out in alarm. A van we were tailing was swerving in and out of oncoming traffic. We all yelled, as if that would do any good, and finally the van ran head-on into an approaching subcompact car and bounced the little blue Honda back eighty yards. The Honda looked like an accordion on wheels.

The bus stopped. John Teahan, our ambulance worker, sprinted to the smashed car. I followed behind—quite a bit slower, due to fear as much as my own lack of speed—lugging our bus driver's fire extinguisher. I was certain the two passengers, slumped over the dash, were dead. Miraculously, they weren't. They were badly shaken up, but not even bleeding. Neither was the driver of the van, who was very apologetic. We waited, holding up traffic in both directions, until the ambulance and police showed up. The van's driver, twenty-five years old, claimed he'd blacked out.

One hour later, we arrived at the Belfast team's gym, which was on a college campus in Jordanstown—a good name for the location of a basketball match. While the team was changing I found a quiet place in a dark hallway and gave myself sort of an anti-pep talk: "This is a low-level game. You've been in eight NCAA tournaments as a coach. This is meaningless, so relax. You're in Ireland to be a writer and nobody back home cares how the Tigers do. Hell, hardly anybody in Ireland cares either."

That last part was confirmed minutes later when I walked in the gym.

During my seasons at UTEP and NMSU we'd play in front of ten thousand fans on any given night. I had no illusions that Ireland would be the same. Still, it was disheartening to walk into a gym with only two hundred fans—although they pretty much filled the place. The Belfast coach, Danny Fulton, carried himself like the elder statesman of Irish basketball, which, it turned out, he was. He'd been the National Team coach—Bill Dooley's job—years ago, and was well-dressed, dignified, and humble.

Right away his Belfast team slammed us like the van had done to the pitiful compact Honda. Before we knew it, we were down 22–4.

Chris Davis apparently had a blackout like the ill-fated van driver, because whomever he was assigned to guard—we kept switching to find someone he could possibly contain—either scored or drew a foul. By Junior Collins's calculations, Davis personally gave up 25 points by halftime.

I was miserable and anxious on the sidelines, but I was determined to handle our first-game jitters stoically. During timeouts I talked to the Tigers about sticking to our offense and not getting riled up or frustrated. Belfast had a tall team, and they had their own third American, John Leahy, who (like our Ricardo Leonard) was married to an Irish woman. He'd played at Seton Hall University, and drained threes like they were layups—5 for 6 on the night.

The Frosties Tigers kept hustling, and the Belfast lead slowly dissolved. We had cut the lead to 6 points at halftime. In the locker room, Chris Davis announced that the soles of his shoes were slippery. He said he thought we'd be playing at the *other* gym in Belfast, and that was why he'd brought these faulty shoes.

After the break Barnaby got hot, pouring in the bulk of his 24 points. John Teahan made some big baskets, and we took the lead with two and a half minutes to go. The gym sank into a solemn quiet while the Belfast boys let things slip. It looked like a miraculous comeback for the Tralee team.

With two minutes to go, our double-post offense found Chris Thompson in the low post, where he was fouled on the shot. He missed both free throws badly. The seasoned Belfast boys knew what to do. They fouled Thompson again the instant he caught the ball on our next possession. Thompson missed four more free throws in the final minute, and we lost, 90–89. It was a dramatic comeback on our longest road trip of the season. Still, we were 0–1.

Sleeping on the ride back was out of the question, as much because of the pregame car crash as because of the lousy way we started the game. We got back at 4:30 A.M.

And that was my first game in the Irish Super League.

The next night I played the Sunday session at Betty's Pub in Tralee. Betty's happened to be the pub where the fans of Micheal Quirke's Gaelic Football team hung out after matches, and so if I missed a Sunday football match, I always heard about it in the evening.

Ciaran Dalton, his wife Colette, and two other musicians were there. Betty's had the open fireplace going, which the musicians avoided because the intense heat played games with our steel strings, affecting the tuning.

Ciaran was always interested in talking about American old-time music, but I badgered him to play Irish tunes. I suppose I was worried that he'd ask me to begin an Appalachian tune on my own, which could mean several fine musicians not playing a note, just listening to me. I wasn't ready for that.

We started in on the music. Ciaran had solid forearms, wide sideburns, and in the soft pub lighting his face had the power and tint of an American Indian chief. He always wore an earthy wool sweater that looked like a vestige of the 1800s. I'd learned you could get on his bad side—I'd heard of it happening to other musicians—if you were arrogant, irreverent, or inconsiderate. He was stubborn about his music and a purist in a way that was fairly unpredictable. Also, he couldn't care less about basketball, or sports in general for that matter. To me, Ciaran was like the Chieftain of the Tralee music scene—he'd founded most of the sessions in and around Tralee. Some had been going continuously for decades.

Ciaran liked nothing better than to talk between tunes about the traditions within Irish music. "There's quite a few tunes that came back," he said that night, "Irish tunes that went to America during an exodus of poor Irish folks, only to migrate back with a fiddler or 78-recording at some point, slightly different. It was as if the tune was changed by the overseas experience. Some tunes are practically identical, but with different names, Irish and American."

Ciaran had many examples: "The Belle of Lexington" was the American version of "Kitty's Wedding." Ireland's "Miss McLeod's Reel" was called "Hop High, Ladies" in America. "Anything for John-Joe" sounded very close to the eastern Kentucky tune "Devil Ate the Groundhog." The West

Virginia tune "Waynesboro" was called "Over the Moore to Maggie" by the Irish. The list went on, and the tune names were part of the fun: fascinating, or disturbing, or curious, or melancholic.

Irish tunes were circular, like the American old-time numbers. They usually had an "A" and "B" part, each played twice. Both forms were originally dance music, either to a "set" dance or a "called" dance, like an American barn dance or square dance.

In the American old-time tradition, musicians play the same tune for perhaps five minutes, which transforms the musicians into a trance-like groove. Also, the longer jams allow you to learn tunes on the fly.

The Irish, on the other hand, played a tune through three times, then it was on to the next tune, without a break. They'd often play three or four in a row, not missing a beat or taking a breath. That made it harder to learn because just when you thought, "I've got this one!" they were already off to the next one. It also meant there were three times as many titles to learn. I'd never learned a single tune without a title to go with it—until I went to Ireland. I was surprised to find that some Irish players didn't have names for their tunes. Or if they did, the tune had been played three tunes previously, and nobody could recall. Local fiddle wizard Kerry Barrett told me, "We know thousands of tunes. We know thousands of names. But we don't know the names and the tunes together."

Late that evening, Ciaran leaned over and asked me to start up an old-time tune. I was hesitant, because the leader or best musician usually kicked off the tune.

I began flipping through my mental index cards for a simple number. I sawed out a few bars as a sample and asked Ciaran if he knew it: "Johnny, Don't Get Drunk."

"Go ahead and play it," he said without cracking a smile, "but it will never catch on here."

After I played "Johnny, Don't Get Drunk" once around, the others joined in as though they'd been born playing it. That was a relief. Afterward, we toasted the mythical Johnny, downed our pints, and waved for more.

That left a natural spot for a short break in the tunes. We had drinkers crowded around us, and one of them broke into a sad song, in Irish. Ciaran said it was a sad one, anyway. We had time to rest as we waited for our fresh pints.

American old-time ones often involve the name of a river, or mountain, a farm animal, or often a lady's name. "What's the story behind the titles of Irish tunes?" I asked.

Ciaran said there were a lot of common themes. "Cooley's Fancy. Anybody's fancy. Plenty of roads, too. The Road to Limerick. The Rocky Road to Dublin. The road to anywhere," he said. "Roads and travel are very Irish. And people's names in the titles, especially Paddy. Like Paddy on the Railroad. Paddy Go Easy. Paddy anything, really."

"Let's not have a lecture," Colette said. "Let's have a tune."

"When things go wrong," Ciaran said, looking at me, "someone creates a tune out of their sadness." Ciaran put a hand on my shoulder. Irish men were much more affectionate than American men are. They'd wink at each other, or put hands on the sides of a cheek, as if they'd never see each other again, or might go blind and needed to memorize a face. "How did your team do in Belfast?" he said. "The Tigers, is it?"

I was surprised he knew we'd played. Could he see it in my face that the Frosties Tigers had lost a heartbreaker?

"We came in second," I said.

"There's a fiddle tune named for every sorrow," Ciaran said, ignoring my humor. "And for every joy. It's just that there's more sorrow in Ireland." And as he said that, the bar got quieter, as if everyone were listening, although that couldn't have been true. Maybe the singer had finished and we had a gap.

"Enough talk, lads," Colette said, looking at Ciaran.

We took up our fiddles and flutes. Ciaran reached for his mandolin but he didn't play. It was as though he were trying to decide and, despite knowing a thousand tunes, he couldn't think of a single one. He turned and leaned close to my ear.

"You're on the road to something, right? In Ireland? You'll have your own fiddle tune by the end of your work here."

Ciaran started plucking out a tune I didn't know. Although I'd at least *heard* hundreds, I was sure I'd never heard that one. Or had I? The first part—it was another two-part tune—was lively and sweet. The second half was modal—nearly a minor key—and seemed profoundly sad. But the sad second part ended unresolved, which pulled it right back into the first, and happier, part. I set my fiddle back on my knee. Then I had to pay close attention, to figure when the second section ended and the first came around. One seemed to flow into the other. By the time I figured it out, Ciaran had gone on to another tune, one I recognized called "Farewell to Whiskey."

I tucked my fiddle under my chin and played along, but my sights were on the rearview mirror, thinking of the great ditty before.

At the end of the evening when I asked Ciaran the name of the first tune, he couldn't recall what he'd played, even after being reminded that he'd followed it with "Farewell to Whiskey." I thought maybe he was being coy. He asked me to whistle the first one, but I couldn't call it up. He laughed and said, "Well, you could name it yourself if you could ever remember it." We were standing by the boot of his car, which he closed on his five instruments. Then he and Colette drove off.

There I was, stuck with no tune, and no name either.

But walking home on the damp streets, the tune fell back into mind: I could hear it again, and started whistling to the rhythm of my own steps. The tune needed a name, so I had to think of one. Paddy something, I thought. Paddy the Visitor. Paddy on the Walk Home. No. Paddy Lost His Way.

Paddy on the Hardwood.

I laughed out loud, and a couple of old men standing under a storefront, out of the drizzle, looked at me strangely. Nobody would know what "hardwood" referred to here in Ireland. The Tigers' floor wasn't even made of wood. Laughing, walking by myself, I realized I was a bit drunk. Drunk and more or less happy. Whatever was going to happen in Ireland would happen.

Waking the next morning I tried to whistle the tune again, but it was lost.

The Cuckoo's Nest

On October 6, in order to publicize our first home match, we had our Media Day, which the Irish call a "Press Launch." Meet the press, take pictures with our Tony the Tiger mascot, invite the local muckety-mucks. Give away a few boxes of Frosties.

I made the mistake of spinning the ball on my finger. When the photographers saw that they pulled me back for another ten minutes of snapping.

Martin Ferris showed up, the County Kerry TD, and our hosting the equivalent of a congressman was a welcome surprise, even if he had spent ten years in prison for running guns to Northern Ireland for the IRA. Before educating himself in prison, then getting into politics, he'd been a fisherman as well as an outstanding Gaelic Footballer. He was regarded as a Robin Hood sort of character in Tralee.

The Tigers were poised for our first home game October 11, but there were no printed schedules anywhere around town. No cards, no magnets, no posters. The committee had made a media guide, but they included players on our roster I'd never heard of, even after being in Tralee six weeks. They were guys who'd been on Tigers' youth teams in the past. When I pulled Junior Collins aside to ask him about that, he told me, "That's to make our team look larger, and more impressive, like." An interesting theory.

I later noticed more than a few misspellings in our press release. Specifically, I suppose, what bothered me most was my name: *Ross Bradburde*? Our own committee had put the press release together. So, of course, in the next day's local papers there were stories on the Tigers, some of whom I hadn't had the pleasure of meeting, along with my new name.

William Main called me the day of our first home game and asked if I could type up the rosters for both teams to insert in our program. The insert came out fine, but I worried that I'd have to do it every game. I was the only one associated with the Tigers with a working computer, although I didn't have a printer. I went to the Internet cafe and whipped up the insert, even taping a cut-out image of Tony the Tiger on the bottom. I did not include the phantom players Junior had in the media guide. Also, I took the liberty of spelling my name the way I always had.

Watching the Killester team get off the bus from Dublin was quite a shock. There were four big, black players when the limit was two Americans. Each one was bigger than the previous one. Two of them, Junior whispered, had lived in Ireland for decades, and married Irish women. As I took a closer look, I saw plenty of gray in their moderate Afros. I realized that those two were near my age.

Another shock: learning the hard way that we'd be sharing the bathroom, before the game and at halftime, with the ladies. I wasn't surprised to find the Frosties Tigers would use the women's locker room. That's common for games in sports, except at the very highest levels. But the women were always notified, so there was never an embarrassing moment. In this case, we had the locker room all to ourselves. But the Sports Complex didn't have enough toilets. So even though nervous bowels and bladders are a common sports ailment, we'd be lining up all season for relief with the ladies.

I'll admit our dingy Sports Complex looked much better with a full and lively crowd. We had nearly four hundred fans, mostly teenagers. Admission was five euros for an adult, three for kids under sixteen. Of course, the fans were spread across only one sideline, seven rows deep. The team benches were on the opposite side. The official scorer's table, manned by Junior Collins, was between the benches.

Our mascot, Tony the Tiger, paced in front of the stands, dishing out high fives. Since our warm-up tops had not arrived, the Frosties Tigers wore, well, a little bit of everything. We didn't really look at all like a team. From behind our bench, a DJ blasted the classic rock anthem, "The Eye of the Tiger," then followed it with hip-hop. The place was still damp and cold, the backboards still wooden, the walls dark green, yet the hall came to life, much more than I had anticipated.

I had warned Alan Keane the previous day that if he missed any more practices I would dump him, even if he was our best long-range shooter. Introverted, moody, and dedicated to the pool—I could live with that, but he'd been absent a hell of a lot. He didn't have a family or reside an hour away like Teahan.

For our first home game I started Aidan O'Shea, our diabetic 5'6" back-up-to-the-back-up, sub-to-the-sub point guard. The Irish players needed to get some confidence, so I'd promised myself to play as many as I could, even if it was just in spots. Aidan had never played in the first half before, only garbage time. He promptly lost track of his man, who made two wide-open three-point shots, and then Aidan accidentally threw the ball to Killester, which resulted in a breakaway layup. We were down 8–0 within the first minute. I subbed Aidan out. I couldn't tell if his confidence was bolstered from starting the game or not, but we had a game to play.

Near the end of the second quarter I could sense that Killester wasn't as impressive as they looked. They seemed heavy-legged. We were able to cut the gap and trailed by 2 points at the half. Although Barnaby could never seem to get our offense going, we pounded the offensive boards, putting in easy baskets after our own misses. John Teahan wasn't scoring the way I'd hoped, but he grabbed every loose ball, often yanking the ball from the grasp of a bigger player. The lead changed hands several times.

Naturally, after telling Alan Keane that he was dispensable, I should have known what would happen: Keane came off the bench and shut me up, drilling four bombs in a row to break the close game open. Geez, I thought, can Keane shoot threes—maybe it was fine for him to miss practice once in a while.

And when Killester threatened to come back, Kevin O'Donoghue hit a timely basket from the top of the key to seal the victory. It was a great day for the Irish players.

Frosties Tigers 82, Killester 75.

The fans pounded the bleachers and swarmed our bench afterward. And our mascot, Tony the Tiger, waddled over to give me a couple awkward hugs. The players jumped around, high-fiving their mothers, cousins, just about anyone. We were 1–1.

John Teahan got some dreadful news after the Killester game. His infant son Sean had gone into convulsions. They did some emergency tests and discovered that Sean only had one working kidney. The family, which also included a four-year-old daughter, would be commuting the five hours to Dublin twice a week for more tests and subsequent diagnoses.

It was a brutal blow for Teahan and it quieted our giddy locker room instantly. Although Teahan didn't live in Tralee, he was the only Irish-born player on the squad with a family, and a sense of worry suddenly draped the Tigers. Between his wife and two kids, and his ambulance work, I hardly saw him during the week. Now making even half our practices, as he had been, would be difficult. Teahan's own mother had died when he was a young boy, which I'm certain compounded his troubles. For little Sean's sake, I hoped that fierceness was genetic.

The Star of Munster

I had been hassling Alan Keane about his sporadic attendance. Then, the day after the Killester game, the phone rang early. It was a kid named Kieran Donaghy.

Donaghy was 6'4" and the most talented nineteen-year-old in Tralee—maybe in the entire county. He was another boy trapped by the division between Tigers and St. Brendan's. Donaghy had outgrown the lowly County League competition, but loyalty had frozen him with St. Brendan's. He had been in the Tigers' fold a few years earlier, but had a falling out with the old coach. Or maybe one of the old coach's many in-laws and relatives.

Back in August, I asked Kieran Donaghy to meet me for dinner. We could chat, get to know each other, and he could think about taking the step over—and up—to the Frosties Tigers. "You pick the restaurant," I had told him, hoping it wouldn't be the McDonald's that had finally opened at the edge of Tralee in 1999.

Donaghy picked a place downtown called the Brogue Inn, a really nice spot. Marriage proposal or prom night nice. And Donaghy ordered the twenty-five-euro T-bone steak, the highest priced item. "With extra spuds," he added.

I did a quick pocket-money calculation. "Just the soup for me," I said. "And a glass of water."

After his giant steak arrived, I got to the point: he'd have to work hard, I said, and be a good listener. I'd give him the first real individual instruction he'd ever had. He listened casually between bites of steak and requests for more chips and ketchup. Donaghy had the face of an eleven-year-old boy, yet he had huge hands. Also, he cursed all the time—he said it was "a massive fucking steak."

I had stressed to Donaghy that he'd have to be in great condition to be able to play as hard as I was going to demand.

"Not a bother," Donaghy said. "I've been off the drink for six weeks."

That late-August evening I had given him my phone number, informed him that our first training was set for the following week, and told him to call me the next day with his decision.

Yet Donaghy had never showed up to training or even bothered to call me, until he saw us beat Killester.

The most frequent comment I got after the Killester game was how great it was to see so many Irish kids playing. The old coach only played his starters, and a sixth man if someone was in foul trouble. Kieran Donaghy watched that first home game, he said, where I played several guys shorter and slower than him. I'm sure that he figured he could earn playing time now in the Super League, so after blowing me off two months earlier, he was calling to meet again.

Great, I thought. Another Irish player to irritate me.

We met for a second time, the Sunday after the Killester game, for a cup of tea—no steaks this time—and I got right to the point. "I told you in

August that I wanted you to play for the Tigers. And I said you were through improving unless you stepped up to the Super League. Now you've missed the first six weeks of practice, you see the Tigers win, and you want to jump on board."

Donaghy nodded, his boyish face flushed. I could see he cared what I thought. He apologized profusely as his big hands clamped around a teapot that must have still been hot, as though it was his penance.

"Practice with us for a month and I'll see how it goes," I said. "I can decide if you're serious." I touched the teapot; it *was* still hot and I jerked back my hand. "You're going to have to really work to get in shape like the other guys."

"I'll be grand," he said. "I've been off the drink for six weeks."

That sounded familiar, but I left it alone. Here was a kid who had never made a basket in the Super League, although he was quick to inform me that his nickname was "Star." He was a busboy at his uncle's pub. Donaghy was also a fine Gaelic Football player, though he played for a different local club than Quirke did—Austin Stack's. He'd be the Frosties Tigers' youngest guy, but not by much.

In the United States Donaghy's plea would have been audacity of the highest order—missing the first twenty practices then asking to join up. No self-respecting junior high school coach in America would let a kid miss the first month. If I let him join the Frosties Tigers, I was afraid I'd lose what little leverage I had with the Irish players' commitment. What would Alan Keane do if I began using a guy who had missed *all* our practices?

The next day I put the issue to the team. Should we let Donaghy join us? The players came down on both sides. The most interesting comment came from Alan Keane, who had "personal misgivings" about Donaghy, yet he'd try not to hold a grudge. The Tigers voted: Kieran Donaghy was a Frosties Tiger.

I found out after the meeting that the source of Keane's misgivings was Donaghy's way with the ladies, or one particular lady. Donaghy had stolen a girlfriend over the summer from a St. Brendan's player.

Smash the Windows

The Irish Cup is perhaps the pinnacle of Irish basketball, a single-elimination tournament that starts, oddly, during the third week of the season. That was way too soon, in my mind. It was huge publicity if a team got to the Cup Finals because the games were televised nationally. A few regular season and end-of-year championship games were televised, but it was delayed telecast and they only showed thirty minutes of highlights, which for them meant made baskets. Our season went until March, just like in American college ball. But the Cup was over in late January, if a team got to the final. If you lost in the first round, you would be done with the Cup competition in October—half the teams would be gone. If you lost in the second round, you were finished in November.

It seemed dumb. Why would they play climactic games so early in the season? The regular season national championship and the end-of-season "Top Eight" would still lie ahead, but that competition didn't carry quite the same weight because it wasn't live on national TV.

Our one-side-only bleachers at the Sports Complex were jammed for the October 19 opening round Cup match. Our opponent was Big Al's Notre Dame of Dublin. Big Al's was a burger joint. Nearly all the Irish teams carried the name of their sponsor on their uniform, and often the church parish as well. Our local media referred to us merely as Frosties.

Notre Dame had *five* Americans. Three were veterans. Their player/coach, Anthony Jenkins, a former Clemson University star, was married to an Irish woman, and thus had an Irish passport. Another American player had lived in Ireland for ten years. A third filled their Bosman position. He'd been playing in Portugal for years and although an American, he now carried a Portuguese passport. On top of those three, Notre Dame had two young *imported* Americans.

Although Kieran Donaghy had practiced hard all week, I held myself to my word—I wouldn't play him in the Cup game.

The Sports Complex had an air of excitement, and maybe that's why we played the entire first quarter with jitters. Barnaby was awful. He was 0-for-10 from the three-point line, and appeared to be deliberately throwing the ball away. He'd finish the contest with 10 turnovers, an appalling number. His performance, as a paid import, was starting to cause grumbling among both the team and the committee. Chris Thompson fought his way to a phenomenal 19 rebounds at halftime. But he fouled out early in the fourth quarter. I'd taken a gamble on leaving him in because I thought we'd have no chance with one American.

For the last nine minutes it was their five Americans against one, our Chris Davis. Not the kind of odds I'd expected in Ireland. But Chris Davis came to life, his dreadlocks flying as he made shots from all kinds of angles. We were down only 1 point with 2:03 on the clock when Alan Keane got fouled. I felt confident having our best shooter on the line, especially since he worked forty hours a week at the Sports Complex. He knew those rims intimately— if anyone could claim a home-court advantage, it was Alan Keane.

He missed both free throws. Then we had to foul on purpose to try and stop the clock. The Frosties Tigers never got closer. We lost 88–79. You could feel the despair in the locker room. It was only our third game, but an important part of the season was beyond us. When I came out of the locker room, Kieran Donaghy was sitting in his street clothes, still on our bench.

Upon taking the job, I thought the Tigers had a huge advantage: Ricardo Leonard's Irish passport. But in the last year there was a new trend that the Tigers had helped ignite. The first three teams we'd played had American guys who were married to Irish women, or were Americans somehow carrying Irish passports. Maybe I was worrying about the wrong things—practices, our defense. In the long run the Frosties Tigers would profit more if I could get my American guys to marry local lasses instead.

Roscoe Patterson, our practice player whose terrific career in Ireland was winding down, was planning to marry his Irish girlfriend soon. He'd been waiting for over a year for his Irish passport to come through, and Junior had been claiming since August that Roscoe's papers should be coming any day. The sooner Roscoe married, the sooner he could become an Irish citizen, and help the Tigers as a role player. I told William Main that the Frosties Tigers should offer to pay the wedding expenses. It would be great to add another American, even if his best days were behind him. I didn't understand the Irish immigration laws, but I was getting the feeling that nobody on the Frosties Tigers' staff did either.

The doorbell rang early that next morning. I peeked out the window and saw Junior Collins, likely on his way to or from Mass. He was sitting on

JUNIOR COLLINS OVERSEEING HIS TRALEE TIGERS AT A ROAD MATCH

the hood of his ragged car, arms folded across his chest, looking up at my window. He wanted to rehash last night's epic battle, and point to the next dragon coming up on our schedule. I didn't answer the door; I needed some time away from the Tigers' folks. Sunday was a day for writing and fiddle exercises. Grabbing my fiddle, I staggered through Paddy Jones's assigned tune for what must have been thirty minutes. When I nearly had the tune learned, I went back to the window. Junior was still sitting on his car.

I should have gone downstairs and invited him up for tea, but I didn't.

The Frosties Tigers committee wanted to meet with Ricardo Leonard on October 23. They felt that it was a terrible waste of money to pay a guy who was injured and might never play again. In the NBA, if a guy gets hurt he still gets paid. But the lower-level places in Europe—and make no mistake, Ireland was lower-level—wouldn't pay a badly injured player. They'd send him home. But Ricardo *was* home, in Tralee.

William Main told me, "I'm sure Ricardo will understand."

I was certain he wouldn't. Ricardo had done as little as he could, and gotten paid for it, his entire career in Ireland. He had made underachieving a way of life. The guy should have been at the peak of his career, getting six figures in a higher-paying European country like France or Spain. Instead he was lounging on the Emerald Isle where he wouldn't have to train much but could still get 350 euros a week.

Ricardo was supposed to be working at the sports shop, but he couldn't even do that due to his clunky cast. William wanted to continue to pay him until he could go back to his regular job. That seemed more than fair to me, but I was certain Ricardo would be upset. In fact, I didn't even attend the meeting, knowing it would take hours, and I didn't want to hear Ricardo bitch. Which he did, according to William.

Anyway, William and Ricardo came to an agreement. The Frosties Tigers would pay him until December, when his cast came off and he could return to work at his store.

The Pleasures of Hope

As I was tucking my fiddle away at the end of my Tuesday lesson, Paddy said, "I'd love to visit your New Mexico one day. Carlos Castaneda country! To travel the land where Castenada traveled would be pure joy."

It had been twenty-five years since I'd read *The Teachings of Don Juan*.

I phoned Connie when I got home and told her about Paddy's comment. This was part of my daily habit, too, with the time difference: waking her in the New Mexico morning.

Connie yawned. "Castaneda wasn't even from New Mexico," she reminded me. "None of that book would have taken place anywhere near here." We shared a laugh. There were always tourists in New Mexico looking for coyote art.

I'd lived in the Southwest consistently since 1983, and I'd never heard anyone mention the anthropological fantasist/philosopher. "I guess that's the image that Paddy has of New Mexico," I said.

Connie, of course, took things a step further: "Well, are *you* looking for a magical part of Ireland that doesn't even exist? An Ireland that the Irish would mock?"

On October 26 we traveled by bus to play the Waterford Crystals, who had been the league's regular-season champs the previous year. But at the end of the first quarter, I told the Tigers that Waterford was the weakest team we'd played—despite being on their court, we went up 20–10.

I had to call on John Teahan to guard the other team's best player. It was the third game in a row that none of our three paid players could get the job done. And Teahan did fine, despite his new lower back troubles that he said had been dragging him down. His defensive technique wasn't great, and he violated some of the most basic fundamentals—he'd lose sight of the ball, or nearly hug his man when he was on the weak side. Still, he would get a fiercely determined look in his eye and frustrate the hell out of whomever he was guarding, or "marking," as my Irish lads said. But Teahan wasn't shooting the ball well, and I thought it might be his lower back acting up. Or maybe he was worried about his son.

The Waterford game was Kieran Donaghy's debut. He was terrible: silly passes, missed layups, and he lost track of his man on defense. When he did do something right—he had a sensational blocked shot—things went against him anyway and he was called for a foul.

It became quite clear to me that Donaghy had no confidence in his shot and tried to drive everything to the basket, often foolishly. He couldn't take a hard dribble and stop for the short jumper. It was a shame too, because he jumped well enough to be able to pull up over guys. If he could ever learn to use the pull-up jumper he'd be dangerous.

Chris Thompson played well until he fouled out. Again. Barnaby continued his slide into the abyss. He was 2 for 10 from the three-point line and had 10 turnovers against their zone. That made him exactly 2 for 27 in the last three games.

Then Chris Davis sank a string of dramatic shots, and suddenly we had the Waterford Crystals reeling with three minutes to go. We even went up briefly, by 4 points. But Barnaby forgot to run back on defense twice in a row after we shot, a major screw-up in our simple system, and we gave up two breakaway dunks. We lost by three, 74–71.

Immediately after the match, William Main approached me. We were having tea and sandwiches with the Waterford team in a pub adjacent to the gymnasium. This was an Irish custom that I quickly got used to. Sometimes beer was served as well. "I think we should think about sending Barnaby home," William said. "He's certainly not giving one hundred and ten percent."

I couldn't blame William Main. Of course the club's president would be upset with Barnaby and Ricardo, our highest-paid Tigers. We had the bulk of our salary structure giving us close to nothing. The problem was that if we dumped Barnaby, the Super League rules wouldn't let us replace our Bosman until next season; it was past the October 1 deadline. The Bosman deadline seemed like a weird rule since a team could change Americans as often as it wanted.

The only game Barnaby played well was against Belfast, right after I fined him for being late. I couldn't resort to that each contest, though at times the idea appealed to me.

On the three-hour bus ride back to Tralee, John Folan and I sat together and went over the game stats, like any coach and assistant would do in the States. Folan's pub managing meant his attendance was as sporadic as Alan Keane's or Teahan's. Still, he was pleasant to be around, and I didn't want to harass a volunteer who drove an hour each time he came to Tralee. This small incident warmed my heart: when we stopped for snacks, Folan bought a one-pound hunk of cheese. It was as big as my foot. He finished it by the time we got back to Tralee. Folan told me that one of his favorite things to do is to devour a brick of cheese in front of a televised football game.

The Frosties Tigers were now 1–2. (The Cup games didn't count on your overall record, although it certainly stung like a loss.) Anyway, we'd lost three contests by a total of 13 points. Losing can get into a team's psyche, and I was concerned that my Tigers would soon believe we couldn't beat anyone.

The Sunday after our loss at Waterford, I went to the County Kerry Gaelic Football semifinals in Tralee. Micheal Quirke, our 6'6" forward, was playing.

Quirke hadn't been able to play with the Tigers at Waterford because he had to be rested for the big match on Sunday. That made two road trips he'd missed because the football season had dragged on a month. His Kerry team had qualified for the championship game in the All-Ireland finals. Otherwise, Quirke would have been with us full-time. I thought surely he could have played with us on Saturday night and played football the next day.

Quirke's team won again that Sunday, and qualified for the county championship game in two weeks. "We won't even see him for practice now, let alone for the three games we have before then," Junior said me.

Ireland was obsessed with sports, and Tralee and County Kerry were known to be especially sports-crazy. But Gaelic Football—I don't know why it was always capitalized, nor why basketball wasn't—was tops. When the Kerry team played, the whole town wore the gaudy green and gold. To an outsider, Gaelic Football seemed to combine elements of rugby, American football, and soccer. There was lots of passing and constant action. Gaelic Football had been played for a hundred years, hurling perhaps a thousand.

Their field, the pitch, was about the size of an American football field. There was a soccer-type goal at the end of the field, but the ends of the soccer goal rose up like American-style goalposts. If the ball, a bit smaller than a basketball, was kicked or punched into the goal, it meant 3 points. If it was kicked or punched over the crossbar, that counted as 1 point.

Players advance the ball by kicking or punching it, or passing it to each other in the same manner. You can run with the ball, but have to dribble it every four steps, or kick it off your foot, back to your hands as you go. No easy trick. And you only get one basketball-style dribble, then have to use the foot method intermittently. You can't tackle, but you can slam the ball carrier with a shoulder or wrestle the ball out of his hands, and that gets pretty rough.

It is an easy game for a novice to enjoy. From the stands, that is. I went to watch Micheal Quirke's team play out of curiosity. I felt like yelling at him to protect himself and stay away from the action so he wouldn't ruin himself for basketball.

Hurling is the other big sport, although Kerry is not the power in hurling that it is in Gaelic Football. Hurling is something like a blend of lacrosse and, well, Gaelic Football. The players all have hurleys, which are part hockey stick, part bat and were used to control then whack the ball, baseball style. But they look suspiciously like weapons. Almost as long as baseball bats, they have a flat wedge at the end. Hurlers score the same way: 1 point for over the crossbar, 3 for a shot in the goal.

Players of these two old sports used to take an oath, swearing that they wouldn't play any "foreign" sports. The highly organized Gaelic Athletic Association is even subsidized by the Irish government.

I learned this at the Kerry the Kingdom museum in Tralee. Its tour of three thousand years of Irish history explored the Neolithic Period, the Stone Age, the Bronze Age, the introduction of agricultural techniques, the Norman Invasion, the Celts, the struggles with the British gentry, the Irish Revolution, the Civil War. The tour culminated with a huge exhibit devoted to Gaelic Football.

Tralee had several clubs with their own fields and clubhouses, and featured teams for boys and girls of all ages. Most clubs had a pub and restaurant on the grounds, so they could feed the lads after practice.

Gaelic Football was so glamorous in Kerry that a half-dozen color pages in the newspapers were devoted to the sport each week. An all-star squad was selected from the hundreds of teams within the county for the All-Ireland tournament, which was happening in a few weeks, right at the start of basketball season. And Kerry had qualified for the finals, as it often did, even though thirty-two counties were competing.

Since Quirke, one of the Frosties Tigers' best Irish players, was tied up with football practice, I was strapped. He was not playing for the county team yet, but might be selected. Still, this was typical for American high school basketball, waiting for players to get done with football each autumn, and wishing they'd lose and not make the playoffs. So I was trying not to sweat it.

The great part about Gaelic Football and hurling was that even the superstars played for free. Amateurism was a matter of pride for these guys—surprising and refreshing to a jaded American coach like me.

That was the situation for my Irish-born Frosties Tigers as well. They played for love of the sport, so I could understand how some resentment over the Americans' salaries might be an issue for our Irish players, fans, and media. Even over the 250 weekly euros our Yanks were getting.

Gaelic Football was so much a part of Kerry culture that you couldn't get away from it even during basketball practice. As I mentioned, in Gaelic Football there are two ways to pass the soccer ball–sized football—kick it, or hold it in one hand and club it underhanded with the free hand, the way a novice would serve a volleyball.

At our next practice, I stopped things after a few minutes. The Irish players were still in the bad habit of throwing careless one-handed passes. I was tired of the turnovers and wanted to demonstrate why grabbing the ball with two hands after a jump-stop was a safer way to pass the ball.

"Super Dave," I said. "Let me have the ball, I want to show you—"

Super Dave punched the ball, Gaelic style, over to me. And he wasn't even a football player. This ball-punching happened all the time. After a traveling call, an Irish player would look disdainfully at the referee, then punch the ball underhanded to him. Just shooting around the Irish guys would punch the ball to each other.

That day I declared a new team rule: no more one-handed passes, and no punch-passing the basketball either.

CDoney in Both Pockets

William Main called early one morning to reveal our latest worry. "Rus, our sponsorship with Kellogg's ends when this season concludes," he said. "It's been a three-year deal, one of the best in Ireland, but we'll have to renegotiate with them in the spring, or get dumped."

I knew what he was hinting at.

The Frosties Tigers had to start winning if we expected Kellogg's to pick us up again. And I'll admit my initial reaction, which I kept to myself: Why should I care? I was a writer who was only going to be in Ireland for a single season. But then I suddenly felt guilty. I was being selfish if I didn't care about the impending death of the club that had taken a chance on me, even if my easy job was getting to be a drag.

Nobody had said anything about the sponsorship of the Frosties Tigers before I arrived. Kellogg's was supposed to let us know by Christmas, William said. Even if they did decide not to re-up with the Tigers, we should have time to find another sponsor. Anyway, from that day on, I couldn't think about our season or record without wondering, "How will this affect our deal with Kellogg's?"

We had a rematch with Notre Dame of Dublin on November 2. After the way we frittered away our small lead in the Cup game, I wasn't optimistic. They'd have five Americans and we still had no Micheal Quirke. This would be Kieran Donaghy's Tralee debut after the match at Waterford, where he was nervous, ineffective, and foul prone.

We got off to a poor start in the rematch. Barnaby struggled again; a season-long slump had gripped him by the throat. I wondered if his golf game was as susceptible. He was not a point guard, I was starting to realize —merely a small guy who used to be able to shoot.

I benched Barnaby in the second quarter, tired of his sloppy play and curious to see how we'd do without our highest-paid player. Then Chris Thompson, predictably, got in foul trouble and had to be yanked. Again.

I called timeout. "We need to slow the pace," I said, "and be very selective on offense. Only a layup or an easy shot will do." We had a trio of tiny Tigers on our tile floor. "You three," I said, pointing to Kevin O'Donoghue, Liam Culloty, and Alan Keane. "All three of you run back on defense the instant we shoot. Donaghy, you'll have to guard one of their big guys."

We had to slow down Notre Dame's fast break. We played the entire second quarter with four Irish guys and Rasta-forward Chris Davis against their five Americans.

Astonishingly, we bounced back and took the lead at halftime. Kieran Donaghy was terrific, and I could see the surprise on the faces of the Notre Dame players. He was just nineteen, with three weeks of practice and only one game under his belt. But for a few stretches he took over a game against five older Americans: assists, steals, and some long-range three-pointers. To think I very nearly did the "right thing" a few weeks ago and told him to come back *next* year for the first day of practice. Donaghy also seemed to have his own cheering section, which included a throng of St. Brendan's folks. He was overly emotional. Any call that went against him was cause for violent anguish. Any basket we sank he pumped his fists and slapped palms with the other Tigers.

The second half we hung tough. We had a 12-point lead with five minutes to go. Then Notre Dame got hot, and the pressure was on. Alan Keane missed two free throws at the end—again—giving them a last chance. But tiny Kevin O'Donoghue handled the pressure, made the right passes, and we hung on. Frosties Tigers won, 85–84.

Junior Collins smothered me with a musty hug when I came out of the locker room. "That was the first time in five years that we had four Irish guys on the court at the same time, like." Junior said in the past there had always been at least three non-Irish players on the court. And we sneaked by a Notre Dame team with five Yanks.

Even though we were 2–3, I was proud. I felt maybe I'd outcoached somebody, and I admitted that to Junior. We would, however, see how proud I was after two tough games in Cork the following week.

A few days after beating Notre Dame, Kieran Donaghy—I wouldn't call him "Star" until he'd won more games for us—rang my doorbell.

"My mum threw me out of the house," he said. "For fuck sake."

He had an immense duffel bag on the sidewalk behind him. I didn't have a room for him. "Quit saying fuck," I said. "What happened?"

"I quit my job clearing tables at the Greyhound," he said. His uncle's pub. "That way I could come to every practice and join the Tigers full time." Was he blaming being bounced out on his new loyalty to me? His mother

Another excuse — Kieran Donaghy arrives late for practice

was irate because he wasn't working, he said, and the fact that now he was sleeping late. They had had a huge fight.

Donaghy looked desperate. I told him to come upstairs, wondering what I had in the fridge to feed him.

"Coach, could I move in with the Americans?" he asked.

I knew that occasionally Donaghy crashed on their couch already—I'd run into him some mornings there. I'd had to shake him with two hands in order to wake him.

"It's fine with me if the imports don't mind," I said. This was something I didn't miss about college coaching: managing personal problems, babysitting. Calling moms. But for some reason I didn't mind with Donaghy. "You should help with the cleaning," I added. "There's always a big pile of dishes."

He said if he didn't find a job soon, his father was going to drive the eight hours from Northern Ireland to bring him up there to work. His parents had been separated for years; his dad longed for Donaghy to be a Gaelic Football hero. The pressure was on the Frosties Tigers committee: find Donaghy a job in Tralee quickly, or he could be off to the North. Donaghy had improved. He was blessed with more natural ability than the other Irish players, and we couldn't afford to let him pack up for Northern Ireland. I'd have to meet with Junior and William Main soon.

THE TOP OF CORK ROAD

Neptune was one of the two teams based in Cork, and was 4–1 going into their match with us and featured two older Irish guards who had been in the Super League for ten years. One, Stephen McCarthy, had been a fixture on the Irish National Team. The other guard, lefty Gordon Fitzgerald, was a hardened veteran of the Irish Army. Neptune had won eleven league championships in the last twenty years, easily the most distinguished record in Irish history. Their proud tradition made them sort of the Boston Celtics of Irish basketball.

The Frosties Tigers countered with our only real veteran, John Teahan. But early in the game Teahan started grabbing his lower back. He'd aggravated it again, badly this time. He played half the game, but was scoreless for the first time in ten seasons. Part of his problem was that he sat in an ambulance all day, then drove an hour to Tralee. Then he sat for two hours on the bus to Cork. It would be hard to either heal or stay loose that way. He was getting older, and needed time to warm up, stretch, and heat his back before games. Of course we didn't have the facilities to give him treatment.

The Frosties Tigers were up 5 points at halftime, but had 8 turnovers in the third quarter. We lost 79–66. And now Teahan's status was questionable.

We would return to Cork two days later to play that city's other team, the Demons. Their coach was at the Neptune game, so he couldn't have been too worried about facing us. His name was Pat Price, and he'd had remarkable success in Ireland. As the only other American coach, he indirectly put pressure on me to succeed. It was surprising how young he looked. He said he was thirty-two. I was forty-three, and a guy in his thirties looked like a kid to me. William Main would occasionally mention Pat Price. "Isn't it amazing how well Mister Price is going?" he might say.

If Micheal Quirke lost his Gaelic Football match that Sunday, he would be ours full-time. But if he won, even though this would be for the County Kerry Championship, he somehow had more games to play—the county champions then played each other. There are thirty-two counties, so the process could take another couple of months. The playoff system was complex, a mystery even to people who had been involved for years. I sat down with Quirke one day with a pencil and blank sheet of paper and a calendar, but he couldn't explain it and didn't even know when they'd play next. I feared it might never end. The season before, when his football team hadn't done well at all, he hadn't missed a single basketball game.

Quirke's Gaelic Football coach, Eoin "The Bomber" Liston, told Quirke to stay completely away from basketball until football was over. Fair enough. If a guy was still playing football in the States, we'd let him finish the season. But it was frustrating because we lost a couple close ones in which I couldn't help but think that Quirke would have made a difference.

"The Bomber" had won a half-dozen All-Ireland championships as a player and was a football legend. Here's how big he was: Once, while I was relaxing at the Sanctuary Health Club, he climbed into the hot tub with me and half the water in the jacuzzi gushed to the floor. (I hadn't known it was him until someone informed me later.) When "The Bomber" left, the water level receded to my knees.

I was tempted to corner Quirke and insist he play with us anyway. He was one of the best players on his football team, and surely the coach

A BAD BACK, AN ILL CHILD, AND ANOTHER LOSS — JOHN TEAHAN

wouldn't bench him for playing a few basketball games. But after considering Kerry's hardcore Republican history, I decided not to mess with a coach they called "The Bomber."

To Drink With the Devil

Back home in New Mexico, I had maybe two or three bottles of beer a week, less in the winter. That would have been impossible in Ireland, because the pint of Guinness was like sixteen ounces of heaven, with a foamy head. Smooth and creamy, it even tasted nutritious. "It's a food," the old guys would reassure you, without a hint of irony. Or this one: "Beer has food value, but food has no beer value. It hardly makes sense to eat."

Kieran Donaghy's grandmother told me, "When I was a wee girl I was always sick and very skinny. They gave me a glass of half Guinness, half milk every day for a year. That did the trick."

Guinness legends were part of Irish lore. A tin-whistle player named Barry, who'd obviously had plenty of pints himself, told me that when his mother gave birth to his oldest brother, the nurse immediately put a glass of Guinness in her hand. "In fact," he said, "she saw the Guinness before she saw her son." We toasted his mother.

I hadn't yet tried Beamish's or Murphy's Stout, favorites in County Cork, but I was planning to. The Demons' coach, Pat Price, said he preferred Murphy's.

One night in October, I went out for a pint. I was frustrated by only having eight guys at practice, or maybe because we could only practice five hours a week. Anyway, I ordered up my usual Guinness, took a sip, looked at the glass, and stifled a yelp.

The pints were smaller, smaller than they'd been the night before. I started to signal the bartender, the "publican," when I finally got a grip and realized: I might have a problem. When the pints seem to be getting smaller, a guy is definitely addicted.

One lucky thing for me: if I had more than three, I felt awful the next day. Being vulnerable to hangovers was for the best and would save me money. Still, I looked forward to my pint every night, even in its shrinking glass.

THE OLD BOOT

John Teahan rang me on November 8, the day we were to return to Cork to play the Blue Demons. His back was a mess. He said he couldn't play but he'd ride along with us. I told John that he should stay home and treat it. His wife was a respected physiotherapist, but even she couldn't seem to get him loosened up. Perhaps there was serious damage, Teahan said.

So we were off to play the Demons, Quirke-less and Teahan-less. It meant the Frosties Tigers had just seven players. Quite a bit of resentment was popping up concerning Quirke, mostly from the Irish guys. But with as few players as we had left, I figured I had to be patient.

Demons coach Pat Price told me their club was affiliated with St. Vincent DePaul, a Catholic organization. Many years ago, legend had it, they wrote a letter to Chicago's DePaul University. "We'd like to start a basketball club," the letter said, "and would appreciate any extra gear you can spare." DePaul shipped off a box of old uniforms, all of them embroidered with the DePaul team's *Blue Demons*. The Cork club had been the Blue Demons ever since.

The Blue Demons played their games at the University College's Mardyke Arena. The facility was gorgeous—wooden floor, glass backboards, well lit and warm. The luxury was shocking compared to our Sports Complex, which seemed to have been built around the time of the 1916 rebellion.

We went down 25–10 in the first quarter. When Chris Thompson caught the ball down in the low post, he didn't even pretend to be interested in scoring. Pat Price figured that out quickly and put a small Irishman on Thompson, who remained scoreless at halftime, although the rest of the Frosties Tigers had clawed their way back. In the locker room I told Thompson that he'd have to go to work, meaning he'd have to score. And to my surprise, he did. Liam Culloty and Barnaby did a fine job of dumping the ball inside to our two Chrisses. We found ourselves with a 1-point lead with fifteen seconds to go in the game. If our defense held them, we would win. And since we focused most of our practices on defense, I knew we'd be fine.

But the Demons' best player, an American named James Singleton, drilled a three-pointer at the buzzer, right in Thompson's face. It was a stunner; we lost 63–61. Another close loss for the undermanned Frosties Tigers. This was getting old.

I tried to stay positive and upbeat in the somber locker room. But soon Barnaby began complaining about his gym shoes. The previous season the Nike Factory Store had donated a pair to every Tiger. Barnaby had been saying for the past two weeks that the club should buy him a pair.

I reminded everyone (but had Barnaby in mind) that we were playing in Ireland. Not that anyone was confused about that, but nobody got a shoe contract in Ireland. I told them that the Nike store manager who'd once helped us complained that last season, after picking out their free shoes, only one of our guys had offered a "thank you." And one of the Tigers even tried to sneak by the counter, not with basketball shoes, but *golf* shoes. I wonder who that could have been?

I went out to congratulate Pat Price and trade stories about our frustrations with Irish basketball. When I came back in to round up the team, Barnaby's shoes were sitting forlorn and lonely on the bench. Kevin O'Donoghue, the only remaining Tiger, asked if he should gather them up and return them to Barnaby. I told him I didn't care. O'Donoghue, the consummate team player, scooped up the shoes and packed them in his Tony the Tiger gym bag.

It was hard to know how to interpret Barnaby's gesture. Did he mean to say, "Here's my shoes, they don't work anymore"? Or was it, "Screw you, Coach, if you won't buy me shoes"? Or was it a symbolic way of saying he was ready to depart from the crappy way he'd played so far? (He was shooting 21 percent for the season, although his defense had been tough against the Demons.) Or had Barnaby simply forgotten his shoes?

I could see where Barnaby would be confused. Last year the coach got him everything; this year the new coach fined him for walking in late with golf clubs. It was becoming apparent that Barnaby missed Ricardo Leonard more than anyone else did. Ricardo was a force in the middle, but also a deft passer. Now our opponent didn't have to collapse inside on Ricardo, so Barnaby was consistently drawing a better defender. Although Barnaby was quick to complain about Ricardo's game in our first talks, I soon came to realize Barnaby complained about everything.

After Ricardo's injury, Barnaby was pushed up—our fourth-best player was suddenly our third-best. And the thing was, Barnaby was a really good fourth-best player for an Irish team. But he was revealing himself to be a poor third-best player. Another example of this: Scottie Pippen. When he left the Bulls, he didn't look so good without you-know-who to make him (and everyone else) a better player.

FIDDLER'S HEAVEN

Junior stopped by my apartment to give me more bad news: "Coach, did you hear that Quirke won his big match yesterday, like?"

"Aww, Junior," I said. "I just cleaned this floor." I grabbed a broom to sweep up what he'd tracked in.

Junior plopped down and said it was the first county championship for the Kerins-O'Rahilly Gaelic Football club in forty-five years. Suddenly we were as interested in Quirke's football season as our own basketball season.

Junior was in the habit of visiting me the morning after games on his way home from Sunday Mass. Although I resisted the intrusion the first few times—I was either writing or fiddling—that day I surrendered and welcomed him up. As the Tigers floundered, Junior became my mass of mute support. He propped me up emotionally, trying to read my moods and comfort me. Also, Junior was the first to notice that it was November, and my heat wasn't working. I'd assumed I would have to adjust to the Irish weather and had taken to wearing a wool cap around the apartment. Junior vowed to call the landlord. Even then it would be December before the heater was functioning.

"We're still doing pretty well," he said, "without Ricardo and John Teahan. Maybe you can, you know, get us to play better before the end of the season, like."

"I'll try," I said. I prepared a couple of cups of tea. Junior doused his with milk, using the last of it. I had to drink mine black.

During the games, Junior sat at the scorer's table, keeping the official scorebook. The scorekeeper was supposed to remain neutral. This, of course, was impossible for Junior. If an opposing coach questioned the time, score, or foul count, Junior often became irate. Later in the year Pat Price would admonish Tralee's scorer's table for a shot-clock malfunction. Junior, in what I understood to be loyalty to *his* American coach, told Pat Price to do something obscene and biologically impossible.

Because of his scorekeeper's duties, Junior was obsessed with the Americans' scoring output. For both teams. "The Demons' Americans outscored ours, 46–34," he said, "but our Bosmans were even."

I tried to explain the game was simpler than that. If we were winning, I wouldn't care who scored what.

That Sunday I took the bus a few hours north to County Clare. It was the Traditional Music Festival weekend in Ennis. The perfect antidote for my

Frosties blues: music sessions in every pub. Ireland had to have the world's highest pub/people ratio in the world. It was not uncommon to have eight or ten pubs in towns of only three hundred—counting children, the infirm, and teetotalers. Ennis seemed to me to have an especially high percentage of pubs, even for Ireland. And (therefore?) County Clare was regarded as a hot spot for Irish music.

Ennis was a soulful place. A river snaked through the heart of town. Narrow streets jammed with storefronts and cafes slanted their way at odd angles. The ruins of a medieval church lay peacefully in a heap near downtown. And pubs. Did I mention the pubs?

During the festival, appreciative listeners whispered over pints and whooped loudly after the tunes. Tralee was a good town for traditional Irish music by American standards, but there are few towns in Ireland like Ennis. Nearly everyone on the street toted an instrument. I played a little and listened a lot. And drank a lot, for me—four pints in one night. Incidentally, I'd noticed that the Tralee musicians did not consider Tralee to be a good town for traditional music. They'd speak longingly of Ennis, Westport, and Galway, where the music was accorded more respect than in Tralee. Sessions in those towns were lively every night, and it wasn't treated as background music. Also, this was a musicians' festival in Ennis, and didn't attract the tourists that the earlier *Fleadh Cheoil* had.

I had arranged to meet up with Sean Ryan, the ex–Notre Dame ballplayer and flute player. Sean had heard about the Tigers' misfortune and laughingly apologized for introducing me to Bill Dooley. We walked along the river looking for the right session. Sean had heard that the entire Boylan family, one of whom Sean had married, would be gathering to lead a session. The Boylans were a large clan of fine musicians from Northern Ireland. We found only a single Boylan—Sile. Sheila, if you couldn't process the Irish spelling. Still, we decided to stay.

The pub was full, but it wasn't noisy. It was reverent. We pulled stools to the edge of the circle of musicians. Just as in a pickup basketball game, great players or tall guys get recognized immediately while the short, slow guys prop themselves up, hoping to be chosen. Sean was soon invited into the epicenter with the elites. I hacked away from the perimeter, along with another novice. I'd been playing for ten years. In Ireland that meant I was a novice. Most of the musicians have spent their whole lives in music, and oftentimes the folks at sessions will have released CDs. Ennis pulled in Ireland's elite for this festival.

Soon, Sean Ryan's wife appeared. Clodagh, like her sister Sile, was a world-class fiddler. Because of Sean's marriage to Clodagh, he could have his Irish citizenship soon. He hadn't been a great player at Notre Dame, but he would have been dynamite at a smaller school. He was 6'5", thirty years old, looked pretty fit, and I started thinking—how about Sean for the Frosties Tigers? When I asked him about it, he reminded me that he and his bride would soon be moving to Chicago. He socked me in the shoulder and laughed, but I wasn't joking.

The next day Junior stopped by again, this time with his youngest son. Ten-year-old Tomas loved to sing me Irish songs he'd learned during his school's daily music period.

Each child, Tomas said, was issued a tin whistle. The teacher then picked a song, and the kids gave it a whirl. It must have caused a horrible racket. Still, Tomas seemed keenly interested in the traditional music. Once when he came over with Junior to drive me to practice, he took one look at my closed fiddlecase and said, "You've got an *accordion*!"

No, I told him. It's not an accordion. It's a fiddle.

"Rus has got a feedle," Tomas gasped.

As I reached for it, Junior said, "Oh God no, please!"

I knew Junior didn't care for Irish music at all because he'd told me as much on several occasions. But I took the fiddle out and played them a jig. Tomas was mesmerized and asked if he could hold it. I showed him how the friction of the bow across the strings produced a sound. I decided then to keep an eye out for an undersized fiddle.

After Junior left, I called Quirke to congratulate him on his big football win. He didn't offer condolences for the Frosties Tigers.

Joys of the Chase

On November 16 we squared off with the Tolka Rovers in Tralee. I liked that name, the Tolka Rovers. It would be a great name for a traditional Irish band.

Unfortunately, they didn't shoot like musicians: they made eleven three-pointers in the first half. For the first time our defense collapsed, and we gave up 51 points by halftime, in our very own Sports Complex. Our fans were eerily quiet and the gym felt like a library.

I was determined not to berate my guys and go on locker room tirades. How could I expect the Frosties Tigers to keep their cool if I didn't? But I felt tempted this time. I even looked around at halftime for something to kick. While I might have had issues with their skills or decisions, I had never been disappointed with my Irish players' effort before. But we got outhustled and couldn't muster the energy to guard their shooters.

"Don't try and get the lead back all at once," was my advice. We were down 16, and it was going to take the entire second half, one play at a time. Sure enough, we whittled away slowly, rammed the ball to our two big Americans—the two Chrisses—and actually took the lead toward the end. Little Kevin O'Donoghue did a fine job controlling the ball and tempo again in the last quarter. Liam Culloty filled in with some heads-up play, and knew enough to throw the ball to our big Yanks. Even our numerous missed free throws in the last five minutes didn't screw us up: Frosties Tigers won, 76–74.

Still, it had been sloppy basketball. I felt worse than when we lost the Demons game at the buzzer. We had gotten off to such a shoddy start and played poorly. I talked to the team afterward about being emotionally committed to the success of the Tigers. I spoke about what it meant to be on a team, and the necessity of being prepared mentally for every single game. A minute into my talk I began noticing Barnaby smirking and shaking his head the rest of my postgame speech. He had one of his better games: 9 points on 3-for-8 shooting, and only 5 turnovers, which was plenty for most guards but a marked improvement for him.

The next day, November 17, a truce was called in the Toaster War: Barnaby bought one on sale, and William Main reimbursed him when Barnaby showed him the receipt.

But it hadn't led to peace. Now William and Barnaby were entrenched in another battle. President vs. Point Guard. Ex-Priest vs. Whiner.

The Sneaker Wars.

William told me, "If we buy Barnaby gym shoes [forgetting that he'd bought him a toaster], we'd have to buy each team member a pair. It would only be fair." That would have cost about 600 euros, a lot of money for our club. William reminded me again how he felt about confrontations.

I'd learned for certain that Barnaby was now Ireland's highest-paid player, American or Bosman, at 350 euros a week. And Barnaby was shooting 20 percent while leading the league in turnovers. Most teams couldn't afford him, and I wondered if the Tigers could.

Barnaby took to wearing an old ragged pair of gym shoes, which I supposed was his way of proving a point. Kieran Donaghy, who was not exactly the elder statesman of Irish hoops, suggested the Tigers chip in and buy Barnaby a new pair, then tape a lollipop or a baby bottle onto the box. The Irish players, Donaghy said, had no sympathy for Barnaby on this issue. If they had to buy their own shoes, why shouldn't Ireland's highest-paid player?

March of the Leprechauns

With the idea of building a young fan base, I began doing free clinics around Tralee once a week at the local elementary schools. The Irish seemed stunned by this because every other sport charged children at least a nominal amount. Often one of the tall, black Americans tagged along, and that excited the town kids beyond belief. They began stopping me on the streets to introduce me to their mums or ask when the next match was.

Kids began coming to the games in droves, boosting our average game attendance by at least a hundred, despite our record. These youngsters were enthusiastic fans, and considering our record, that was welcomed. The games were a cheap ticket for them: three euros.

The downside was that some of these kids felt compelled to come over and say hello to me. During the game.

In the second quarter of the Cup game someone tapped me on the shoulder. Little Seamus and Cahill said, "Hi, Coach!"

I didn't want to be rude, or ignore them, so I gave them each a high-five and pointed them back to the stands across the floor. Their mates must have seen the warm reception Seamus and Cahill had received because pretty soon more kids came over. Because the team's bench was in full view of the audience, I couldn't do anything but be kind. We didn't have ushers or security, so the parade of little ones seemed like it would never end. While I called plays or tried to confer with players, a wee Bernard or Bernadette would find his or her way over for a high-five from Coach. At least the kiddies didn't run across the court when the game was in progress; they went around the baseline.

Also, the instant timeout was called, other youngsters stormed the court to shoot baskets until the horn blew. Dozens of kids crowded around the hoop and heaved up shots. At the timeout's conclusion they scrambled back to their seats.

At halftime of the Tolka Rovers match, one little boy grabbed my sleeve and shouted, "Coach, who's winning?"

The Frosties Tigers had a reputation for underperforming and self-destructing. Now we were missing 40 points a game from last year's lineup due to injury or football. On top of that, Barnaby was averaging just half what he did a year ago. So my task was to *over*achieve, and hold things together. We hadn't been blown out and every game was close. I was playing two guys all the time—Kieran Donaghy and Liam Culloty—who'd never made a basket in the Super League before, and 5'6" Kevin O'Donoghue was getting plenty of minutes, whereas he'd previously played mostly garbage time.

Still, I'd had a couple rival coaches ask me, "Will the Tigers' committee give you time to build a program?" I didn't know the answer to that. I certainly wasn't even thinking about *next* year, not from a basketball standpoint.

William Main still prefaced many of his comments with, "Now, I don't know the first thing about basketball, but . . ." Anyway, abrupt firings were common in basketball, and more common in Europe. A bad season quickly led to the coach's dismissal. In other European leagues, as little as a missed free throw could trigger a pink slip.

One rainy November morning, I was staring down at the street below, watching shoppers scurry past. I'd been stuck on the same line in one of my short stories for two hours. I wasn't making much progress. Just as I was about to give up for the day and go out for a pub lunch, I noticed that I'd scribbled diagrams of offensive plays on the side of my manuscript. The stories were about how college basketball swallowed up the lives of coaches and players, but I was starting to get the idea that maybe that wasn't only an American phenomenon.

Still, each morning I continued to spend thirty minutes fiddling, concentrating on Paddy Jones's skills and drills. I picked up the fiddle throughout the day during writing breaks, too. I left the case open. At night I was often at a music session. It added up. Some days it meant playing three hours a day, and that was a lot. Paddy was teaching me some of the classic County Kerry tunes: "Mary in the Woods," "The Hare in the Corn," "Munster Buttermilk," and "The Star Above the Garter."

Paddy, by the way, was not at all interested in hearing American tunes, or any other style, the way Ciaran Dalton was. Paddy was completely devoted to Irish tunes. Once Paddy told me that he thought Cajun music was boring and redundant. I happened to love Cajun music, and I said, "Paddy, have you ever *danced* to Cajun music?" I knew Paddy was single and on the lookout. "Try dancing to it next time."

Paddy said he would. "Speaking of women," Paddy added, "I'm looking forward to meeting Connie when she gets to Tralee."

I was too. Her upcoming holiday visit was supposed to be a break from a monk-like writing marathon.

I was plodding through a new story that I had started writing in September that I hoped would finish my collection, bring some closure to it. When I tired of that last story, I'd go back through the others, sentence by sentence, to polish them. The *Colorado Review* had accepted a story for publication, a first for me and a substantial step. Months later, *Aethlon* would take another story. Then the *Southern Review* took a third.

Virtually all I had in Ireland were my clothes, fiddle, computer, and books. But even with this minimalist arrangement, I found myself staring at the laptop mulling over our Tigers' losses.

Paddy's Trip to Dublin

One of the television stations invited me to Dublin to be the color announcer when Ireland played Germany in the qualifying-round game for the European Cup. I suspected they wanted to have an American voice on the air.

The game was played in Ireland's National Basketball Arena. Legend had it that the gym was named so that young boys could aspire to play in the NBA.

Bill Dooley was no longer the national coach, having gone back to take a job at Delaware Valley College near Philadelphia. That was how highly regarded Irish basketball was: the national coach, a shrewd teacher who had done a remarkable job, was rewarded with a Division III job at a school of 1,400 students.

Germany was ranked Number 3 in the world, but we (was I Irish now?) made it a great fight. Nine of our twelve Irish players had been born in the United States. They were American college standouts now playing for big money as Bosmans with their Irish passports—and European Union citizen status—in places like Italy and Spain. Two of them, Marty Conlon and Cal Bowdler, had NBA experience. That was a controversy in Irish basketball—shouldn't our national team be playing with only Irish-born guys?

Yet the last names of some of the Germans seemed, well, not too German. Arigbabu? Okulaja? Willoughby? Or how about Papic, Pesic, and Tomic? Yugos for certain. Germany was playing the passport game as well.

Irish basketball continued to send the message that it was better to be American. In the Super League, the Americans got paid and led their teams in scoring. The pressure was always on the American players to produce, and that sent a not-so-subtle message to the Irish: the Americans should be the heroes.

Now, this critique is coming from an American coach, who wouldn't have had a job if it hadn't been for that perception. I wouldn't have this gig as color announcer, for that matter. I'd noticed when I got introduced at clinics around Tralee, folks were quick to point out to the kids, "Rus is from *America*."

On a related topic, here was a minor controversy I'd stirred up: I didn't allow the Frosties Tigers' Americans or our Canadian to talk to the media. Instead, the newspaper and radio journalists would hear an Irish voice when they spoke to the Tigers. My theory was we had to make stars of the Irish guys. If kids were ever going to dream about playing in the Super League, and be dedicated enough to practice, they had to be able to envision themselves in the shoes of our Irish players.

Of course the result of this philosophy would be that the Tigers' committee someday would realize they didn't really need an American coach. I was setting myself up to be unnecessary if all went well. By that time I'd have completed my story collection and mastered the subtleties of Irish fiddling.

Ciaran Dalton gave me a travel tip for my time in Dublin. I took a few hours to visit Kilmainham Jail. Or Gaol, as they spell it.

Kilmainham Gaol had not been used for more than sixty years and was now a national museum. It was an imposing two-hundred-year-old structure whose massive stone walls contained a lot of Irish history, and revealed a great deal about the Irish mindset. Many of the leaders of Ireland's centuries-long struggle for freedom and independence from England—or, the Crown—were imprisoned there. And most of the leaders of the 1916 Easter Rising had been tried and executed in the Gaol's yard. That rebellion failed but the swift executions by the British turned the participants into martyred heroes, and inspired the successful guerilla war that followed. Nearly successful, perhaps, since Northern Ireland was still under British rule. The compromise of giving Britain the North resulted in a vicious civil war in Ireland that people still had a difficult time discussing.

Kilmainham was eerie. The ghosts of a powerful nationalist sentiment governed the place. Many cells still had the original graffiti over their doors. One defiant prisoner scrawled "No Surrender" above his door. (Ironically, that slogan is popular in the loyalist/Protestant areas in Northern Ireland.) Another cell had written over it, "For Rent." Some were marked with plaques to commemorate the legendary leaders imprisoned there: Padraic Pearse, James Connolly, and Joe Plunkett, who married his wife, Grace, in a ceremony in the jail minutes before he was executed. Legend has it Grace stood outside the massive walls and listened for the shots before she walked away. Eamon De Valera was jailed there on two occasions; he was later elected president of Ireland and served three times longer than Franklin Roosevelt in the States.

The last stop on the tour was the Stonebreaker's Yard, where the firing squad executed the 1916 heroes. Our tour guide read the names of the martyrs and gave a brief story about each one's life and death. James Connelly was dragged to the yard, wounded from the uprising, too ill to walk. They tied him to a chair, put the blindfold on, and pinned a white circle to his heart. When it was time to leave the Stonebreaker's Yard, many of the folks on the tour were in tears. I was one of them.

Kilmainham gave me a different perspective on the Irish mentality, like John Teahan's rock-solid hardheadedness. Or was it his iron will?

The part about the leaders getting executed still concerned me. Although I took heart from Eamon De Valera's story, which Ciaran Dalton filled me in on when I got back to Tralee. "He was convicted and headed for execution, the same as the others. But he was born in America," Ciaran said. "It was feared that if he was killed, it would turn American sentiment against the British."

Saved by his U.S. passport.

The Woods of Old Limerick

Two hours before our next game, at Limerick, Barnaby said, "I don't think I can play. My hip is bothering me, but I don't have any idea why."

I had sunk to one of the lowest suspicions a coach can have: Barnaby was faking an injury, or maybe even getting ready to quit the Tigers. Barnaby and William Main were still feuding about sneakers. I stayed out of it but I feared that this disagreement, however petty, might be affecting his play. The other Tigers mentioned it constantly: Barnaby *used* to be a great player.

Despite his slump, we needed him. We had only seven players and were underdogs even when he was healthy. William grudgingly got a Limerick sports therapist on the phone. Barnaby missed our warm-ups while he was getting a rubdown. He limped out at game time and said he'd give it a try.

The first play Barnaby Craddock waddled downcourt, grimacing in pain, and drilled a three-pointer. Maybe he was hurt, but maybe it was going to be our night.

Chris Davis seemed possessed by the spirit of Bob Marley and scored in all kinds of creative ways. He tallied 36 points. Even Chris Thompson's recurring rash of foul trouble couldn't stop us. The pride of St. Brendan's, Kieran Donaghy, continued his rapid rise, adding 14 points. Donaghy had begun mimicking Chris Thompson's intense defense in practice, and it was now carrying over to the games. Donaghy did a fine job guarding their American for a quarter and showed uncommon heart for a young guy.

We won 94–73. Our first road win, and we were now 4–4. This was after playing five of our eight games on the road, so I knew things would get easier.

It appeared the Tigers were ready to make a move. Micheal Quirke was to play another Gaelic Football match the next day. If he could simply lose, Quirke would be joining the Frosties Tigers the following week.

I was starting to get the idea that the "F" word was the national word of Ireland. Kieran Donaghy said it all the time. You couldn't walk down the bustling streets of Tralee without some ladies, schoolgirls, businessmen, or couples tossing around the expletive. Sometimes they said "feck," instead.

I'd had my own little struggles with cursing, but had made a conscious effort to stop after working with Coach Lou Henson, who never cursed. The ethics of cursing didn't bother me. It was more the idea of being completely under control, emotionally. I wanted that emotional control to rub off on my team. And specifically, I wanted Donaghy to get himself under control.

Every Tuesday I walked the forty yards from my apartment to the mighty music session at Baily's Corner. The musicians hunkered down in a little wing of the bar called a snug. The sound was pure bliss, due to the wooden walls and compact spaces. This pub was made up of several snugs. If the drinkers did squeeze in, they knew to be silent. It was a less boisterous session than most. In fact, it was academic, in a casual way. I was getting more confidence—working on Paddy Jones's drills and tunes was paying off. That meant more playing, less sitting idly with my fiddle on my knee.

Guitarist Paul DeGrae held court, surrounded by three or four of us fiddlers, including his lovely wife, Dee. Maybe it took that many fiddlers to match his astonishing dexterity. The first time I went to this session there were *seven* fiddlers gathered around DeGrae, the lone guitarist. I pictured Bruce Lee or Jackie Chan in a karate-action film: the hero, cornered by flailing weapons and sticks, calmly deflecting the attackers.

Paul DeGrae's guitar playing was incredible. I was supposed to be concentrating on fiddling, but I often couldn't take my eyes off DeGrae's hands. Hearing outstanding musicians can be frustrating, but DeGrae's playing was inspiring, so rich that Irish music took on an even deeper dimension.

Perhaps Tralee's finest young fiddler was a fellow named Sean Abeyta, who possessed a rhythmic, driving, hypnotic style. He also had feet that were nearly as big as his fiddle. I noticed because Sean tapped—or thudded—one foot incessantly in time to the jigs and reels. His foot seemed to be driving his bow. Sean looked like he could be Greek or Italian (black hair, olive skin) but with that last name and my years in the American Southwest, I had to ask him if he had Hispanic blood. Sure enough, Sean's father was part Native American, part Mexican, from Colorado. Sean told me he had lived in the States as a small child before his mother moved him back to her home in Ireland.

Sean said home was the island of Inishboffin, a tiny, isolated spot miles off the coast of County Galway. The island had perhaps a hundred inhabitants and was one of the most remote spots in all of Ireland.

"What do folks do on Inishboffin?" I asked.

"Well," Sean said, "in the summer, we fish and we feck."

And in the winter?

"There's no fishing."

BAILY'S CORNER PUB, EVERY TUESDAY NIGHT

Junior Collins came by to visit the next day, his son Tomas at his side. "He's been throwing up at school," Junior said. "He's wicked sick, like. He can't stop the heaving."

Tomas slumped his head on my kitchen table. I looked around for a towel and bucket, just in case.

"I've got some good news and bad news," Junior said. "First, the good news."

Quirke had lost his big football match to a team from Cork, Junior said. His team was eliminated, ending a dream season. And Quirke played poorly, with the famed County Kerry coach, Paudie O'Se, watching. So, maybe the rumors of Quirke being selected for the Senior team—the biggest honor in any Kerry kid's sporting life—would fade. We would only have him for a month total if he got the call up.

The bad news: Alan Keane, the Frosties Tigers' swimming ace and three-point marksman, tore a chest muscle trying to bench-press 250 pounds, a really dumb thing to do. Weightlifting should always be tapered off during the season, done as maintenance. Keane would be out for weeks. We were running out of able bodies.

Young Tomas lifted his head wearily from my table. "The Tigers aren't having a good year," he said. Then he plunked his head back down.

We sat and stewed over this news for a while. When Junior got up to leave, hoisting the pale Tomas to his feet, he said, "Don't forget our next game is against Marian. You know who their star player is, like."

Marian had a winning record and was led by former Frosties Tiger Jermaine Turner—the guy I had decided not to bring back despite pressure from John Teahan and William Main. I was afraid that Jermaine would get ten slam dunks and taunt me after each one.

As if there wasn't enough bad news, Kieran Donaghy had his last football match scheduled for Saturday afternoon, just five hours before our game against Marian of Dublin. He'd be exhausted before we even tipped off. Kieran assured me he'd only play half the match. I already knew Donaghy well enough to know that he'd play as hard as he could regardless of what he was doing later.

And the worst news: John Teahan came by, on an unrelated ambulance run to Tralee, to tell me his son had been finally and conclusively diagnosed. Little Sean would need surgery to remove the inoperative kidney.

I made him lunch. Like the other players, he'd never eaten a grilled cheese sandwich. The Irish players seemed to like them. Or maybe they were just being polite. "I'll still come to training and encourage the young players," Teahan told me.

"Like hell you will," I said. I wanted him to get his back healed, spend time with his family. "Get young Sean and your back in shape, and we'll still be here," I said.

Then Teahan surprised me with this: "Let's make Kevin O'Donoghue captain." Being captain in Ireland was a much bigger honor than in the States. Teahan, more than anyone, was moved by our tiny guard's devotion. O'Donoghue was finally getting to play some, and Teahan was passing the torch in his own way, without fanfare.

I had come to appreciate Teahan's street-fighter mentality; now that he was hurt, practices were lackluster. I was even learning to decipher Teahan's accent. Bill Dooley had been right about most everything, but he was especially right about Teahan. With a recurring back problem, health issues with his infant son, and being over the age of thirty, I feared Teahan's career might be over, like Ricardo Leonard's could be.

· The injury was frustrating because we'd won two in a row and appeared headed in the right direction. We'd either be 4–5 or 5–4 after Marian. It could be our first time to brag about a winning record.

Night of the Fun

The day of the Marian game, November 30, Junior rang me. "The match might be canceled, like. The roof at the Sports Complex is leaking."

·"Maybe it's good news," I suggested hopefully. "We can play Marian when everyone is healthy. When did you find this out?"

Junior said he knew the day before, but he didn't want to worry me. Instead he gave me forty minutes on game day to get it fixed, or phone Marian and tell them not to make the trip from Dublin. And then have it announced on the radio that the Frosties Tigers' Super League game was cancelled.

We finally got a very cranky janitor to go up to the ceiling on a rolling scaffold, lay a long plank across the beams, and put a bucket on top.

Perhaps it wouldn't rain too hard.

A few hours before the game, I learned Kieran Donaghy had played the entire seventy minutes of a Gaelic Football match that very afternoon. Not a huge surprise, I guess.

Donaghy would be zapped, but I had to play him. Quirke finally joined us, but I knew he'd be out of sync. Liam Culloty, who had filled in nicely off the bench for an eighteen-year-old, was present but nursing a fever and sore throat. Barnaby hadn't practiced all week, resting his sore hip. Chris Davis found out his mother in Florida had suffered a mild stroke. And Chris Thompson had been fighting on the phone with his girlfriend in America.

On top of that, a highly motivated Jermaine Turner was coming back to Tralee with a point to prove.

Jermaine Turner was a leaping fool, gathering 20 rebounds and adding 20 points. He certainly proved his case: he was clearly better than Chris Thompson, and on a good day, better than Chris Davis, too. I felt foolish; it was obvious that I'd made a mistake.

Davis had 7 turnovers. Thompson contributed a paltry 7 points and was called for goaltending four times. His usual tough defense was nonexistent. We lost, 76–67.

The two sportswriters hounded me afterward, trying to get me to just come out and say it. I didn't need to. I'm sure every one of Tralee's four hundred fans in the Sports Complex knew: Thompson couldn't score enough as a paid American, even in Ireland. "He's the lowest scoring imported player in the country," one writer informed me.

At least the rain bucket held up, and the leaky roof hadn't bothered us. We were now 4–5, and I bet William and our committee would want to make a personnel change. The Bosman deadline was past. And we were stuck with our Irish players. That left the two Americans. Unless the Frosties Tigers wanted to change the coach.

After the game, in what I'll admit now was a fit of frustration, I complained to Junior Collins about the state of our Sports Complex. The cold, the dark walls, the crummy yellow tile floor. The wooden backboards. Typical bitching after getting beat. "The rims aren't even ten feet," I finally concluded.

Junior insisted they were. "We paid three hundred quid to have those rings put on," he said. "Of course they're regulation height."

By this time Kevin O'Donoghue and John Teahan had come out. When Junior borrowed a tape measure, I marched them out to hoist me up. I'd prove it to them. But when they tried to raise me, I wobbled from side to side, and had to grab the net to keep from crashing down.

"Forget it," I snapped. "I'll break my neck."

Junior went and got the janitor's ladder. Sure enough, I was right: nine feet, ten inches.

By that time I'd been taking fiddle lessons from Paddy Jones for twelve weeks, playing in three weekly pub sessions, and practicing every morning for an hour. At the sessions I'd play along with more than half the tunes. Some I was familiar with, others I played quietly, trying to pick up the bones of the tune. My hesitancy was a good thing—nobody seemed to mind that I was showing up regularly. In basketball, who wants to play with the new guy if he shoots it all the time? I was reserved at the sessions, learning slowly.

Paddy Jones was an old-school disciplinarian and he'd gotten me motivated. First thing out of bed every day the fiddle case was cracked open for scales and drills, the intricate cuts and rolls, to improve my Irish technique. I slowed myself down, listening to every note. I was Paddy's first student every Tuesday, and I marched in with the kids coming for lessons on other instruments, right after school. Paddy and I sat in a sparsely furnished room, just two chairs, and he had me play for him my assigned tune for the week.

There's a phenomenon the Grateful Dead's percussionist Mickey Hart calls *entrainment* that happens rhythmically between musicians—subconsciously, two or more begin to adapt the same timing and emphasis. I've read that if two women become roommates, their bodies will adopt the same menstrual cycle. Strangely, if you put two ticking metronomes in the same room, they will eventually entrain and be on the same beat. It had happened to me many times sitting next to better fiddle players in West Virginia. And then again in Tralee. Anyway, Paddy played along with me; the concept was that his style would rub off on me.

Paddy was from the heart of Sliabh Luachra (say "sleeve LUKE-rah"), a hilly area not very far from Tralee that had produced some of the finest and most distinct players of traditional music. You couldn't actually find Sliabh Luachra on most maps, and many musicians would tell you it was more a state of mind than an actual place. It was on the border of east County Kerry and west County Cork, and included the villages Knocknagree, Ballydesmond,

Scartaglin, and Gneevguila. The Sliabh Luachra had a style of its own. The rhythms were more varied than what was commonly played in most Irish sessions, where the 4/4 reel was the dominant form with a few 6/8 jigs thrown in. The Sliabh Luachra players enjoyed playing polkas and "slides" (or "single jigs"), and their style had a lively and peculiar lift.

Not only was Paddy a great teacher, he was a terrific storyteller and, like Ciaran Dalton, a rich source for area folklore. Paddy's great posture and broad chest seemed to give him a distinct stature. He was 5'9" but, like Ciaran Dalton, seemed taller. An avid reader of fiction and poetry—he loved Guy de Maupassant—Paddy also studied more spiritual authors like Ouspensky and Carlos Castaneda.

That December he said, "To really learn Irish fiddle you have to ingrain yourself in all things Irish. Walk the bogs. Feel the rain on your face. Talk to the old folks in the villages. Listen to the words of the songs, and empathize with the pain of the singer. Stand on our beaches and gaze into the sea. Sit by the turf fire and take in the old stories."

I told him I'd try.

"Have you walked the bogs in the rain?" he asked.

I had not.

"You have to *live* the tune to really learn it," Paddy insisted.

I was trying, yet was it possible for me to entrain not only with the music, but with an entire country? I was not even Irish by heritage. No matter how hard I tried, I couldn't switch my ancestry.

The Rocky Road to Dublin

Barnaby's agent, in what was either an oversight or unmitigated gall, sent the Frosties Tigers a copy of a mass-mailing/e-mail advertising Barnaby as "available." I took it to mean that Barnaby's days were numbered; he was poised to leave Tralee. My hunch in Limerick had been correct. Barnaby's heart was not with us.

Pat Price from Cork's Demons phoned to say they'd received the same e-mail. I let it pass, didn't say anything to Barnaby. What could I have said? Please stay, we'll give you a better toaster?

Two days later Barnaby confessed: he was taking a job in Iceland of all places, leaving Ireland before Christmas. It put the Frosties Tigers in a bind since it was past the October 1 deadline for acquiring a Bosman.

I immediately felt remorse. So what if Barnaby was toaster-crazy and demanded new shoes? Maybe I should have tried harder to be nice to him. Now I was stuck. Ricardo, Teahan, Alan Keane, and now Barnaby—all gone. And Quirke too, for the most part.

Then things took an odd twist. Barnaby said, "I'm still too hurt to take the road trip to Dublin for the St. Vincent's game. But I want to play in our game against Killarney on December 21." Then he'd be off to Iceland. That was weird. A guy quits the team but wants to play in one more game. Barnaby also mentioned he needed to keep going to the therapist, the "physio," for his injured hip and back, to get ready for Killarney.

It would be up to our president, William Main, and our esteemed committee. I had mixed feelings. We were going to have to play another dozen games without Barnaby, so we might as well get used to it. On the flip side, we were already shorthanded and we might not win too many other contests. Maybe we should let him play, I thought, to give us a better chance to beat Killarney, which had won merely a single game.

I tried to handle his departure with class, telling Barnaby he was a good player and wishing him luck. It wasn't all his fault. He was a victim of bad timing. Without Ricardo, he wasn't as effective and he couldn't adjust to my new system.

William Main stopped by and I told him Barnaby's story. For the first time I heard bitterness in William's usually optimistic tone. He was glad Barnaby was gone: the highest-salaried player in Ireland was not producing.

When I mentioned Barnaby's request to play one last game against Killarney, William saw through it right away: "If we keep Barnaby around for two more weeks, he will collect two more paychecks."

Not only that, but Barnaby would avoid the first game at rugged St. Vincent's of Dublin, including the ten hours of round-trip bus travel, then play in the rivalry game against nearby Killarney. "He's milking us for more money, and likely some free physio appointments," William complained.

William said it would cost us at least 800 euros to keep him around, including physios. In fact, William suggested we kick him out of his apartment that day. "I want players here that are willing to give one hundred and ten percent," he said. William's dreamy math was becoming a recurring theme.

The players had mixed emotions when I told them about Barnaby. The

Killarney game was a big deal in County Kerry. They didn't want a traitor wearing the Frosties Tigers red and white. But they also wanted us to field our best team against Killarney.

The Irish complained about the weather constantly. "It's desperate." Or, "It's lashing rain." Or, "It's horrible out." But I was raised in Chicago. The Irish climate seemed pretty mild to me. Not as nice as New Mexico, sure, but not like the Windy City. What I didn't count on was the lack of sunshine. In the dead of winter, the sun rose at 9 A.M., and sunset was about 4:30 P.M. It made for a short day. So the rain was a drag, especially if it was ruining our very-limited daylight.

Thinking about the weather reminded me of what happened my last day in New Mexico. I had been checking e-mails and the latest basketball news at the university English Department. I looked at the web page of the Tralee Tigers to see if they had anything posted about their new coach. They hadn't. (My name wouldn't be posted until our season was nearly over.) I logged off the computer and started for my car. The department secretary called something to me on the way out. Did she say "Good luck?" When I got to the double doors, I realized what she really said: It's raining. Pretty hard, which didn't happen much in the desert. I doubled back to the computer to send a couple more e-mails and wait it out.

Then it hit me.

I won't walk ten steps across the parking lot to my pickup truck while it's raining, but I'm moving to Ireland. Southern New Mexico got seven inches of rain a year; Tralee got seventy.

We had to travel to Dublin for a mid-December match with a fine St. Vincent's squad that was near the top of the Super League, and had perhaps the best Irish players. Three of St. Vincent's tough and crafty Irish guys had played small college ball in the States.

The day before we left I received more bad news, this time from our 6'6" footballer, Micheal Quirke. Quirke seemed to be the bearer of bad news quite frequently. I thought his football season was over, but he informed me that the *town* championship still had to be played, and that it was scheduled for the very same day as our Dublin trip.

I didn't understand the Gaelic Football system, which had a town championship, a league championship, a county championship, and the All-Ireland championship. Little of their schedule was planned out in advance, but it still took precedence over the Frosties Tigers.

Then our diabetic sub, the tattooed, 5'6" Aidan O'Shea, missed practice to go to a party. So I told him he couldn't play Sunday either. He seemed relieved, likely since he'd seen St. Vincent's play before. Maybe I was being hardheaded, but Aidan had missed plenty of practices. A few weeks earlier he told me he missed our Friday practice because he'd overslept. For a *10:00 P.M.* practice. (Aidan would quit the team just two weeks later, the only Irish fellow to quit, dissatisfied with his role.)

We'd have only six players for the trip to Dublin against one of Ireland's top teams.

The next morning, Kieran Donaghy called with some great news: Quirke's match had been postponed until after Christmas. I rang Quirke right away, excited that he could now join us in our time of need.

Quirke said, "The thing is, Coach, that I really have too much studying to do for college, so I still can't make the trip."

I was dumbfounded. We were planning on taking the train; I told Quirke we'd put him in first class, and he could study in peace. Five hours up and five hours back in luxury. He still declined. At New Mexico State, a player might miss a *practice* in order to study a couple times a year. Never a game. Ever. It had to be the first time in basketball history that a player missed a game in order to study.

CRONIN'S HORNPIPE

It was two weeks before Christmas, still dark at 9 A.M. when we left for Dublin with our six players: the two American Chrisses, Thompson and Davis; young Kieran Donaghy; 5'6" grocery man Kevin O'Donoghue; college student Liam Culloty (joining us again for the weekend); and sixth man Super Dave Cronin. Super Dave couldn't start for a high school team in the United States, but he was going to get his first real minutes on a professional basketball team that weekend.

Six players on a team would be unheard of in American college hoops. At UTEP we finished the 1988 season with eight players. But one of the players was future NBA star Tim Hardaway, and he was worth five guys by himself. Every Irish team nearly always had a full roster, ten players for a match.

That morning, Quirke left a message for Kevin O'Donoghue, saying he had woken with a stomach virus. Great. Football. Studying. Stomach flu. Three excuses in less than twenty-four hours.

When I hung up with Quirke, I said it out loud for the first time: I can only coach in Ireland for one season. Two would put me over the edge.

I told Super Dave Cronin he had to do two things before the game. First, he had to replace his gym shoes, which seemed to be twenty years old. They were held together by tape and shoelaces, piecemealed together. I offered to pay for them, but Dave declined. He worked for Clifford's Cash & Carry, a local bulk-goods outlet, when not taking classes at our local college, Tralee's Institute of Technology, the same school that kept Quirke so busy. Also Super Dave's dad was an accountant in Tralee with a nice home. I was certain they could afford the shoes, or I wouldn't have asked.

Next, Super Dave had to get a strap for his glasses. I didn't care if they fogged up, but they'd get stomped on by one of St. Vincent's guys if they fell off.

William Main decided that the train would be too costly, and not having Quirke was a good reason to nix the idea. We didn't really have enough players to warrant a bus, so we hired a big van instead, which came equipped with a driver. But we got hopelessly lost on the way to St. Vincent's. This was a recurring phenomenon: the Frosties Tigers couldn't find their way on road trips.

Junior's sense of direction wasn't as strong as his movie trivia, so while he suggested possibilities to the bus driver, the Tigers argued about missed turns. St. Vincent's was near a cemetery, they agreed on that much.

After thirty minutes of going in circles, the driver pulled over. He jogged across the street to ask a woman pushing a baby in a stroller. They both gestured wildly, spinning back and forth.

"I can't believe this," I said.

Then the driver dropped down to one knee in order to coo to the infant in the stroller.

Kieran Donaghy said, "Now he's asking the fucking baby for directions."

St. Vincent's gym was nearly as decrepit as the Tigers' home court, although I envied their glass boards, wooden floor, and white walls. They had a surprisingly noisy crowd of fifty, but it was a chilly dump, like our Sports Complex. It sort of felt like home.

Maybe that's why we got off to a great start, up 25–23 at the end of the first quarter. But I knew that was too fast a pace for a team with six guys. The faster the pace, the more my depleted squad would tire. A low-scoring game would be more to our advantage.

We were down 6 points at halftime, 8 going into the last quarter. Then we cut it to 4 points with five minutes to go. Chris Thompson seemed to take our undermanned quest personally. He broke out of his scoring slump with 25 points, grabbed 17 boards, and blocked 8 shots. Chris Davis was valiant with 35 points. Kieran Donaghy tossed in 20 and two of St. Vincent's players left the game bloody after tangling with him under the boards. But the two big Americans and Donaghy combined for 80 of our 89 points. Our other three combined for just seven. We were still down 6 with two minutes to go, but ran out of steam and lost, 106–89. Still, it was not the disaster I'd anticipated.

Super Dave didn't score. But he kept his glasses on and he played solid defense, considering he was guarding some of the Super League's best Irishmen. He missed his two shots, but one of them caromed in and out. Super Dave had played more than half the game, and he held his head high when he came out of the locker room.

We were 4–6, with Killarney our last game before Christmas. We had to get things turned around, and not just for my own mental health. We had the Kellogg's sponsorship to worry about.

I was halfway hoping William Main would change his mind and let Barnaby play against Killarney. But William wouldn't budge. "Strictly a financial decision," he told me. "It's nothing personal against Barnaby."

Without Barnaby on the Frosties Tigers, Chris Thompson's inability to score from beyond three feet would be further exposed, although he had been terrific at St. Vincent's. We should have probably fired Thompson then, sent him home for the Christmas holidays. But he worked hard, and was fun to coach—once the game started. I say that because he was a below-average player in practice. He couldn't seem to get himself motivated on a day-to-day basis and had poor practice habits. Then, by Saturday night he was nearly always live-wire intense.

I sent out a handful of "feeler" e-mails to agents and coaches, wondering if a big guard was available. One coaching friend laughingly suggested I call Antoine Gillespie.

Antoine Gillespie shattered NBA star Tim Hardaway's scoring records at UTEP. I recruited both players out of Chicago, and was still on good terms with them. Both had been largely unrecruited; Gillespie hadn't even been the best player at Gordon Tech High School. Tim Hardaway was largely ignored as a prepster; signing Hardaway at UTEP, when I was just twenty-six years old, bolstered my reputation as a hot young coach. Guys like Hardaway insured that UTEP continued its run of NCAA bids, television exposure, and sellout crowds.

Hardaway's success in El Paso had a Pied-Piper effect on Chicago kids during my years at UTEP. Antoine Gillespie was the last of the Chicagoans. At 6'4", he was a clever scoring guard and became a legend in El Paso for his dedication. Stories circulated about him dribbling through campus, weaving around the light poles and parking meters. I loved that part, the dribbling across campus.

Gillespie's trademark move was the pull-up jumper off the dribble. This is a skill that can only be perfected with relentless practice. Footwork, timing, balance, ball skills, quick release—they all come into play, and Antoine Gillespie had it down after years of repetition.

Gillespie finished at UTEP in 1995, narrowly missed making the NBA, and by the time I arrived in Ireland, he was in the midst of a lucrative career in Europe.

I'd lost my job at UTEP in 1991, dumped after being accused of driving some players to their summer jobs, a minor violation of NCAA rules at that time. I was guilty, and didn't think it was a deathly serious charge. But the higher-ups at UTEP thought so, and my up-and-coming career screeched to a halt. Years went by before my career—or my heart, anyway—got over what I saw as an unjust firing. I've been mad at UTEP ever since.

I was away from college coaching for three years, so after recruiting Gillespie, I never got to coach him. My first year back was at New Mexico State, when Gillespie was a senior at UTEP. Any college guy gets asked by NBA coaches and agents, "Who's the best player you've seen this year?" I never failed to mention Antoine Gillespie; I genuinely believed that with his sweet shooting and uncommon work ethic he'd land in the NBA someday.

Gillespie never made the NBA, but he'd been playing for more than $70,000 a year in France, nearly ten times what we were paying in Ireland. That's why that agent's joke was, just call Gillespie. Hah hah.

I called Gillespie anyway. Sure enough, he'd signed in September for big money with a team somewhere in the south of France. But he'd been hurt, and his team signed another American. Because of the social welfare system in France, he was still getting part of his paycheck from the French government. His groin had healed, and he was practicing again and looking for a team. Still, his compensation payments from the government would keep on until, presumably, he found a team in France next season.

In other words, he could come to Ireland to play for the Frosties Tigers for the last three months of our season. This may have amounted to some kind of abuse of the French government's kindness, but what did I care? The Frosties Tigers needed help.

It seemed too good to be true. He asked a few questions about the town of Tralee. "It's heaven," I said. What kind of offense did we run? "Whatever kind you like, Antoine." It was an emotional conversation, at least for me.

"Man, wouldn't it be great," Gillespie said after a long pause, "if we could finally join forces?"

It sure would, I said. Gillespie had to decide whether it was worth it to play for peanuts in Ireland in order to help an old friend. He could get himself back into shape for his comeback in France, where his real career was on hold. Or he could stay in France and hope for a better offer.

Paddy's Surprise

Paddy Jones's reverence for Irish music made fiddle lessons something to look forward to. But the way the Frosties Tigers' season was going, I should have figured that something would go wrong with Paddy as well. Sure enough, when I arrived for my last lesson before the holidays, Paddy looked glum.

"I've got very bad news, Rus," he said. "I've hurt my hand." Paddy had injured a tendon in his hand throwing out some trash. The hand had swelled up on him, then turned black, then purple. Fiddling hurt, and the doctor told him not to pick one up for a few weeks.

First, half my team went down with serious injuries. Then my fiddle teacher.

The focus in Paddy's lesson was on playing his new tune of the week together. It was important, especially in Irish music, to play with people. My guess was that it made Paddy's day more tolerable. We usually worked our way through his homework, playing the jigs, marches, hornpipes, and reels I'd been assigned. "But with my injured hand," he said grimly, "I'll just have to listen to you. Solo. Go ahead and play."

That made me unnecessarily nervous. But I went ahead.

It was awful.

He had me reading music from the page, which I can hardly do. I play by ear, and Paddy knew it. But the music in front of us substituted for his fiddle—it gave him a written basis to judge my playing. I stumbled through the new tune, or tried to, but never got past the first line because he kept stopping me to start all over. The tune had to be played exactly as it was written. In fairness to Paddy, he was likely in a foul mood with his fiddling future in doubt. It was the first time I wished our lesson would actually hurry up and pass. I'll bet he did, too.

When it was all over, he told me to be patient, but still work hard every day. Being a good player was going to take time, and I shouldn't get frustrated. It was the worst half-hour of my musical life.

John Teahan rang me December 18, the day Barnaby Craddock left to spend the rest of his winter in Iceland. Teahan's back was feeling better after a month of rest, and he thought with Barnaby gone, maybe he'd try to play in the game against Killarney.

Then Micheal Quirke stopped by to say he was sorry he left us to travel to Dublin with just six Tigers. He said he'd do his best not to miss any more matches. Unless it was for Gaelic Football, of course.

Finally, Kieran Donaghy found a job. That meant he wouldn't be leaving Tralee. He'd be working part-time at a clothing store, forty yards down Ashe Street from me. I could stop in and make sure he was keeping his Young Men's section tidy. Soon, Donaghy began using his lunch breaks to come visit me.

With eight players available—everyone except Barnaby, Ricardo Leonard, and Alan Keane—I thought we'd have a good chance to defeat Killarney, even if Quirke and Teahan had hardly practiced in the last few months. Still, Killarney beat us 73–64, only their second victory of the season. We dropped to 4–7, and it ruined my Christmas spirit. We wouldn't play again until after the holidays.

Chris Thompson had another low-scoring game. Any loss seemed to bring a rash of finger pointing from two newspaper writers and our committee. And the target was always the paid players; since Barnaby was gone, that meant the two Chrisses. In most of our losses, Thompson had come up short on the offensive end. He finished the Killarney game with just 10 points. He was by far the lowest-scoring American in the Irish Super League. Without Barnaby it was obvious. The Frosties Tigers needed a guard who could score.

Connie came over from the States a week before the Killarney game to spend Christmas in Ireland. It was the first time she'd been around me when I was coaching. Losses meant sleepless nights, and the night of the Killarney game I didn't even shut my eyes. The next morning she found me studying the Tigers' schedule. "Realistically," I said, "we might not win another game."

Then Connie counted on my wall calendar. "One hundred days until you can come home to New Mexico and look for a real job."

Besides Connie, I only bought Christmas gifts for Junior Collins and his family. Books for his wife, Jackie, who was an avid reader, and books for his sons, who were not. I hoped these would get the boys started. None of Tralee's four bookshops had a copy of *Don Quixote* for Junior.

Also, I found young Tomas a fiddle at Buskers, the music store in Tralee.

It only cost a hundred euros, so I snatched it. It wasn't a very good one, but this was a start. Tomas's eyes lit up like a Christmas tree when he opened it, Junior said.

A Visit to Ireland

On December 22, Antoine Gillespie surprised me with a phone call.

"Gillespie is coming to Ireland!" I shouted after I hung up. I imitated his trademark jumpshot off the dribble.

"Calm down," Connie said. "You're bouncing off the walls."

I'd finally get my chance to coach him. And the Frosties Tigers had hope.

Maybe Gillespie was pulled by a twinge of loyalty. Right after my dismissal at UTEP in 1991, Gillespie phoned me at the junior high school in El Paso where I'd taken a gym-teaching job. "Can you meet me on Sunday nights at UTEP's arena?" he asked. He was a freshman, sitting out games and practices because, despite a good SAT score, he had lacked a core class and that made him ineligible.

I swallowed my pride, and considerable hurt, and went to work with him on his ball-handling and shooting. It was the only time I'd ever returned to the UTEP gym—always in private and under the cover of darkness—until I was hired at New Mexico State in 1994. (Our NMSU teams were 8–5 against UTEP, not that I was paying very close attention to the rivalry, mind you.)

Coaching Gillespie would be a good way to put my anger toward UTEP behind me, even if it was ten years later. Gillespie and I would be reunited, able to work together, something my firing preempted. Gillespie, by the way, claimed he needed to go to a massage therapist every day for a groin injury. It was forty euros an hour and would add up quick, but he'd be worth it, he assured me.

The unpleasant business of firing Chris Thompson was ahead of me, but I needed to wait until Gillespie actually arrived, just to be sure.

In the meantime, Connie and I were off to County Clare, then Westport and Donegal for the holidays. We wanted to see the country, and we would be visiting some of the areas known for great Irish music. Before we left, John Teahan stopped by in his paramedic uniform to tell me that MRI tests revealed joint damage in his back. He was going to miss the rest of the season. "Happy Christmas," he said when he left.

Connie was interested in the poetry that was inspired by Lough Derg, where a Catholic retreat rested on a small island in the middle of a lake. The local priest had told her that she could come by anytime, someone was always around. We found out, however, that "always around" did not include Christmas day. Still, we had a nice time, going for long walks around the lake, but wishing we could get across to the island.

Antoine Gillespie arrived from France an hour before our first game in the Castleisland Blitz. The Blitz was a nearby post-Christmas tourney that would not count on our record, yet was an Irish basketball tradition. There were boys and girls of all ages playing all day, all weekend. The games were only twenty minutes each, with a running clock, so I didn't expect Gillespie to do much. It was his first game, he'd just met his teammates, right off the plane, and he hadn't played competitively all year.

He scored 20 points in the first mini-game. A point per minute and that was with a running clock. We lost by one to Notre Dame, with its five Americans. Then we beat Limerick on a last-second three-pointer by a healthier Alan Keane. In our third game of the day, to ascend to the finals, we lost in the last second to Killarney. Still, Gillespie was fantastic. Two people told me afterward that he was the best player they'd ever seen in Ireland.

The problem—and there was always a problem in Irish basketball—was the Rasta-forward, Chris Davis. He didn't show up for the Christmas Blitz.

Seems he went to Austria to visit his fiancée (not the Dublin woman who was not his girlfriend), where he learned that a cousin in Florida died. So Davis had to stay in Austria five more days, because of the death in Florida. If that makes sense to you, you're more equipped to coach in the Irish Super League than I was.

Davis was highly perturbed the next day when he found out he wasn't getting paid for the week he missed. The Florida-Austria-mourning thing made sense to him, but not the concept of no play–no pay. I was tempted to fire Davis instead of Chris Thompson, but Davis was the better scorer, and now I had to live with him and his complicated social life. I'd had several talks with Davis about his night-owl lifestyle, but he swore he had things under control. We were stuck. It would break the bank to fly in another American.

Anyway, I played Thompson in the Blitz instead, as sort of a last hurrah.

He was his usual self: blocking shots, playing great defense, missing four-footers and free throws.

The next day, just as I was about to tell Chris Thompson the bad news that we were letting him go, the coach from Marian, Jermaine Turner's club in Dublin, called. "I've heard a rumor the Tigers are sacking Chris Thompson," he said. The coach thought they'd take Thompson. He said their other American, Mike Trimmer, was disappointing, and far too old to win with. Trimmer, nearly forty, was the oldest American playing in Ireland.

This was a surprising request, because Chris Thompson was awful when he went against Jermaine Turner. They were the two players at the heart of the "Who should the Frosties Tigers hire?" controversy. But now they could wind up teammates. The Marian coach asked a lot of questions about Thompson's character and team spirit, which I said were impeccable.

When I told Chris Thompson we were making a change, he took the news well. He missed his girlfriend and their baby terribly, he said. They'd been going through a rocky stretch, and he was relieved to be going home to Louisiana. He was not the least bit interested in finishing the season with the Dublin team that was far ahead of us in the standings.

We finished the first half of the season at 4–7. Belfast's team, Star of the Sea, had to start the new year with the seven-hour journey to County Kerry to face the Frosties Tigers. I wanted to feel optimistic but it was difficult, what with four Tigers starters disappearing like a Nixon file.

Hopefully Gillespie would not get a big offer from someone else in Europe. Alan Keane was almost healthy, and that could help our offense. Quirke was back full-time, since Gaelic Football was over, although the new football season started again before basketball was through. Unfortunately, his local team did so well that it was taking the entire bunch on holiday to the United States for ten days as a reward for its great finish. He'd probably only miss one game, though, he assured me.

When I walked Connie to Tralee's bus station, I told her I thought we should get married when I got home to New Mexico. We were a perfect fit; nobody knew better than I did how rare that was. Despite our anguished goodbye, our story might have a happy ending that defied logic and my own history.

As for the Frosties Tigers, well, nobody knew yet. But we had Antoine Gillespie, so we had a chance.

PART TWO

THE MAN WHO DIED
AND ROSE AGAIN

Belfast was alone in first place at the Christmas break, so I knew our January rematch was going to be difficult, Antoine Gillespie or not. Belfast's third American, John Leahy, had been terrorizing the league with his three-point shooting, just as he had done against the Frosties Tigers in our league opener. Three of their guys were actually on the Irish National Team, including Leahy, whose marriage had earned him an Irish passport. They also had a gutsy 5'8" Bosman player from England who could dunk or pop threes.

Belfast came roaring out of the gate so fast that we gave up an astronomical 40 points in the first quarter. We only had 15.

Assistant coach John Folan aided me with a quick calculation: "If the game keeps up at this pace, Rus, we'll lose by a hundred points."

Chris Davis was awful. I wasn't opposed to the Rastafarian way of life on a philosophical level. Being laid-back is a wonderful trait off the court, but it didn't really fit my vision of the Frosties Tigers' defensive scheme. Davis was back to being out of shape after his long Austrian holiday break and skipping the Christmas Blitz. He was exhausted and had a coughing fit during our first timeout. Kieran Donaghy whispered to me, "Smoker's cough."

Fortunately, Antoine Gillespie went to work.

He was a funny player. Not fast at all, and he couldn't jump. But he was so smart and crafty. And a deadly shooter. He had 20 points at halftime, and we had cut the deficit to 10 points. Each time Gillespie scored our crowd grew more frenzied. On the way to the locker room, I told Junior Collins this was the most fun I'd had all season.

In the second half, Alan Keane stepped up and knocked in a few long-range threes. Still, Belfast held the lead. Kevin O'Donoghue gave a great effort against an experienced backcourt but couldn't stay near their little Bosman, who was on fire.

"Let me guard the Bosman, Coach," Gillespie said. Then it was as though Gillespie ran off to a phone booth and put on a cape. First he shut down the feisty Brit who was destroying O'Donoghue. Next Gillespie began drilling jumpers from all over the court. It was as if it was his own private game, and he didn't want to get bored shooting from the same spot all the time. After each of Gillespie's buckets, the Frosties Tigers' benchwarmers would shake their head in wonder. "Where did you find this guy?" Super Dave asked.

Finally, Gillespie's twenty-eight-footer with less than a minute left put us ahead for the first time all night. They had one final chance, when their point guard drove into the teeth of our defense and pulled up for a short jumper. But Kieran Donaghy, shadowing him the entire length of the court, rose with him and smashed the shot back down. The Tigers won, 95–92.

The Tralee fans mobbed the court as though we'd won a championship. Donaghy hugged Gillespie, jumping into his arms. Gillespie finished with 45 points, 10 assists, and 11 rebounds, the most statistically impressive game any player had in the Super League all year. I had to pull him away from autograph seekers after twenty minutes so we could have our postgame meeting. The win was an energizing start to the second half of the season. Next we were off to Dublin for two games. One was a rematch with Jermaine Turner's team.

Most days you couldn't find the word "basketball" mentioned in the national press, but the Kerry papers always mentioned the Frosties Tigers after six full-color pages of Gaelic Football. The sportswriters in Ireland had a strange style. There was nothing wrong with the quality, mind you, it was simply different. For instance, here's how Timmy Sheehan of *The Kerryman* described a key play in our win over Belfast:

> Gillespie's assist provided Davis with his first basket at the outset of the second quarter and with Charles Mason withdrawn for a period and Micheal Quirke extremely hardworking, the locals resurrected their challenge with a brace of threes from the prolific Alan Keane.

The headline to that piece proclaimed *Frosties Bash First Place Belfast!* I clipped the article and mailed it to the folks at Kellogg's.

Kieran Donaghy was at my door even before Junior the next day. He didn't want to talk about the Belfast game so much as he wanted to talk about Gillespie.

"Ohhhh," he said, "when he made that bomb in the fourth quarter! I said to myself, 'for fuck sake, this man can shoot.'"

I surprised Donaghy with this fact: "In high school Gillespie played *center*. He never got to shoot three-pointers."

"Go away," Donaghy said.

"It's true. Here's what you need to know, Kieran," I said. "Gillespie is a totally self-made player." I'd already heard stories about Gillespie finding brief openings in the gyms around Tralee so that he could get in his shooting drills, sometimes for just fifteen-minute intervals. And he'd been in town less than two weeks.

"He's a lot different from Chris Davis, boy," Donaghy said.

I told Donaghy he had a rare opportunity. "You ought to latch onto Gillespie. Do *everything* he does, every day. Get completely dedicated."

"I'm already dedicated, Coach," he said. "It's been six weeks now I'm off the drink."

I'd been hoping that Donaghy would find someone who was a good influence. Chris Thompson was a fine guy, but he had no sense of how to improve his own game. Donaghy, I already knew, could be easily influenced, so I was thrilled to be able to turn him loose with Gillespie. During practice, Donaghy usually insisted on guarding Gillespie, often muttering curses to himself as Gillespie drilled shot after shot.

"He lifts weights every morning at *eight*," Donaghy said, as if rising that early were inhuman.

From that day on, Donaghy was Gillespie's shadow. He even took to wearing one of Gillespie's South American wool caps with the earflaps. Perfect for the Peruvian mountains or the damp streets of Tralee.

We'd beaten Killester at our place, despite its four Americans, one Irishman from the national team, and an Australian Bosman. Killester's home games were played at the IWA, the International Wheelchair Association in Dublin, where it borrowed the court for home matches. A wheelchair game was being played before ours, which put my worries in perspective.

Killester was Chris Davis's old team. They didn't rehire him, so I was hoping he'd be pumped up to prove them wrong, as Jermaine Turner had been against us.

Killester had quite a crowd, and it became apparent that most of it was there to check out Gillespie. They politely applauded his every basket, ooohing and ahhhing. Gillespie didn't disappoint; he was on fire again, tossing in 43 points and adding 10 assists.

Unfortunately, Kieran Donaghy played poorly for the first time since his debut at Waterford. Killester's Irish star, Damien Sealy, smoked Donaghy for 25 first-half points. At the halftime buzzer, Sealy bashed him in the back of the head for good measure. It was a blatant cheap shot that would stick in the Tigers' collective psyche for a long while.

Chris Davis, sadly, wasn't motivated for revenge in the least, and his man—a mean-spirited power forward named Clyde Ellis—scorched Davis for 30 points on just 17 shots. It was a pretty efficient ass-kicking.

Gillespie, double-teamed much of the game, found Quirke for easy baskets. Quirke put in 22 points, mostly on layups. The Tigers were down 2 points with 2:43 left. But we ran out of steam and lost 113–105.

Road games were always tougher, but we'd had such a dramatic win against Belfast that I was certain we were headed in the right direction, and that made it even more disappointing. We joined Killester for sandwiches and tea afterward. No beer this time.

Then Davis irritated me by jumping in a car with the same lady who originally brought him to Tralee—the one who was not his girlfriend. Really. He disappeared for a few hours, but made it back for curfew.

We played Marian the next afternoon, January 12, on the other side of Dublin, with less than twenty-four hours' rest. Marian didn't have a Bosman, only its two Americans, and I was certain that at least one—Jermaine Turner—would be tough.

Kieran Donaghy bounced back with a great effort. But Quirke played poorly. Football conditioning was just different than basketball and that may have been why Quirke looked out of sorts. Liam Culloty gave us scrappy minutes despite the fact that Chris Davis now felt like it was his job to occasionally yell at young Liam during the games. Maybe Davis figured since he was not contributing much as a player he'd try to help coach.

We didn't have enough energy. The score was close, never out of hand.

But Gillespie, who had quickly become a one-man team, was zapped. I could sense his fatigue from the start. He played his first poor game, and even missed several free throws. Every jumpshot was short, and he missed ones he normally made. It was a shame, because if he played decently we likely would have won. We didn't: 92–81.

We were 5–9 for the season. We'd been 4–4 not so long before.

COME NOW OR STAY

Both our weekend losses came on the verge of the Tigers righting the ship. After the Marian game, John Folan told me that Chris Davis was going to stay overnight in Dublin.

"Like hell he is," I said.

I'd talked to Davis several times about his mission in Tralee, and how it *didn't* include weekend soirées in Dublin. He was nearly thirty years old, and every job he'd had since college paid less than the previous one. His career was in a tailspin, and partying in Dublin wasn't going to help. When the Boston Celtics lose to the Knicks, I'll guarantee they don't allow one or two guys to hang out in New York afterward and party. Our rule was we travel together, to and from the games.

Then Gillespie approached me and said that he and Donaghy would like to stay in Dublin, too. He didn't know my pattern of talks with Davis, or, more importantly, Davis's pattern of behavior. But wait. Gillespie was rooming with Davis, maybe he did know his history. That was even scarier.

On top of that, Donaghy was just nineteen years old. I couldn't leave him with two older American guys to party in Dublin.

I said no.

Gillespie yo-yoed back and forth to talk to the other two about it. They thought Gillespie had my ear because he'd known me for so long. And he did. But it irritated me that Gillespie wouldn't tell them both, "If Coach Rus wants us on the train, we need to go home to Tralee."

Instead I got the distinct impression that Gillespie was telling them the opposite. Leading a mutiny. Gillespie was surprisingly divisive in the locker room after the Marian loss. He'd made comments like, "We shoulda played zone," or, "This is a messed up club." When it was time to get on the train, Gillespie and Donaghy were indeed there.

But no Chris Davis.

The lure of the nightlife in Dublin and the woman who was really not his girlfriend was just too great. I couldn't fire Davis—the club was nearly broke, and a flight for a replacement American would cost the Tigers hundreds of euros. William Main agreed that we should fine Davis, though. It left me with an ugly feeling.

On the train ride back to Tralee, I looked up to see Gillespie and Donaghy sitting across from each other, wearing those identical woolen Peruvian hats with earflaps. They were reading the sports section. Then both were eating a sandwich. Then they both took gulps of their Lucozade sports drinks. Then both leaned against the window to sleep.

Hushed Be Sorrow's Sigh

The next day I went to the local Christian Brothers School to start another free youth basketball program for their third graders. My new idea was to institute a mini-dribbler team to perform during halftime at the Frosties Tigers games. I'd run similar programs in El Paso and New Mexico for nearly twenty years. I had new shirts printed up out of my own pocket, my modest contribution to the future of Irish basketball. I even came up with a cool name: The Tiger Tykes.

I knew one of the teachers at the Christian Brothers School, so I stopped by her room with my shirts to show them off and get the kids pumped up. When I unfurled one, a kid with freckles and no front teeth said, "How about that, lads? What do you reckon they'd say, a St. Brendan's fella wearing a Tigers shirt?"

The rival club, St. Brendan's, haunting the Frosties Tigers even in the third grade.

Still, the kids loved the idea, especially when I mentioned a free basketball to go with the free after-school program. The teacher said, "Grand, but you'd better go get approval from Brother O'Connell. He has some reservations."

I marched down and introduced myself to Brother O'Connell, told him about my fabulous idea to teach kids discipline and basketball fundamentals, and promote team spirit. Free of charge, of course. Basketball, uniform, expert coaching. All free.

"Sure, and it's good for the boys to get some exercise," said Brother O'Connell. "These days they get rides everywhere. No one even walks to school anymore, so. Would you be wanting to do this program during school or after school, is it?"

"After school," I said.

He sighed. "You couldn't be doing it *after* school, so, because of insurance reasons. And we'd have to get a teacher to stay after with you, and that would mean trouble as well." Brother O'Connell shrugged.

"Well, we could do it during school hours, then," I said.

"You couldn't be doing it *during* school because our programs are filled up, you see." It was his peculiar way of telling me hell no.

I left him a Frosties Tiger Tykes jersey anyway, in case he changed his mind, and trudged away through the falling rain, my cardboard box turning to mush. The kids' shirts were soaked before I made it home.

The rematch with the Waterford Crystals was a game we could win. We'd lost in the last seconds back in October. They were now tied for last place, despite having won the Super League the previous year.

We came out dead-legged. It looked like we were running in wet turf. Chris Davis's guy had 18 points at halftime, and I had to switch the footballer, Quirke, onto Davis's assigned American guy. Whomever Davis was guarding became an instant star. The word must have been out on Davis. Teams were attacking him, exposing his poor defense and relaxed style.

Gillespie looked tired again as well. He'd gotten a big rep after the first upset win over Belfast, but he was the least effective American on the court that day. Teams had taken to putting their best Irish defender on him, letting their American defend Super Dave or Kevin. Then their American double-teamed Gillespie and dared our youngster to shoot when Gillespie dumped the ball off. It was an effective strategy because our kids didn't have the firepower to make them pay by popping in open shots. Being trapped every time he caught the ball wore Gillespie down.

Mysteriously, Kieran Donaghy and Quirke both took big steps backward. They were awful and stumbled around as though they were moving a piano.

Waterford won, 80–73. In a season of lows, this was the lowest. Junior Collins was waiting for me at the scorer's table after I lectured the team. He was becoming my only friend. We shared the stats and grumbled about the game.

Junior said, "This was a bad game, like. We should forget about it."

I told him I wished I could.

"Are you losing weight, coach?" he said. It was possible. I hadn't had a great appetite the last month.

We were taking our beatings, with hardly the strength to dust ourselves off before the next adventure. Or the next beating. Halfway through *Don Quixote*, a man named Unamuno says, "The triumph, my Don Quixote, was ever a triumph of daring, not of succeeding." I'm not sure who the hell Unamuno coached, but I'd bet his team wasn't any good either.

The next morning Junior came by for his cup of tea, on a break from after-church shopping. He looked at my calendar, where I had begun boldly X-ing out the days until I could return to the States. Junior harrumphed. Then he said, "I found out why the Tigers were so poor, like. Both Donaghy and Quirke played an entire seventy minutes of Gaelic Football the very afternoon of our Waterford match."

No wonder we looked like we were running in mud. I was hugely disappointed, but I knew that telling County Kerry kids not to play football would be like telling the Irish not to go to Christmas Mass.

"The two of them probably felt guilty," Junior continued, "but figured the Tigers could win even if they were exhausted."

That didn't explain Chris Davis's continuing slide into the abyss of mediocrity. Davis hadn't played well since the Limerick game before the holidays, but that couldn't be blamed on Gaelic Football.

Then Junior asked, "Do you think Kellogg's will keep us?"

Two nights later, Chris Davis couldn't practice. He claimed to have bruised a rib at the end of the Waterford game. Now he'd slip even further from being in basketball condition, if that were possible. Our next game was against Notre Dame in Dublin, and I knew what that meant—Davis would be more interested in the nightlife afterward than he would be in the game.

I was already thinking of hiring Mike Trimmer, Marian's former American who still lived in Dublin, just to replace Davis for that single game. A team could replace Americans in the Super League anytime, like changing socks. The game was one we probably couldn't win anyway, but maybe the threat of a pink slip would send a message to Davis. He was on thin ice.

The Charms of Music

Screaming and browbeating guys after a loss was not my idea of coaching; not that I didn't have the urge. But the Frosties Tigers were young enough that they'd take it to heart and then get even worse. Instead, I usually jumped in a cab and zipped out to the Saturday night session at Kate Brown's Pub. This was out in Ardfert, an old village six miles from Tralee.

Ciaran Dalton hosted that session, too, the only one where I had to pay for my own beer. Ciaran always insisted on buying the first one. Kate Brown's Pub had an open fireplace and giant flagstones for a floor. The walls were adorned with ancient spears and armor and there was fabulous Valentia Island slate everywhere. Even the bar itself was made of slate.

I'd become a fixture at four Irish music sessions in the area. They were great scenes, fairly unpredictable, and a charming slice of a vanishing Irish tradition. Most pubs were happy to have Karaoke nights or Christina Aguilera on the jukebox. I'd been around enough to do my own surveying: only a small percentage of pubs had live traditional Irish music. In Ardfert the crowd often got shhhushed, and the place quieted down, quiet enough for someone to break into a song, sometimes in the old Irish language.

After the Waterford disaster I raced to the music session as soon as I could. I got changed, picked up my fiddle, and grabbed a taxicab. It was rare that any musician would ask me about the game's result, but Ciaran had gotten curious about the oddity of my odyssey—an American coach interested in Irish fiddling. Or was I a fiddler interested in coaching?

That night, after pushing coats and cases over to make space for me, Ciaran had a question: "What's the most frustrating part about coaching in Ireland?" With two simple nods, he signaled the waitress to bring me a pint.

How much time did we have? I couldn't go over all the frustrations before the pub closed. Instead I figured I'd keep it simple.

"The Irish concept of time," I said. Nothing started on time in Ireland. The games, the practices, movies. I'd had a season-long battle to get the Tigers to be punctual. Even Irish train and bus schedules were a mess. Of course, pub closing times were very fluid, too, so it wasn't all bad. "New Mexicans," I added, "had sort of a 'land of *mañana*' mentality. Everything could be done tomorrow, and even tomorrow was a remote concept. But still, the Southwest's sense of punctuality isn't as bad as Ireland's."

Ciaran nodded.

I asked him, "Is there anything in the old Irish language, a word or concept, that would be roughly the equivalent to *mañana*?"

He bit his lip, deep in thought. "No," he said finally, "we wouldn't have a word in Irish that would convey that kind of urgency."

The Frosties Tigers practiced Tuesdays and Thursdays, the same nights as the best music sessions. The Thursday session was in Ardfert, at a place called Jo's. Actually, it was renamed the Abbey ten years ago, but the locals still referred to it as Jo's. This was a rowdy session, like a big family with lots of good-natured teasing. I was always a bit late because of practice, but they immediately slid some chairs over to make room. It was a ten-minute cab ride from Tralee to Ardfert, but I could count on a lift home from a musician.

Once I'd heard a genuine "seanachi," or storyteller, stand up and captivate the crowd with a long, rambling story. The pub got as quiet as a church.

The pubs emptied out an hour after closing time, lights went on, but we musicians continued to flail away, full pints of Guinness in front of us. I always stayed put for this time, until the bartender asked us to leave. Since I had no work commitments in the morning, I was dedicated to closing down each session.

The most interesting aspect of the traditional music sessions was the camaraderie and banter between songs—what the Irish would call "good craic." My only friends in Tralee, besides Junior Collins, were musicians. Any free night I hunted down a session. My entire social life was music-centered. By January I was often playing five nights a week, so I wasn't exactly lonely—until the end of the evening, when I'd get out my phone card and call Connie.

The Star of Munster

Kieran Donaghy (I still wouldn't call him "Star," like everyone else) had done a decent job for us at the small forward as the youngest starter in the Super League. He showed flashes of being a strong player, especially for a nineteen-year-old who, by his own admission, had been playing basketball just once a week since he was a boy. I should have known a teenager would come with some baggage.

He'd quit the Greyhound Pub, but so far he'd retained his job at the men's clothing store. Recalling his history of spotty employment, I wondered how long the new job would last.

Barnaby Craddock's departure before Christmas for Iceland (where his team would finish 5–17, then fold) had opened up a room at the imported players' apartment. Donaghy had been hanging around a lot anyway, so with no Bosman player to claim the open room, he moved in.

I didn't mind. He was lifting weights more and working on his shooting with Gillespie. But his mother minded plenty. She didn't want him sleeping until 11 A.M. like the Americans. They were getting paid. Donaghy was not.

That was the start of the Plumbing Wars.

Donaghy was a bit lazy, mischievous, and had little interest in working full-time. Because he was a good footballer, he had near-celebrity status in Tralee.

His mother signed him up to be an apprentice plumber in Tralee, but Donaghy wasn't looking forward to a life on his back, fixing pipes and toilets. During the three-year internship he'd make ninety-five euros a week—as little as it sounds.

I reminded myself that Donaghy was the Tiger most in need of a role model. His dad hadn't lived with the family for years, and I noticed how easily influenced Kieran was by the older players. Donaghy continued to borrow Gillespie's clothes. At least twice a week he'd show up at my doorstep without any clear reason. I'll admit Donaghy's need for direction was part of why I liked him. And liking Kieran Donaghy was an important step for me. I'd grown overly frustrated with the Tigers and needed to reconnect on a personal level if we were ever to show improvement.

His mother rang me one afternoon. "Could you come over tomorrow and help me talk to Kieran?" she asked.

"About what?"

"About what he's going to do with his life," she said. She explained her plumbing position, and she wanted me there to mediate. I understood. Together we could make Kieran Donaghy a plumber. It didn't seem like a part of my job description, but I said I would.

We convened at her kitchen table. There wasn't the usual pot of tea for us—this was all business. Ms. Donaghy started by saying how frustrated she was. "All you do is sleep late and play basketball," she complained. She meant to add "like a lazy American," I figured.

I agreed that Donaghy needed to do *something*. His sitting around all day wasn't good for the Tigers either. "I think that within the next year, Kieran will be good enough to get a basketball scholarship in America," I said. Donaghy nodded in triumph, as if that meant he could always sleep as late as he wanted.

Ms. Donaghy didn't seem too excited.

"He'll be good enough to get some kind of scholarship to the States," I reiterated, knowing it would likely be a junior college. Still, that had potential: a four-year school could follow, and then perhaps a degree.

"Kieran won't study for a minute," she said. "You know yourself, Kieran, you hated school."

"Fucking plumbers are out of work all over Ireland!" Donaghy hollered. He must have done some research. He quoted some unemployment statistics. Soon they began shouting at each other.

It was difficult to hear a young man use the "f" word around his mother. I pulled him by the arm back into his seat. "Calm down, Kieran. Let's figure this out rationally." A basketball referee would have slapped Donaghy with several technical fouls.

His mom said, "You won't be able to leave Gaelic Football to go to America; the allure of Gaelic Football is too strong for any Kerry boy."

"How the fuck can you say—"

I had to stand this time to hold them apart.

Finally we hammered out an agreement: Donaghy would try the plumbing apprenticeship. If he hated plumbing he could quit after six months, but only if he had another job first. And if I could find him an American college scholarship in a year and a half, she'd allow him to go. Ms. Donaghy said she'd accept this.

The accidental plumber — Kieran Donaghy at halftime

Then I made my single demand: I insisted he stop using the "f" word in front of his mother. We all shook hands.

She offered to make everyone ham sandwiches and tea. Donaghy and I accepted.

I told Chris Davis the next day that his conditioning was terrible. I didn't mention the fact that Antoine Gillespie told me that Davis started his day with a Marlboro Light and in fact smoked cigarettes all day long. Davis denied that he was in poor shape and that his priorities were screwed up and said that he'd be ready for our January 25 game against Notre Dame, in Dublin, to which he was all too anxious to go.

I told Davis he wasn't going to Dublin for the next game.

I'd hired Mike Trimmer, the semiretired American in Dublin. Trimmer was going to meet us at the arena and play one game, then we'd reevaluate Davis's status. Davis was pretty quiet after that. We were off to Notre Dame in the morning. We'd lost six of our last seven. Notre Dame had won seven in a row.

Before I turned in for the night, the massive Micheal Quirke came by my apartment.

"I can't go to the game in Dublin," he said. "I have to study for my recreation exams." *Again*, he could have added.

Quirke's suspicious school requirements left the Frosties Tigers with only one post man, Mike Trimmer, who'd never played with us, and only six other players—again—since Liam Culloty was nursing an ankle back in Cork.

What could I do? What would you do? Call Quirke a quitter and a coward for leaving us like this? It was tempting. And what could I do with a player who didn't want to play? Sports and Leisure was not exactly as demanding a major as pre-med. In fact, I was certain it wasn't a difficult field—Sports and Leisure had been *my* major in college.

The Morning Star

Although Keiran Donaghy was staying with the Americans, his family's home was a five-minute walk from the high school where we practiced. He was there early evenings to take advantage of his mom's home cooking, which was not something he could count on at our imports' apartment. I usually stopped by his house on the way to training to make sure he was ready and not sleeping or AWOL. At first I figured it was a necessary responsibility, but part of the attraction was Donaghy's grandmother, his "Nan."

The Donaghy house was divided in half. Mary had her own side, with a fireplace, kitchen, and bath. She kept a roaring fire that roasted anyone seated on her couch. While Kieran collected his socks, shorts, and shoes, I'd sit with Mary and listen to her stories about growing up in rural Ireland. (She was the one who drank the Guinness/milk tonic as a child to avoid anemia.) Mary would tempt me with an Irish coffee, but I couldn't have whiskey before practice. I'd settle for a cup of tea and a scone that she buried in fresh cream.

Despite Donaghy's off-the-court slacker persona, I'd grown to enjoy and respect him, especially the way he hustled and scrapped during games. Something his Nan said made me like him even more:

"Every night, no matter the hour he comes home, Kieran comes into my room and gives me a kiss on the forehead," she said. Any guy with that kind of devotion to his grandmother just had to be a good lad, I thought.

Okay. I'd overlook the "f" word with his mother if Donaghy gave his grandmother a goodnight kiss every evening.

Then, about the goodnight kiss, Nan added: "Even when he's had far too much to drink."

We were scheduled to leave at 8 A.M. for the game against Notre Dame in Dublin. But we couldn't find our future plumber and starting wing player anywhere. I called Donaghy's cell phone repeatedly, hitting "redial" each time after four rings so I wouldn't be charged the outrageous rate of fifty-seven cents a minute for the privilege of leaving a message. No luck.

Neither of Donaghy's American roommates was around. Gillespie was already in Dublin, where a woman was flying in to see him. He planned to meet us at Notre Dame's gym. And Chris Davis wasn't playing, so who knew where he was? Dublin already, likely.

At 8:01, I rang their doorbell repeatedly, the bus warming up with the other players on it, except Quirke, who presumably had his nose in a book and a hot tea at his side. No answer.

From 8:03 until 8:08 I threw rocks at Donaghy's window. This had worked instantly the day before, when we had had a rare mid-morning practice. Still no answer.

Nothing to do but ring his mother. I was tempted to use the "f" word myself this time. But his grandmother answered.

She said, "I haven't talked to Kieran since he rang me a few hours ago at 4:30."

"You mean *four-thirty* A.M.?" I asked.

"That's right. He was outside the Brandon Hotel," his dear Nan said. She didn't know what he was doing up at that hour. He hadn't kissed her on the forehead, which meant he'd either stayed at the Americans' place or he was missing.

I was sure Donaghy was sound asleep, not hearing the doorbell, or phone, or rocks, but we left his apartment anyway, partly because I was afraid I'd break the window.

Halfway to Limerick, an hour out of Tralee, Donaghy called Alan Keane's mobile phone. He'd overslept. He'd already bought a bus ticket to Limerick, and he'd meet us at our cafe breakfast stop. I should have taken the phone and told Donaghy to go back to sleep. I know I should have. But it would have left us playing the league's hottest team with just six Tigers. And his grandmother would have been disappointed.

Notre Dame was finally playing as well as anyone in the Super League. Having five Americans caused it some chemistry problems early in the season. Most imports wouldn't want to come all the way to Ireland to be a fourth or fifth option, although that was the kind of problem I would have enjoyed coaching through. We had *two* Americans—Antoine Gillespie and the newly added graybeard, Mike Trimmer. Also a sleepy, hungover nineteen-year-old, 5'6" grocer Kevin O'Donoghue, student Liam Culloty, swimming whiz Alan Keane, and the bespectacled Super Dave Cronin.

We played great. It was one of the Frosties Tigers' finest efforts. Alan Keane got hot, hitting five three-pointers in the first half. Kevin O'Donoghue dropped in a couple of shots, which looked absolutely dramatic—a tiny guy popping in shots over players a foot taller. Even Super Dave nailed a three, over Notre Dame's captain, 6'8" Anthony Jenkins. Jenkins was regarded as the greatest player in the Super League's last fifteen years, so it was another confidence builder for Super Dave.

The Irish players hugged, knocked foreheads, and bashed each other on the back every timeout and free throw. It was a war, but they were grinning.

And I was beginning to realize: I *liked* these guys. I very nearly said it out loud after one timeout: "Hey, you guys are great. You mean a lot to me." But how would that have helped?

Of course Kieran Donaghy was absolutely awful. He played like he had been out partying until dawn and hadn't slept. Imagine that. During a timeout he was struggling to get his breath. "Okay, big boy," I said, getting nose to nose with him. "You want to stay out all night? Let's see what you can do with the game on the line."

Donaghy was sweating a drinker's sweat, and I could smell the alcohol the way I often could on New Year's Day practices back in the States. He reached for a water, gulped it down, then snatched Super Dave's cup from right out of his hands.

I backhanded the second cup of water and it splattered in Donaghy's face. He looked like he might thank me. When the horn blew, the Tigers dragged him out of his chair like he was a punch-drunk fighter going out for another round of beatings.

We were down six at halftime, then six again after the third quarter. The Tigers were threatening a major upset. The aging Mike Trimmer, our fill-in for Chris Davis, played well, but ran out of gas badly at the end. Trimmer hadn't played in a game for a month, and he was crowding forty but still in better condition than Davis, who had—surprise!—showed up in Dublin to watch with the woman who wasn't his girlfriend.

Unfortunately, Gillespie was cold, and he took most of our shots. He finished with 17 points, his lowest output so far.

We lost 90–78.

A loss, but another moral victory for the young, short, under-manned Frosties Tigers. Too bad they didn't list moral victories in the league standings.

We were now 5–11.

Our studious footballing forward Micheal Quirke had been "called up" to practice, and perhaps play, with the County Kerry senior team. Whether he ever made the starting lineup didn't matter in some sense because just getting the call-up was an honor.

Hadn't Gaelic Football just ended? Yes, it had. But in Ireland football catches a basketball coach on both sides—the beginning and end of our season. This problem was acute in Kerry. No other Super League team had lost players to Gaelic Football.

The good news: Quirke wouldn't be able to vacation with his *local* club in New York and Florida. He'd have to be available to train for the County Kerry team. But the bad news: Saturday afternoon matches with the Kerry team meant Quirke could be exhausted for some games. Or, if he was a benchwarmer, as nearly everyone predicted, he would be fresh and rested for the Tigers, and not on the Pirates of the Caribbean roller coaster in Florida with his club team.

"Did you know Pat Price in America?" Junior Collins asked. He passed me the quart of milk for my tea.

"No," I said. I was tired of hearing Pat Price's name, which served only to remind me that there was another American coach, in Cork, and he was winning big.

Of course, we'd lost our opening Irish Cup game in October. At the end of January, Pat Price's Blue Demons won the Cup in a dramatic overtime game.

Still, the Frosties Tigers lost to the Demons in November on a last second three-pointer in Cork. And we had beaten the other three Cup finalists once. So, as I regularly told my lads, we were not that bad.

Besides the odd idea of playing the Irish Cup games early in the season, Junior Collins informed me of another Cup tradition: "The winners usually go on a weeklong drinking spree to celebrate, like," he told me. "There's only been one time in Irish Super League history that the Cup winner won the regular season title." Presumably winning both was impossible because of the nasty hangovers.

Our next opponent, on February 8, was the 2003 Cup Champ Demons. I hoped they'd been out celebrating big time.

Apples in Winter

That Friday was clear and the sun stayed out all afternoon. I finished working on my writing early. I was in the process of combining a few of the stories into a novella, and I had painted myself into a corner. Different strategies, different points of view—still, I couldn't make the story fit into a coherent piece. I closed up my laptop, fiddled my homework from Paddy a dozen times, then changed into my walking shoes.

Tralee town was busy as always. I was planning on a brisk walk in the town park, and maybe sharing a joke and chat with Johnny Moynahan, the caretaker. He was worth his own book. A hulking man who resembled the American actor Peter Boyle, Johnny had sharp wit and a majestic laugh. He'd never owned a car or a telephone, let alone a mobile phone, and he bicycled everywhere. A hopeless romantic, he was in love with a different woman every week. But he was married and wouldn't have dreamed of cheating on his wife of thirty years, Josie, who—Johnny swore—sequestered herself in prayer eight hours a day. Johnny was also a poet and often recited his poems to me.

It was a fine day, and Johnny wasn't around, so I continued on beyond the park and took the walking path to Tralee Bay. The path turned grassy pretty quick, but not muddy, as I kept straight along the canal that began at the edge of Tralee. I usually stayed in the town park because if it began raining, I could zip home easily.

This day the sky got bluer as I passed the windmill in Blennerville. To my left were the Slieve Mish Mountains, and on my right the view went quickly from condos to farmland. Within minutes I was out of Tralee traffic, in the midst of the rolling Irish countryside. Straight ahead was Tralee Bay, and it was so sunny that the usual gray-green water was a peaceful blue. The sea was high tide, I realized when I got to the bay; I veered right and kept the water near me to the left, postcard beauty surrounding me. The mountains. The bay. The sheep. The beach.

My mind was clearing. The confusion of the story had given me a slight headache, but it was gone already, and I had a light sweat going beneath my ever-present raincoat. I thought about Pat Price's Demons. Were we catching them at a good time? Would they be hungover and uninterested, or in a groove and confident? Should the Tigers start in a zone to avoid early foul trouble? I'd have to have one more talk with Chris Davis and try to get his attitude right for our last few games. Certainly my young Irish guys had gained important seasoning despite our collapse.

I stopped walking. Behind me was the market town, Tralee. Ahead? The seaside village of Spa and then the fishing port Fenit. I was in an incredibly peaceful place, and all I could think about was basketball. Should we be trapping the Demons' Americans? Or might that make heroes out of their Irish guys by leaving them wide open? Should I have Donaghy guard an American and have Davis help him out?

I realized that I couldn't concentrate on my stories unless they were sitting right in front of me. Ireland was not the easy coaching gig I'd hoped for, mostly because we were getting clobbered. I had intended to be engrossed in my writing, but I was spending much more time thinking about the Frosties Tigers.

What surprised me was that I realized I enjoyed it. The challenge appealed to me: how could the underdog Frosties Tigers have a fighting chance? How could the coach keep his cool, promote positive vibes, and build for the future, setting the table for the Tigers to be good next season? Assuming I didn't quit or get fired. The Tigers had to keep the score close and by some miracle get hot and win. In the midst of this basketball nightmare, somehow the game had become fun again: a challenge, a puzzle, and a call to leadership. As a college coach, I spent hours thinking about business—recruiting, class attendance, travel, scheduling. Although now it was clearly going to take longer for me to complete my collection of stories than I'd initially hoped, I didn't mind.

I made only one major change in my schedule that February: if Junior Collins didn't stop by, I made sure to call him. He still held high expectations for our Frosties Tigers. We might qualify for some sort of Purple Heart, but little else. I stopped and wrote myself a note: Call Junior.

Go to the Devil and Shake Yourself

We looked pretty good at practice that week. I was feeling optimistic about playing the Demons, who would surely be overconfident.

They soon had a real reason to be overconfident. On February 6, I came home to a recorded phone message from Antoine Gillespie. He was back in France. Gone. No handshake. No goodbye. No hug for old times' sake. A French team had made him an offer—likely ten times more than the Tigers could pay. His phone message said, "Remember, basketball is a business."

I felt betrayed. The Frosties Tigers had spent the last of our money flying him in, even buying an extra ticket because he had so much luggage, and then his massage therapy bills had been almost as much as his salary. He was the highest-paid player in Ireland and we were 1–4 with him. Then he dumped us. Also, he took his home uniform—wait, *our* home uniform—one of our basketballs, and *my* nausea-inducing mobile phone that I'd loaned him the day he'd arrived.

I knew I was not supposed to take it personally. Basketball *is* a business. Gillespie was right. It's a business. It's a business.

The worst part was hearing what I already knew from William Main: "The Frosties Tigers Basketball Club doesn't have the money to fly another player in from the States," he said. "I'm sorry, Rus, but you'll just have to make do."

So I had to call the aging Mike Trimmer again, who filled in for us in Dublin. What would Kellogg's think when it found out about Gillespie?

Donaghy stopped by during his lunch break, looking as though someone told him there'd never be another Christmas. He was still wearing Gillespie's South American hat with the earflaps.

"When did you find out?" I asked him. I put down the Super League master schedule I was studying. We had seven more games to play.

"He told me last night he was leaving."

Last night? "*Last night!* I didn't find out until I got a phone message," I said. "I was around all evening."

"Gillespie said he was going to tell you face to face," Donaghy said.

"Well, he didn't," I said. "You ought to get rid of that stupid hat."

"We had a long talk before he left," Donaghy said, pulling the hat off. His face was red, the way it got when he was upset at the referees. "Gillespie said you helped him to become a player. And that *you* taught him all those dribbling drills. And that you could teach me. Gillespie said you taught—"

"Fuck Gillespie," I said.

Donaghy ignored that one. "He said you worked with Tim Hardaway all the time, and that you were a great dribbling teacher." Then, after a pause, "Who taught you to dribble?"

"Nobody," I said. "I taught myself."

"But who put the *idea* in your head? What made you think, you know, to practice and to believe you could be good at it?"

I tried to explain that part to Donaghy—how I wanted to earn a spot on my college squad, simply to be a part of a team. And how I wasn't good enough to make the team in high school, but I put the idea in my head myself. If I practiced like a maniac, good things would happen. I told Donaghy about me getting cut my senior year of college. "I was closer to Super Dave or Kevin O'Donoghue than to you," I admitted.

"But you could see," Donaghy said. And then he finished his own thought. "You could *see* something that nobody else could see."

I didn't have the patience for Donaghy's flighty logic. "All I can see now is Gillespie walking away."

Donaghy didn't say anymore. He left that Peruvian hat on my kitchen table and walked away. I could see the Frosties Tigers losing the rest of our games.

Smash the Widows

As if things weren't bad enough with Gillespie back in France, Junior Collins delivered this grim news at my kitchen table two hours later: "Quirke has a Gaelic Football match on Sunday."

"Big deal," I said, sweeping up the floor where he'd tracked in some mud. "We play *Saturday*. Surely he can do both."

"But now he's on the Kerry team, like," Junior said. "The big boys. You don't understand the football mentality, like."

I told Junior I was beginning to.

Our scholar/forward was the last man on their team. They were actually required to list them in the newspaper, #1–25. Fifteen men made up the starting lineup. Quirke likely wouldn't play one minute, but he couldn't take the chance of getting tired or hurt. A lad in Kerry would play seventy minutes of Gaelic Football the very same day of his basketball game, but would not play basketball a full day before the football match.

We were again stuck with seven players, one of whom was at the University of Cork. I did make an adjustment for Liam Culloty. Since he couldn't practice with us during the week, I called the Neptune coach and asked him if Culloty could practice with them. Neptune had only nine guys and was happy to add a smart player so it could practice five-against-five, even if Culloty was on another team every weekend.

Friday night, at our one-hour practice, Kieran Donaghy was a no-show. Junior did a little sleuthing and found Donaghy watching a lower-level game involving his old teammates at St. Brendan's. I knew he was likely as depressed as I was about Antoine Gillespie, but I couldn't let him get away with skipping training.

The Frosties Tigers couldn't afford to bench Donaghy against the Cup champion Demons the next day. But this was the same child who had overslept our last game, and I needed to wake him up for this one. So to speak.

I let him wander out for the jump ball, and sent Super Dave Cronin out there as well. Super Dave said from behind his thick glasses, "Coach, excuse me, we've got six of us out here."

I motioned for Donaghy to come off the court, and he did, with a face as crimson as his Tigers jersey. He needed the strong message and I didn't mind giving it. He sat the entire first quarter, and his legs bounced up and down like he needed to pee. The Frosties Tigers did fine, up six at the end of the first period. Donaghy continued squirming. Assistant coach John Folan warned me that he feared Donaghy was going to quit if I didn't put him in the game immediately. I knew he wouldn't: Donaghy needed me.

We went up ten in the second quarter, and took a lead of six at halftime. Undersized, underaged, underAmericaned, and probably undercoached, but there we were, giving the Cup winners a scare. Donaghy burst off the bench for the second half and played terrific.

In the fourth quarter, when we were down eight, Chris Davis got a technical. It counted as a personal foul in Irish ball, and it was his fifth. The fool had fouled out. I noticed Micheal Quirke in street clothes sitting in row 2 during a free throw, but I couldn't put him in the game. We had just our tiny squad—short and sparse—and our borrowed old Dubliner, Mike Trimmer.

Still, we scrambled back and cut the lead to 2 points. The Sports Complex was in a frenzy. So were the Tigers. So much of a frenzy that Alan Keane made two bonehead passes against their desperate press, and we lost our way. We went down, 85–72.

Junior put his arm around my shoulder as I returned from the locker room to our quickly emptied gym. Because of the green walls it was especially dark when they shut it down. Trudging off under Junior's arm, it occurred to me—here I was, with my sterling coaching pedigree, getting my brains beat out in a land that cared little about hoops.

Kieran Donaghy slunk over to us. We were the only three in the gym. He extended his hand. "Coach," he said, "my bad"—an expression he'd learned from Gillespie. This was the second weekend in a row that Donaghy's immaturity had hurt our team. Gillespie abandoning the Frosties Tigers hadn't helped either Kieran or me.

I was turning into a tragic hero, surrounded by the foolhardy Frosties Tigers. Junior, Kieran Donaghy, and I shuffled out of the gym together.

Is It the Priest That You Want?

Micheal Quirke's Gaelic Football career was on hold. The big guy sprained his ankle that week. We hadn't seen him in basketball gear since the January 25 "I-have-to-study-on-game-day" story. The second one, I mean. Now he was too hurt to play—or sit on the bench—in either sport.

The account rep from Kellogg's rang William Main and said she'd like to sit down with us in two weeks, just before our season concluded. Kellogg's wanted William and me to travel to Dublin for the meeting they had been putting us off. We were supposed to know right after Christmas about sponsorship, and we'd been left hanging.

"This has to be positive," I said to William, smiling. If Kellogg's were going to dump us, they wouldn't drag us five hours to a meeting in Dublin. As with most Frosties Tigers adventures, I would have to pay my own way: train fare, hotel, taxis, and meals. On scouting trips, Cup Finals, you name it.

But now good news was right around the corner. Still, I wanted to shake us out of our six-game losing streak.

Farewell to My Troubles

The Christian Brothers schoolteacher in Tralee (who'd sent me to be rejected by Brother O'Connell) told me about a spiritual guru named Mooji who was coming to Dublin. Fair enough—I needed a spiritual boost. She described Mooji as someone who was "enlightened and centered." He was from Jamaica but lived in London. So I went to Dublin a day ahead of my team, before our rematch with the Tolka Rovers, to get some answers from Mooji.

At the hall near Trinity University I stood in line with a crowd of nervous types who were all—and I mean all—chain smoking. They were chattering about getting a cup of coffee and where there was late-night espresso. One lady went in while the rest of the line didn't budge. So I ducked past and went in myself. Inside a small room was a big sign with the Alcoholics Anonymous 12 Steps.

Wrong hall.

Mooji's talk was in an apartment around the corner. A sign at the door suggested a five-euro donation. Inside, the incense was so syrupy I had to lower my head to breathe.

I was one of the first ones to arrive, and was seated all alone at the scheduled 8 P.M. start. Nothing started on time in Ireland, not even spiritual enlightenment. The room gradually filled with an interesting mix of people over the next twenty minutes—Grateful Dead types, muscular lesbians, computer nerds, old ladies, elderly couples.

Mooji came in and sat cross-legged in an armchair. He was about my age, with flecks of gray in his dreadlocks. Perhaps he'd once been a soccer player or an athlete of some sort. He looked around the room slowly and smiled. The heater went on, and you could hear the warm air blowing through the vents. It went off. A few minutes later, the cycle repeated. Then Mooji began speaking about awareness. Awareness of your thoughts, of your attachments to material or ephemeral things. "Who we really are," he said softly, "at the core of our being, is not our job, or career. We have happiness and peace within." Everyone had been spiritually enlightened by being born, Mooji said, although we'd lost our center. Occasionally he'd pause, reflecting on what he'd said, then he'd talk some more.

Then Mooji took questions. I thought of asking whether the Frosties Tigers should play man-to-man or zone against the Tolka Rovers the next night. But a fellow with square glasses asked him how to stop worrying about everyday stuff. Mooji's answer turned into a circular logic masterpiece about caring and not caring, attachments and unattachments.

When it was over, the Tralee teacher introduced me to Mooji. He hugged me, wouldn't let go, and kept patting me on the back. I counted: one pat for each of the Tigers' losses. I liked it; I hadn't been hugged in a long time. Mooji had an enticing combination of power and calm. Also, he was a very good hugger. Besides that, he had huge dreadlocks. I should have gotten him together with Chris Davis, to teach Davis how to be aware of where his man was on defense.

The Tolka Rovers were the team that lit us up with threes in mid-November, going up by twenty in the first quarter in Tralee before we stormed back to win.

While the players were jogging through our little seven-man layup line, an obviously disturbed William Main approached me on the sidelines. He asked if he could speak to me alone, outside, for a moment.

"I've never been so insulted in all my life," he said. His face was red, and he looked panicked. Had Kellogg's called without my knowledge?

"What was the problem?" I asked.

"That man there," he said, pointing to a chubby youngster at a card table by the entrance. "He wants to charge me admission to get into this game. Five euros!"

William was embarrassed because he didn't have any cash, I thought. I'll admit my head was somewhere else—thinking about what our starting lineup would be. Of course, I had only seven players to choose from, so that decision wouldn't take me long. I reached into my pocket for a fiver, but he stopped me.

"The point is," he said, "that I'm the Tralee Tigers Club Chairman, the *President*, and I shouldn't have to pay."

I told him not to make a big deal of it, to buy a ticket, come on in, and enjoy the game. But he insisted on calling a taxicab and leaving. It seemed odd. Here was a guy who led meditation weekends.

William stomped off, mumbling to himself, and took a taxi away into the wet Dublin night. Mooji wouldn't have done that. Mooji would have stayed and cheered for the Frosties Tigers.

Mike Trimmer suited up for us again. The arrangement was oddly convenient; he met us just for the weekend matches. Maybe this seems like a strange situation, but not in Irish basketball. Trimmer didn't practice, but we paid him a hundred euros a game on Saturdays. If it was a Dublin game, like many of our road trips, so much the better for him. We hadn't had to pay him the customary fifty-euro win bonus yet.

Alan Keane got hot against Tolka, the way he had at Notre Dame. He dropped in 6 three-pointers. Kevin O'Donoghue, our version of Little Big Man, was good, knocking in 9 points. Super Dave played substantial minutes in the first half and was respectable. Even Liam Culloty appeared confident.

But Chris Davis was disappointing again. He had only 19 points and 6 rebounds. That was not enough for a paid import who played forty minutes. Davis was completely exhausted by halftime, even though we were playing zone most of the way.

We were tied at the end of three quarters, but Chris Davis didn't score or get a rebound in the crucial last five minutes—a time when your paid player was supposed to take over. We lost 94–87.

After the game, Donaghy told me that Davis's training habits were limiting his stamina. The Tigers were 5–13.

The Boys From Old Limerick

Our best win of the season thus far had been at Limerick in December. But in those days we had two full-time Americans, a Bosman, and a ten-man roster. We'd won by twenty.

A lot had changed. We'd lost Barnaby, dumped Chris Thompson for Gillespie, then had to settle for Mike Trimmer when Gillespie bolted. In the meantime, Limerick had picked up Cleotis Brown, a dynamite guard out of University of Illinois, who was voted the best American in Ireland a few years ago. Limerick had won six games in a row. Only Notre Dame was hotter than Limerick that February. No team was colder than the Tralee Tigers.

We got off to another poor start. Then we labored away, getting closer step by step, until we finally took the lead. Kieran Donaghy was stifling their star, Brown, who didn't get an open look at the hoop all evening. With just two minutes to go, we were up by 5 points.

Chris Davis finally played great, dropping in 42 points. Limerick had trouble containing him both games. It would be nice if Davis played that well during our final three games. Maybe he was getting back into shape after all.

Then they threw a press at us. We'd only faced one press all year. Alan Keane, who fell apart against the Cup-winner Demons, immediately handed the ball to a Limerick player and fouled him as he laid it in. It was suddenly a 2-point Tiger lead, and they smelled blood. Is it necessary to tell you the rest? Another couple of turnovers, a few layups, and the Tigers lost again, 88–83. Our record was 5–14.

Something happened in the fourth quarter that stuck with me. Cleotis Brown beat Donaghy on a backdoor cut, but by the time Limerick got him the ball, Liam Culloty and little Kevin O'Donoghue had smothered Brown, trapping him to prevent an easy layup. Brown grew frustrated and lost the ball. And I thought—my guys are getting it. We wouldn't have helped each other like that back in October.

Junior was buoyant when I got out of the locker room. He was impressed that we were *almost* winning with our leprechaun-sized Tigers and our weekend warrior Trimmer. "I'd say we're getting better, like," he beamed. Junior was starting to mix up truth and fantasy. Had we just lost or won? Were we having a titanically bad season, or were we slaying dragons?

The Homeruler Hornpipe

I'd learned that Frosties Tigers misfortunes came in waves. Great big waves.

Chris Davis was a no-show at practice the following Thursday, and this was a guy who hadn't been worth a ha'penny since November. You don't have to be a basketball fan or a coach to know this was a major screw-up. He finally played a good game against Limerick, then decided to take a night off. You wouldn't have thought that our five-hours-a-week training was that demanding, but Davis must have. No phone call, he just didn't show up.

Then Alan Keane sprained his ankle badly. It looked like he was out for the season, and he was the only one who could hit three-pointers. He ended up 34 percent for the year—not great, but the best the Tigers had.

Later that evening, Donaghy said he'd gotten a phone message from Davis: it was Davis's birthday and he was in Dublin celebrating with—well, you know who.

My birthday was a huge deal to me—when I was nine, not twenty-nine. The Tigers had little left to play for this season but pride and dignity. We'd been close in every game, although our record might not have given that impression. The attitude of the remaining Irish players had been great, and I couldn't allow a paid player to blow off the team like that.

At our next practice session, Chris Davis showed up an hour late.

I fired him.

Davis came by to see me after a few days, assuming this was my way of motivating him at the end of the season. It wasn't.

We'd play with thirty-nine-year-old Roscoe Patterson, who was still hoping to join us as an Irish citizen next season. He could, of course, play as one of our two paid Americans. Roscoe had to hustle home on the bus from the Nike outlet store in nearby Killarney. At the very least, the word would get out in basketball circles, and next year we'd never have an American miss practice. If we had a team, that is.

Exile's Lament

On March 2, Kieran Donaghy stopped by during his lunch break. My apartment was becoming the grilled cheese capital of Ireland. He had forty minutes to get back to the men's store and make certain that all the pants and shirts were neatly folded.

I decided to use the time for a serious talk. The coaches from Arizona Western and South Plains College, two of the top junior colleges for hoops in the States, had sent me questionnaires for Donaghy in response to my letter. Donaghy, still not interested in plumbing, was now considering going to America for school. I wanted him to go.

"I'm worried about your personal habits, though," I said. "You'll have a lot of freedom if you go over, and maybe too much free time."

He grinned. "I'll be grand, boy," he said. "Bring on the American girls. Wooooo!"

I was still miffed at him for staying out until 4:30 A.M. the night of the Notre Dame road trip, then missing our one-hour practice before the Demons match. I told him so. "In the States," I said, "they'd bench you or send you home for the stunts you've pulled. You can't go out drinking the night before a game. Every team will have rules about that. You'd have to get yourself under control."

"I've been off the drink for six weeks," Donaghy insisted again.

"You sure?" I asked.

Donaghy's face went dark. "You're always giving out to me about drinking. But you waste your money! *Waste* it!" He was shouting now.

"What are you talking about?" I asked. I was trying to counsel a nineteen-year-old, and he was accusing me?

"You waste your money drinking," he said again. "I've seen you."

"Bullshit." Had he been hearing rumors?

"You go out every night for your music, Coach, and you'll have one or two beers. Am I right?"

"Well, yes," I admitted. I had one or two each evening, sometimes three. Four meant a throbbing headache, I'd learned the hard way.

"But you don't get drunk on one or two," Donaghy said, accusingly.

"Of course not. Who gets drunk on one or two?" Not even a lightweight like me.

"Hah!" he said. "A waste of money."

"What?"

"It's a waste of money to drink and not get drunk. You're tossing money away. When I go out, I'll skull eight or ten pints, and my mates and me have a big laugh and stumble around. It's fun. The next day I can't even remember what happened."

"Wait a second," I said. "You're saying that I'm wasting my money by *not* getting drunk, and you're downing ten pints—that's thirty five quid—so you *can* get drunk. And that's a good investment?"

"But at least I get drunk," he said, as if that were checkmate.

"I don't drink to get drunk," I said.

"Exactly. A waste." And with that Donaghy bit into the grilled cheese I'd slid his way.

At least he didn't say the "f" word. That was some kind of progress.

Our March 5 opponent was league-leading Neptune of Cork that had overtaken Belfast in the standings and would win the regular season championship—if Neptune could get by the crippled Tigers. It was a pivotal game in the Super League, because if we somehow pulled off an upset in Tralee—as we had with Belfast—Neptune wouldn't be Super League Champs. St. Vincent's would likely be crowned.

With Mike Trimmer and Roscoe Patterson, the Frosties Tigers had by far the oldest Americans playing as imports in Ireland. And we had the youngest Irish players. Kevin O'Donoghue was twenty-one, while Kieran Donaghy, Liam Culloty, and Super Dave Cronin were all nineteen. Alan Keane was twenty-four, but he was hurt. We were like the guy with one foot in the fire and the other in a bucket of ice: on the average, we were about right. Still, we'd have a fighting chance since Neptune would have to beat us on our own peculiar court.

Or that was what I thought until Junior Collins called.

It was a rare Wednesday game. And the Tigers committee hadn't really pinned down the folks at our state-of-the-art Sports Complex until it was too late. We had no gym. Volleyball and badminton and indoor soccer, and probably round-robin pinochle, all had time slots, none of which wanted to surrender to professional basketball.

So we had to go to Cork to play Neptune. I'd been working in basketball since 1981, and I'd never heard of a team giving up a home game and playing an opponent twice on the road. Neptune's season had been about sustained excellence, and there was no chance that it would be taking our rematch lightly.

We squeezed into our bus again and made for Cork. Junior said it was a ninety-minute drive. I'd been to Cork twice, but I didn't register the fact that Junior was mistaken. We got off the bus two hours later, just twenty minutes before game time, and hurried through warm-ups. I delivered the pregame talk as the Tigers were lacing, pissing, taping, and stretching.

We went out and played our undermanned butts off. Roscoe Patterson looked terrific—he was clever and efficient and finished with 27 points. We were down 5 points with six minutes to go. But we puttered out again, our gang of six players. Tigers lost, 85–72.

The 13-point difference made it one of our biggest losses of the year. There hadn't been a single blowout, a single 20-point loss. That's the way a coach starts thinking when his team stinks. It was eight losses in a row, but I was seeing progress. Maybe I was the only one.

BANISH MISFORTUNE

By March, the sun began rising earlier and the days became noticeably longer. That lifted my mood. St. Vincent's, our March 8 opponent, was tied for second place. St. Vincent's needed to beat us in Tralee—we'd actually get to play on our own court this week—to have a chance to tie for first place. The Dublin team was 15–5 coming into the game. We were 5–15.

Alan Keane was still out with his turned ankle. Liam Culloty had played in a basketball game with his University of Cork team that morning. (College basketball was even less demanding than the Irish Super League; most teams trained once a week.) Kieran Donaghy informed me that he was required to play in *two* Gaelic Football matches that very afternoon.

This time I feared a blowout.

I was proud that we'd been close every game. This had been an educational year—too damn educational—but teams don't learn much from a thrashing, either the winning or losing side. Though there wasn't much fear of the Tigers beating anyone badly. I prayed that we wouldn't embarrass ourselves.

During warm-ups we seemed unusually bouncy, and I asked the DJ to play "The Eye of the Tiger "again and again. St. Vincent's, on the other hand, looked tired. This was supposed to be a box of chocolates for these guys, a walkover.

Super Dave Cronin hit a three to open the game, and our crowd immediately came alive. The Tigers played St. Vincent's even, frustrating them by getting back on defense and stifling their fast break. We were small and slow, a bad combination, but we bunched up and helped each other defensively, forcing St. Vincent's to attack from the perimeter. A bad foul call on Kieran Donaghy for a blocked three-pointer led to three free throws and a narrow 44–42 St. Vincent's lead at the half.

For the first time all season, I got emotional in the locker room. A cornerstone of UTEP coach Don Haskins's philosophy was not to "go to the well" emotionally. If your team loses, it could collapse. The Tigers needed to give a consistent effort each night without false melodramatic prodding. Now late in the season, we were way past collapsing. But that was not why I got emotional. I couldn't help myself.

"We've come a long way together, lads," I said, my voice cracking. I praised them for their courage and reminded them of our most important defensive rule: sprint back on defense after a made or missed shot. If we didn't give up fast-break baskets, we'd improve our odds. We were young, short, and shorthanded, but we were fighting. I could feel it. The Tigers were picking up my system. We were helping each other on defense so well that every St. Vincent's bucket had been contested. The Tigers had the confidence to aggressively go after a bigger, older, and more talented team. Kieran Donaghy—the Super League's youngest starter—gathered them together in a huddle and pleaded with them to keep battling. Super Dave polished up his glasses and out we went.

In the third quarter we took the lead. Our fans, who refused to abandon us, were stomping in the bleachers. It sounded like thunder. Donaghy was exhausted—140 minutes of Gaelic Football before a basketball game will do that—but terrific. What guts (or "bottle," as the Irish said) he had for a young kid. Donaghy tallied 25 points on just 14 shots attempted.

Donaghy had gotten Liam Culloty so pumped up that Liam swished a couple of threes, the second of which put us ahead and lifted the Tralee crowd to its feet for the entire fourth quarter. I took Donaghy out of the game to briefly rest him. He couldn't have much petrol left, and I wanted him fresh for our stretch run.

Then a strange thing happened.

Liam Culloty, Kevin O'Donoghue, and Super Dave were all under six feet. And St. Vincent's Irish bunch was far bigger and stronger. But, from where I was sitting on our bench, it appeared as though those three—our smallest Tigers—had grown, and were in fact the same size as the St. Vincent's guards. Maybe even bigger. I was certain of it.

I hadn't been sleeping well with the season going to hell. I rubbed my eyes and turned to Junior Collins at the scorer's table.

"Junior," I said, "does it look like Kevin O'Donoghue is bigger than the guy he's guarding?"

Junior reached for the program, but I snatched it out of his hands. I wanted his eyes to tell him the truth, like mine had.

"Kevin has gotten taller," I said, pointing. "And so has Super Dave and Liam. Look!"

Junior said, "I don't know what you mean, like." He looked at me waiting for a punchline, but I had none.

I said, "We're taller than we used to be." It wasn't in the stats, but it was true.

With four minutes on the clock I was swallowing back tears. And I thought of something that Paddy Jones had made me consider during fiddle lessons: *entrainment.*

Paddy had never been to a Tigers game—none of my musical pals had. But the Tralee Tigers had become entrained as a team.

Sure it was only for a single game in our pathetic losing season, but we were playing together, and the sum total added up to a great deal more than our puny parts. We were helping each other on defense. Sharing the ball, moving it like a hot Irish potato, finding the open man. If we could pull this win off, it would be the biggest upset of the season (we'd upset Belfast, but we'd had Antoine Gillespie then) and an inspiring finish to our home schedule.

We went to a 3–2 zone on defense for the last quarter to conserve energy. I put Roscoe and Mike Trimmer on the blocks down low and told them not to leave; they only had to cover the low post and then rebound. Roscoe and Trimmer were wilting, but who wouldn't at their age? It would be up to the Irish guys—Donaghy, Kevin O'Donoghue, Super Dave, and Liam Culloty—to scramble on the perimeter and cover their shooters.

John Folan checked the stat sheet with two minutes left: Mike Trimmer had 20 rebounds. Super Dave's 6 points were a career high; he had dropped another one from beyond the arc. O'Donoghue was steady in his role as leader, with 9 points and 3 assists.

With fifteen seconds to go, the Tigers were up three. Then St. Vincent's American star, Mike Chadwick, nailed a big three-pointer against the zone.

Overtime.

A collapse seemed inevitable. We'd only had six guys; they looked as though they'd been standing in the rain and appeared to be running in soggy turf. We huddled up for one more run. Super Dave looked delirious. Donaghy pounded Roscoe and Trimmer on the back, trying to hammer some young life into their tired muscles. "No easy shots for them," I reminded everyone, "and we'll have a good chance."

With thirty seconds left in OT we took the lead again. The St. Vincent's guys looked worried, but they were too tired and experienced to be panicked. They zipped the ball around the perimeter, looking for a gap in our zone. Finally, they found Chadwick again, who hit another three; this one with Donaghy draped to him. The bucket pushed St. Vincent's up by 1 point with eighteen seconds to go.

We took a timeout. The Tigers would get the last shot, do-or-die.

I drew up a play for Roscoe Patterson—our "triangle," which was a "pick-for-the-picker" play. Roscoe was a poor 5-for-22 shooting for the night, but he had a reputation as a great clutch player. Several of his shots looked good but had rolled around and out. While it was a risky move, I figured the odds were with us. Trimmer was dead on his feet, as was Kieran Donaghy. Surely Roscoe wouldn't miss again.

The Tigers ran things perfectly. Donaghy drove the ball hard from the point to the wing. Little Kevin dove backdoor and emerged on the opposite wing. Then Roscoe screened across the lane for big Mike Trimmer—the decoy—so Roscoe's man had to help to prevent Trimmer from getting an easy layup. And in that split second, Super Dave timed things perfectly. He came down from the top of the key and screened Roscoe's man, who was frozen in a help position. With the clock expiring, Roscoe popped open, all alone, near the foul line. The crowd went silent.

Roscoe missed. St. Vincent's 93, Frosties Tigers 92.

The Bag With the Money

William Main and I took the early train to Dublin on Monday, then a taxi to Kellogg's advertising agency. On the train we'd shared the three biggest newspapers in Ireland, *The Irish Times*, *The Irish Independent*, and the *Examiner*. Once again, the word "basketball" was not mentioned, let alone our dramatic loss to St. Vincent's.

The papers didn't mention that we were now 5–16, either. Or that our fans gathered around and hugged the lads' necks as though we had won. Our two local Kerry papers had been more than fair; they'd been downright positive, and there were even color photos of our St. Vincent's game. We were paralyzed by a nine-game losing streak, yet no players talked back or pouted, and—most important—no one gave up.

"Look," William said. "Equestrian sports get a full page. Here's rugby, along with pictures. Swimming, soccer, hurling, and Gaelic Football are all covered. But no basketball." Cork's *Evening Echo* was the only paper in the nation to consistently cover basketball, but the *Echo* wasn't available at the Tralee train station.

At the ad agency, two young women met us: the account rep for Kellogg's and her advertising partner, both of whom must have spent every lunch hour in tanning booths. It was a peculiar thing in Irish culture, the tan. The nation got twenty minutes of sunshine a week. Still, a small percentage of Irish women had glowing tans that made them look like aliens.

We chatted for half an hour. The office secretary—also bronzed, but much older—brought us cappuccinos and cookies.

These ladies were big-city gals and curious about how I was adjusting to tiny Tralee. William mentioned his favorite dining spots in Dublin, then collected names of the best Asian places where he and I could lunch later.

Then the tanner one suddenly said, "Unfortunately, Kellogg's won't be picking up the Frosties Tigers sponsorship again after April 1. But we think it's been a *great* three years. It's been so great. Really. Just super. And we're more than willing to write a letter of recommendation for the Tigers when you go hunting another sponsor."

Gee. A letter of recommendation. And could we maybe have some more of these cookies, wrapped to go? William looked as though he'd been slapped in the face.

And that was it. Our funding would end one week after the season concluded. I was certain my coaching in Ireland was finished, not that I thought I'd spend twenty years here. Kellogg's had been giving us sixty thousand euros a year, for three years. That covered our American and Bosman salaries and rent, as well as the coach's salary and apartment.

Most frustrating was that we would have been much improved next year. That was what was keeping me from going crazy as we lost one close game after another. I had it all mapped out. We'd find a Bosman who wanted to be in Tralee, and who would bring his own toaster. John Teahan would be healthy. Hopefully Quirke would have his homework completed and his football club wouldn't go as far in the playoffs. Kieran Donaghy wouldn't be a teenager any longer and would be with us from the start. Streak-shooting Alan Keane would have a solid year under his belt, as would Kevin O'Donoghue, Liam Culloty, and Super Dave Cronin. Old Roscoe Patterson could have his Irish citizenship by then. We'd hopefully merge with St. Brendan's, which had two players who could help. Ricardo Leonard's Achilles would heal and he'd keep the weight off. We would *have* to be better. We could not be worse.

But with Kellogg's gone we likely wouldn't get the chance. We were dying a slow and painful death.

I didn't believe that William—or Junior or John Folan or myself—could hustle up a sixty-grand sponsorship for next year. We couldn't even get a schedule printed and posted around town. Or a gym to practice in more than twice a week. Now we'd have to go impress some corporate moguls?

William claimed he was not as crushed as I was, but he was still too depressed to have lunch, an unusual occurrence for him. Especially with a list of fine Asian spots in his shirt pocket. As we wandered away on foot, too fidgety to sit in a taxi, William said, "It's a positive for us, a new beginning." He said it as though he were reading it off a script. "We'll find someone who will back us one hundred and ten percent."

But I didn't want to have to write letters and interview with a bunch of suits about all the great benefits of being the main sponsor of the, well, the Guinness Tigers. Or the Renault Tigers. Or the Kerry Gold Tigers.

William trudged off to his aunt's place nearby. I checked in at the Brewery Hostel, the cheapest place in town. We had one game to go.

We were just the regular Tigers now. No more Frosties.

Our last game was at Killarney, March 12. A local derby, they say, and it was traditionally a big rivalry because the towns were only twenty miles apart. Early in the year it looked like this would be a crucial road game to stay at the top of the standings. Instead, we now needed to win to stay out of a three-way tie for last place. Because Waterford had beaten us twice, if we lost a second time to Killarney, the tie-breaker system would leave us dead last.

We played hard; it was a decent game, but our old Americans were no match for their twenty-five-year-old imports. We lost, 80–70. That's all I want to say about it. Not that I got thrown out of the game, or did anything embarrassing. (Only one technical had been called on me during the season, for stomping my foot. A dramatic stomp, admittedly.)

I thanked the Tigers for playing hard all season, and said the town of Tralee should be proud. Then I walked around the locker room and shook everyone's hand. Roscoe Patterson, who had practiced most of the year, but only played the last three games, made positive comments about how much he'd seen us improve. Kieran Donaghy asked me if I was going to come back and coach the Tigers next year.

"I want to," I told him. Like a fool, I'd fallen for basketball again and I'd gotten burned; there was no possibility of a happy ending.

None of the players knew about Kellogg's.

Here was how the final standings looked. Or at least the bottom part that I was interested in:

Waterford Crystals 5–17
Killarney Lakers 5–17
Tralee Tigers 5–17

We were listed in dead last because of the tie-breaker rule: both Waterford and Killarney had beaten the Tigers twice.

The next morning I took the train to Belfast, wanting to get out of Tralee to find some perspective, some distance. I hadn't saved up enough from the season to take the big holiday I'd planned, staying in hotels around the country, hunting the great music sessions. Instead I went north to see the Boylan family. Sheila, one of the daughters, promised roaring music sessions and great *craic*.

During the days I walked the sad and ragged streets of Belfast, my preferred way to see a city. It was sunny but cold, so I set out, city map in back pocket.

Belfast was much more peaceful than it had been twenty years ago, which was a good thing, because the streets could be pretty threatening on foot, even today. The murals made it obvious when I was in a Protestant (read: Loyalist) or Catholic (read: Nationalist) neighborhood. The Loyalist areas flew the British flag, the Union Jack, at the top of the streetlights, or flags with the "Red Hand of Ulster," which was, well, a severed, bloody hand. Sometimes the curbs were painted red, white, and blue, the colors of the Union Jack. And murals were everywhere. Murals with men in ski masks, wielding AK-47s. With sayings like "Never Give an Inch" and "Who Shall Separate Us?"

When you crossed over an expressway or passed a few factories, the colors changed to the Irish Tri-color. Green-white-orange. And the Catholic murals depicted dead hunger strikers and murdered lawyers. They weren't quite as intimidating, or maybe that was my take, but I'm not even Catholic—I'm probably closer to Mooji. Still, I felt more threatened on Loyalist land. Did I think of myself as a Kerryman now? Each neighborhood had its own taxicab companies, and they wouldn't deliver you to the "other" neighborhoods.

I walked for an hour, all the way to the Milltown Cemetery, the old

SAINT PATRICK'S DAY, TRALEE, COUNTY KERRY

Catholic graveyard crammed full of history. The yard was crowded—with tombstones, that is—and very uneven, but with glorious Celtic crosses, old but well maintained. Every so often, a headstone read something like *Murdered for His Faith*. Or *Killed By a Car Bomb*. Or *Assassinated by British Soldiers*. Some of them even had the IRA's battalion division and rank on the tombstone, which seemed odd because it was a secret organization.

The Irish Republican Army had its own section, very plain, but startling. Some of the Hunger Strikers from 1981 were there, including Bobby Sands, who received worldwide attention as the first of the ten hunger strikers to die that year.

At night, the Belfast music was great, of course. I was confident I'd be good enough to at least fit in, but a whole different group of tunes was played in the North—those typical regional differences and preferences. Still, I followed along as best I could. They didn't play any of the polkas or slides from County Kerry that I'd learned. Belfast fiddlers had a harder-driving style. They played almost exclusively reels, which were quicker and have more kick. Walking into a session with Sheila Boylan gave me immediate access, but left me wondering if folks would have been as friendly had I come in alone. One thing I was certain of, my musical home was in Tralee.

I had a week left in Ireland.

I Lead Such a Troublesome Life

On my way home from Belfast, I stopped in Limerick for the Super League's year-end tournament, the "Top Eight." It was like an expanded Final Four, I suppose, except that it was not yet as popular with the fans, media, coaches, or players as the televised Cup. My last-place 5–17 Tigers hadn't come close to qualifying, though we'd beaten some of the top teams: Belfast, Limerick, Killester, Notre Dame. More stilted logic from a beaten and weary coach.

Limerick had a beautiful gym, but lacked even a sign outside to notify the public of the games. No *"This Weekend! The Super League's Top 8!"* No wonder it was not a big deal.

Although Neptune had been crowned regular-season champs, I wanted to see who won the playoff championship. Unfortunately, not too many folks felt the same. Fewer than one hundred fans came to the final game.

In the title match, St. Vincent's drilled Notre Dame by 30 points. Two short weeks earlier, our six-man squad took St. Vincent's into overtime before running out of gas. It was heartening in some ways, until I thought seriously about how close we were to being very good, even with all of our injuries, defections, and football issues.

Then I grew depressed. The Tigers had no sponsor so I had no job.

Why was I still thinking about returning to Ireland? I couldn't bear to do the simple math: *No sponsor + no money = no team.* Would the Tigers have more than six players? Would Ricardo go on the Atkins diet and lose the eighty extra pounds he was again dragging around?

We hadn't exactly collapsed. The Tigers had fought every inch, the Sisyphus of Irish basketball. The challenge was a much bigger load than our team could push up the mountain. Anyway, in my view, the manner in which we were handling the sponsorship issue seemed foolish. William Main didn't want anyone to know that Kellogg's had dropped us, least of all St. Brendan's. Only William and I knew. But everyone in Irish basketball, including our Tigers, knew the three-year deal was up. And people kept asking me, even in Limerick, "What's the story with Kellogg's?"

We lied to them.

I resolved to call Junior Collins upon returning to Tralee, invite him over for tea. I'd level with him about Kellogg's. Maybe he'd have some ideas on sponsorship possibilities.

When You're Sick, Is It Tea That You Want?

I came home to Tralee to find that William Main had yet to lift a finger to find a sponsor, but still didn't want the press to know about getting dumped by Kellogg's.

Not one letter or proposal had been sent out. Not one phone call made. The Tigers were five months away from next season starting, and we had not one nickel to our name. I can't say for certain why nothing had been done, except that William was embarrassed to admit publicly that Kellogg's had dropped us. He'd longed to have a sponsor in hand before admitting the last one dumped the Tigers. Kind of like the guy who wouldn't go out in public after his girlfriend dumped him. He wanted to show up with a looker on his arm.

One evening when the rain was blowing so hard it ripped my umbrella to shreds—the fourth one—I phoned Connie. While I was sitting in soaked pants, it was seventy degrees in Las Cruces. She had been fixing up our old adobe apartment and making plans for our modest wedding ceremony. After I gave her the Tralee update, she said for the first time what I wouldn't admit: "It's starting to look like the Tigers won't exist next season."

And I had to do *something*, job-wise. Would there be work in New Mexico? Maybe I'd have to go back to college coaching, but I was seriously considering a triumphant return to Tralee. Was it my ego prodding me to come back to redeem our lost season? I still hadn't finished my book of fiction and wanted more time. And there was the music, and my feeling that even if the Tigers hadn't made quantifiable progress in basketball, my fiddling was improving. I knew that in the States I'd never be able to play with fine musicians four nights a week the way I had in Tralee.

The next morning I said it to myself: I wanted to come back to Ireland. I repeated that a few times, but didn't have the heart to tell Connie. Not yet.

It cost about sixty thousand euros to run a Super League team. Our team, that is. Most ran cheaper, because the coach wasn't imported from America. I wanted to release our "problem" to the press and ask them to put a positive spin on it by saying, "What a shame it would be—the Tigers are so young, paid their dues this season, yet might not have a team." The sports pages were free advertising, and a full-page article was, in essence, a full-page ad.

When William Main stopped by, I made him sit down with me and go through the phone book. We looked for potential sponsors and he recorded their addresses. He phoned each one to ask for the name of their marketing chief. We went across the street to the Internet cafe and wrote personalized letters to each one. Then we walked to the post office for stamps and envelopes and those clear shiny cases that grade-school kids use to make their book reports look professional.

By this time of year I was supposed to be wandering Ireland with my fiddle on my back and Junior Collins's wished-for championship ring on my finger. Local folks were going to take me in, teach me to play the jigs their great-grandfathers played. "You're the championship basketball coach," I'd hoped they'd say. I was going to listen to their stories, help them cut fresh turf in the bog, and begin the long process of preparing for the Irish winter.

At one point, William said in frustration, "I'm going to walk away from the Tralee Tigers! It's not worth all the headaches." William spit this out occasionally, like sour milk. We had run out of Kellogg's money sometime in February, and William was dipping into his own pocket to get us through.

I told him, "Look, William. I take that kind of comment seriously. This is the time of year when dozens of college coaching openings are going to pop." It would be my chance to get back into Division I, rested and ready. Perhaps a head job at a smaller school would open. Without William helping the Tigers there'd be no team at all. Maybe I'd be better off getting back to the real basketball world, or finding a job in the States that would give me time to write.

And this: Kellogg's called from Dublin and left a strongly worded message. They wanted their Tony the Tiger suit sent back immediately.

The next day I had my last lesson with Paddy Jones. When I told him I was off to America in a week, Paddy shook my hand, grabbing and squeezing it with both of his. I'd miss him. We'd gotten closer than a teacher and student should. I attributed this to the fact that too many of his pupils were children, and it got to be a long, lonesome Tuesday for him with one eleven-year-old after another. I handed back his books and we exchanged addresses.

Paddy was exactly what I needed to tighten up my loose and sloppy playing. I told him how I was still a bit frustrated. I hadn't picked up all of the subtleties of Irish music, although I was a regular at four of the weekly sessions.

"The fiddle is an old man's instrument," Paddy said. "A sportsman begins declining when he's in his thirties. But a man with a fiddle! A man can get pleasure out of his fiddle until he dies. You're on a long road, Rus."

Sports were long gone for me as a competitive participant. Now I had fiddling and writing. Was writing an old man's game as well?

"How long will it all take?" I wondered.

"Do you see that chair right there, Rus?" Paddy asked, pointing. "That chair probably took ten minutes to make in a factory." Paddy leaned forward on one foot, and I thought for a moment he might rear back and kick the offending chair into splinters. "I have a friend who toils away as a chair maker. He goes to a lumberyard to look for just the right wood. Then he makes each chair by hand, one at a time. They take him two years to finish. *Two years.*" He sighed, as if he was exhausted from the work as well.

It was impressive, but what did Paddy mean? Could I become a good fiddler in my second year with him? Could I get the Tigers pointed in the right direction if I came back a second season? Recalling how I yapped much of the time during our first lesson—that was still preserved on tape—I waited patiently for more.

"There's a woman in town I know as well," he continued. "She plays the concertina, a superb musician. She can hear any tune, it makes no difference, and immediately play it on the concertina."

Pretty impressive, I thought. But what does that—

"But there's no depth to her playing," Paddy continued. "Because it comes easy to her, she has no power to her music. She hasn't had to struggle with any tune, and because of that, she has no passion for it. And she can't remember tunes *minutes* after she's played them. It's a struggle for you, as you have to slowly work out each tune like a musical craftsman." Paddy moved closer. Our shoulders were touching, sitting side-by-side. "Ahhhh, Rus," he said, "you should see the care and love in my friend's chairs. The detail in them is astonishing. It means so much more to him because it's taken him longer."

So it was better that I was a slow learner? Could the same be true for the Tigers? I could hear a piano student down the hall, fumbling with "The Dawning of the Day," the way I had in September. The student kept hitting the wrong note at the end of the first phrase. I was tempted to run down and correct whoever the child was, although surely a teacher was there, listening patiently to the same sour note.

Paddy said, "I have to work out every tune as well. It's true. It takes me months to learn a tune. Sometimes years. But then I have it, and it means so much more to me than if I'd gotten it right away. I don't forget because I have them in here," he said, and thumped his heart behind his deep chest. And it sounded as if he *did* have a bunch of tunes in there. The sound was thick, full. Not hollow at all.

CRONIN'S FAVORITE

Two days later I met with Charles O'Sullivan, the director of the Tigers' in-town rival St. Brendan's. We sat in his idling car outside the Women's Resource Center and talked about the future of basketball in Tralee. Years ago O'Sullivan had been regarded as the best player in Tralee. Now he spent four nights a week helping with St. Brendan's various youth teams. He reminded me of the old coaches in Chicago who were around when I was growing up, whose only desire was to teach young kids. Their under-nineteen team had come in second in the nation a few weeks previous. Our Tigers under-nineteen team, he reminded me, somehow did not manage to play a single game all season, an indication of our poor structure.

O'Sullivan said the St. Brendan's folks were impressed with my coaching, which was hard to believe, since we'd only won a single game after the New Year. He'd coached most of my Irish players when they were younger, including Kieran Donaghy, whom he'd had in his stable until this past November. Then he surprised me with this: "Kieran Donaghy says the Tigers could win the championship next season."

"He said what?" I'd heard him, I just couldn't believe Donaghy would say that.

O'Sullivan repeated Donaghy's prediction.

I didn't know what to say to that. Donaghy had his head in the ever-present Irish clouds. "Donaghy is a damn fool, Charles," I said. "Who knows where he gets his goofy ideas?"

We shifted our talk back to the merger. St. Brendan's club looked favorably on all the free clinics I was doing around town, and the fact that local Tralee kids were getting a lot of minutes for the Tigers. They liked the idea of trying to unite and they were seriously considering joining forces with the Frosties Tigers.

"We have just one question," O'Sullivan said. "Are the Tigers set with Kellogg's for sponsorship next season? We don't want to climb on board a sinking ship."

I fidgeted.

St. Brendan's didn't want much money from us, but it didn't want to get burned by inheriting debt. If I told him we had Kellogg's in the bag, he'd find out sooner or later that we didn't, and maybe hold it against me. On the other hand, if I told him the truth—our committee couldn't find a pub in Tralee, let alone a sponsor—he might order me out of the car right that instant. I could slow-play him, but I was scheduled to go home soon. Who would talk to O'Sullivan then if I didn't? He didn't want to talk to Junior or William.

I didn't want to lie to him. But I did.

We needed them. Our youth structure was pathetic; St. Brendan's was exceptional. I told Charles O'Sullivan that the deal was looking good with Kellogg's, and that we'd know for sure soon. We shook hands, and it was close to official, sort of. The Tigers and St. Brendan's would forget a ten-year grudge and join forces. St. Brendan's wouldn't need to sign up with us until October, and if we had no sponsor by then they'd still be fine independent of the Tigers.

Everything was in place for the Tigers to have a better team next year and for years to come. The coach had more than paid his dues. The team would be healthy, refurbished, and deep.

But we had no sponsor. It would break my heart if this were my first *and* last season in Ireland, if I went down in history as Tralee's last coach, and judging by our record, not a very good one.

The New York Times Book Review had a review of R. F. Forster's *The Irish Story*. The review was written by a man named Richard Eder. This part caught my attention:

> Perhaps every nation has its exceptionalist legend, but there could hardly be two more different than the American and Irish versions. For us it is the belief that we are providentially destined to prevail in our personal, national, and movie life: the so-called happy ending, quite opposite to any tragic sense. For the Irish, the providential destiny is for defeat: unjust, heroic, beautiful, to be someday redeemed; and not so much tragic as lyrically plaintive.

On March 23, the Tralee Tigers had our end-of-season banquet. It was my idea; they'd never had one before. Actually, it was only sandwiches and chicken wings. We invited parents and some business folks around town. I wanted everyone to feel as positive as possible going into the summer. Even if I couldn't return to Ireland, I'd enjoyed living there and wanted to leave on a good note. Not an easy task when you finished the season with ten losses in a row, plummeted to last place, and had no money for the following season.

The five Irish players who had hung with me for the entire year received awards.

Liam Culloty earned "Smartest Player." He was a bit slow and averaged 3 points a contest, but he had the fewest turnovers on the Tigers and was a good listener. He showed great dedication coming home from college in Cork each weekend. Culloty scored 19 points for the season, but I was glad to have him.

"Super Dave" Cronin took home "Most Improved Player." Once he bought straps for his glasses and new sneakers, it was pretty amazing how much better he got. He even had 6 points against St. Vincent's in that overtime loss. On one play I saw Dave wipe his glasses just before the ball got to him, look down to square his feet, then drill a three-pointer over a charging St. Vincent's forward. He was not even twenty yet. He had 13 points for the year, but all of them came after Christmas. He also drew the loudest round of applause that night.

Alan Keane won "Newcomer of the Year" and "Best Shooter." He averaged almost 10 points a game for us, and his 34 percent from the three-point line led the Tigers in that category. But he shot 21 percent from inside the arc, which was a strange statistic indeed. The worst thing about Alan was that he overtrained, lifting weights and swimming until he was exhausted. And obviously he should shoot more three-pointers and fewer twos. Keane was also one of the few players I'd ever coached who was actually better than he believed he was. It was usually the opposite.

Kieran Donaghy received "Most Potential." He was the one Irish guy who could maybe play in college in the States one day, although his high school transcript, he finally admitted, was a mess because of low math scores. Donaghy had somehow lost his simple part-time job at the men's clothing store. Without me to prod him, I figured he'd be unemployed indefinitely. Maybe the Plumbing Wars would flair up again.

By the end of the year Donaghy was easily our best Irish player, but I didn't give him the MVP award he likely deserved. I didn't want him to get lazy or big-headed after he missed the first two months of training. He averaged 8 points per game, but he proved himself as a fighter, and I was certain we could win with him next season. If we had a next season. And if I was part of that "we."

Instead I gave 5'6" Kevin O'Donoghue "Most Valuable Player." He only missed one practice, was consistent, and the most dependable. He scored

56 points for the season—about 2.5 per game. Still, he'd slowly grown into a leadership role. We made him captain after John Teahan got hurt, at John's suggestion. He was our best help-side defender, always in the right place, was steady and smart with the ball, and was our best free thrower. Kevin could have been the posterboy for the Tigers: he was young, short, inexperienced, and refused to quit. He'd also gotten a promotion at the grocery store that coincided with his MVP award.

None of the American imports were around. We'd sent Chris Thompson back to the States at Christmas. Then Gillespie bolted. Chris Davis played longer than any of them, but had left Tralee right after I cut him. Not that I expected a player who'd been dumped to come to our ceremony. Anyway, Donaghy told me Chris Davis was in Dublin. With the woman who was not his girlfriend. Maybe I should have given him a "Dublin Tourism Appreciation" award.

John Teahan came to the banquet. Word had gotten back to me that he was telling folks around town what a fine job I'd done, to have been so close each game with our midget youngsters. Although I was sick of losing, it was refreshing that the captain finally thought I could coach. Teahan went from Irish Player of the Year a year ago to scoring 57 points for the season. Total. His back was still a mess, six months after he'd hurt it. He was stubborn, and we'd had problems, but Teahan was correct about nearly everything he warned me about, not the least of which was that we should have brought Jermaine Turner back. Teahan came to the games hurt, sat on the bench in street clothes, and hollered for his teammates. I didn't know if I'd ever really coach him, but I could sense he was a special breed who would lead with his actions.

Micheal Quirke was there as well. He must have gotten his football commitments and studying out of the way. He was a polite kid, a gentleman, but I felt like he completely let the Tigers down. In fairness, Quirke never once was AWOL. He always told me when and why he wouldn't be playing for the Tigers, often face to face. Football hadn't been going as well for him lately. He had been demoted from the big Kerry team, so maybe more basketball was in his future, and now he'd nearly graduated from the college. I'd welcome him back if we had another season, but his reliability would always be a question.

Roscoe Patterson made an appearance. He filled in nicely the last three games as our American. He'd lived in Ireland for a long time, and he might be able to play as an Irish citizen next season, which would be great.

And Ricardo Leonard came. He was late for chicken wings, but I thought that was a good omen. His Achilles must have been nearly ready; he could walk without limping. But he'd gained all the weight back and was carrying around a massive belly. I hadn't talked to Ricardo much that spring. For one thing, it took Ricardo an hour to say what he actually meant. Also, the last time we sat down together, he told me, "Coach, when you mention my weight and diet, it goes in one ear and out the other." Since I considered his weight the biggest factor in his chance to make a comeback, there was not that much for us to talk about. But Ricardo told me he had something important to discuss before I left that evening.

I met with the players as a group, in a little side room away from the chicken wings, before saying goodnight and goodbye. We huddled like we were meeting at half court, as we did at the beginning of practice. I told them they were expected to play pickup games all spring and summer. And that the Tigers had lost enough close contests to think that if we had everyone healthy, we could be good next year.

Then I took Kevin O'Donoghue aside.

"Kellogg's is gone," I said.

He looked like I'd told him his puppy had been run over. His tiny shoulders sank, and his mouth dropped. I shook his hand and told him not to worry. "We're doing all we can so that Tigers will continue to have a team in the Super League."

"What about you?" O'Donoghue asked.

I got the feeling he thought his coach wouldn't be back. I asked him to tell the Tigers, but to wait until the next day, not wanting to spoil what little we had to feel good about that night.

Ricardo Leonard cornered me when I grabbed my trusty raincoat. He had something on his mind, and I was curious. Was Ricardo ready to make the commitment? Train all summer, get therapy on his Achilles, and lose the excess weight? Had he already gone on a revolutionary new diet? Was he going to reveal to me something hugely insightful about our lost season where everything went wrong? Maybe he'd have some simple-yet-profound Yogi Berra-ism that would help me make sense of our season. Or maybe he was going to thank me for journeying all the way to Ireland to take my chances with the Frosties Tigers.

Bigger shorts.

He wanted us to order bigger uniforms; longer and baggier shorts especially. So we'd look more stylish, he said. Also, I suspect, so he could fit his ample rear end in them. He had the phone number of just the right sporting goods company.

I was tired. I simply nodded and wrote myself a note: *Ricardo wants bigger shorts.*

Goodbye to Ireland

Junior Collins was thumbing my doorbell early the next morning.

"Kevin O'Donoghue told the lads about Kellogg's after you left the banquet, like. The players don't want our lost season to be our last season," he said.

I didn't either. The players—the Irish ones—were overly concerned about whether their coach would return to guide them next year, Junior said. I set a cup of tea in front of Junior, the quart of milk next to it.

I told him that our chances of finding a real sponsor were remote. I didn't say the rest out loud because I didn't want to offend him: We couldn't even organize our youth teams. We couldn't find our way to road games without getting lost. We couldn't get the buses to leave on time.

What it amounted to was that I would be risking my career, such as it was, to think there would even *be* a Tigers team next year.

"Sure," he said, "but we could be better next year, like."

I sat down across from him and he pushed me the milk carton.

The Irish weather was beginning to break open into a gorgeous spring; extended daylight, more sunshine. Not the damp chill of the long nights and short days. Every drop of the usual seventy inches of annual rain had fallen, but by the end of the season it had let up. My flight home had been set for months, and near the end of the Tigers' losing streak I began counting the days until March 26.

Ciaran Dalton invited me over for dinner the evening before I left. His was the only home I'd been to for a meal, other than the five I'd had at Junior's place in the autumn. In my seven-month experience, Irish hospitality meant buying you a pint at the pub. I'd never been for a meal to William's home or John Folan's. Or any of the players, save Kieran Donaghy's during the Plumbing Wars, when my guidance with his career and verbal tics was rewarded with a toasted sandwich.

Ciaran's home was an immense archive of Irish and American traditional music. His walls were lined with stacks of old LPs, CDs, and various dusty cassette tapes. The walls not covered with columns of music held sagging shelves of books, mostly about the history and folk traditions of Ireland.

His wife Colette made roast lamb for dinner with three kinds of potatoes, carrots, and mashed turnips. To finish, a homemade apple tart and a pot of tea.

Afterward we settled in around their open fireplace, the logs and turf blazing away. Ciaran got out his banjo, mandolin, and fiddle and we played tunes, sitting knee to knee, which is the American old-time style. The Irish always seemed to have a table in between the musicians, covered with pints of beer. When we took a break, he said, "Tell me this and tell me no more. Why, when so many people play traditional Irish music, don't you just stick with American music?"

I couldn't answer him then, and still can't. Maybe it was the way Irish music captured every emotion—passion and anger, sorrow and joy, luck and misfortune. And every season, even a basketball season.

That night we traded tunes from both traditions. He'd play an Appalachian number on the banjo and I'd follow along on the fiddle. His huge hands bounced in the claw-hammer style as if he'd been raised in the mountains of West Virginia. I knew the West Virginia style: I went for a week of music every August. Any instrument looked like a toy in Ciaran's solid grip, and he'd switch from mandolin to banjo to fiddle every few tunes.

Colette picked up the guitar to back us, but not before she tossed several more huge hunks of turf on the fire. I knew it meant they planned on playing long into the night. Ciaran switched to mandolin for a series of lively jigs from County Clare, and I tagged along in the musical sense. He smiled to himself during the jigs, and I was certain I knew why: I was getting it, picking up the nuances of Irish music. I'd improved and he could hear it.

During one break, Ciaran said, "You know, there are so many tunes that came back." This was his favorite subject, but I didn't mind hearing it again. "Fiddle tunes originally from the Irish tradition went to America, got played over there, then got transformed. They came back to Ireland in the fiddle case of some obscure musician—whom everybody figured they'd never see again. It didn't have to be a famous musician. Any fool could carry a tune in their head across the Atlantic."

I nodded. We'd talked on several occasions about the similar tunes that carried different names.

"The music is like a currency," Ciaran continued, "or form of communication, the most ancient kind."

Colette rolled her eyes and slung her feet up on a stool. "Dear God," she said, "here comes another theory."

Ciaran kept on. "Folks would exchange tunes, pass them on like gifts. Or take them with as keepsakes."

I'd learned about fifty tunes in my time in Ireland. They were my keepsakes. Was I to take them back to the States as a gift? Or did he mean that one rare sunny day I'd return *from* America?

Ciaran told me to play a tune myself; he'd follow. I led off a set of Kerry polkas, the happy and rollicking form unique to our county. Ciaran listened to Colette and me for a while before he picked up his mandolin. I had begun closing my eyes when I played, which was a trademark of the Irish musicians. When I heard Ciaran's mandolin, I peeked for a moment at the ground. Our three right feet were tapping in unison.

Later, Ciaran asked to take a look at my fiddle. He turned it over in his massive hands, caressed the back, looked at it from different angles, held it up to the light, then looked inside, maybe to see where it was made, or perhaps as though my recent improvements were tucked away within the spruce and maple.

They knew I was scheduled to leave the next morning and planned on taking a taxicab. Junior Collins had insisted he'd take me, but the drive was a major chore for him. It was a two-hour ride to the Shannon airport, but only a hundred euros for me to get there in a taxi. Not too bad, as the Irish said about nearly everything.

But Colette, who was a doctor at clinics around the West of Ireland, said she was going past Shannon to do some work in Ennis and would be happy to take me. By chance, we needed to depart at the same hour. I was glad to save the hundred bucks, but also to get the use of a car, because seven boxes of my stuff—blankets, books, kitchen utensils, sweaters, corduroys, raincoats—had to go to the post office to be mailed back to America.

"Would you mind coming to get me fifteen minutes earlier," I said, "so I can mail my packages home?"

Colette was quiet and looked at Ciaran. I realized they'd discussed my situation and were quite likely wondering if I was ever really coming back to Ireland. I'd been honest with Ciaran about the financial state of the Tigers, but he wasn't a sports fan, so I didn't want to bore him. I'd only brought up our sponsor plight once, a few weeks earlier.

Ciaran deedled around on my fiddle. He'd never played it, and said he wanted to give it a try before I left town. He was a fine fiddler although his playing sounded ancient—archaic, even, sounding as though it had come out of another era, like his sweaters.

Ciaran said, "Why don't you just leave the boxes with us, the things you don't need?" It was as though he was talking to my fiddle; he wasn't even looking at me. "And you can recover your boxes if you return in August, so." As the local postman, he said, he could easily ship them back to America if I decided not to come back.

I told them I'd think about it overnight.

When I got home that night, my last in Ireland, surrounded by stuffed gym bags and nearly bursting boxes, I took inventory of my belongings, and also all the wonderful things about Tralee: The fresh fish, four days a week, right around the corner. The brown scones at forty cents a pop. Nothing better than a late-morning scone with my Irish tea. The lively ladies who ran the Women's Resource Center, above which I lived. The town park where my quiet, contemplative walks evolved from "thinking about fiction" in September to "engrossed in basketball" in November. The Irish players. They'd kept a great attitude in the face of our disastrous season.

I'd especially miss Kieran Donaghy. He could be a headache, but his struggle to mature—on and off the floor—typified the Tigers' season. Coaches are supposed to energize players, but that somehow worked in reverse with Donaghy. His exuberance had the effect of a strong cup of tea. He generally stopped by to see me every afternoon after the Plumbing Wars truce. He became a good listener, and I believe he made me a better coach. I had turned on my team in anger before he arrived: frustrated with Ricardo, Barnaby, Quirke, and to some extent Teahan, I needed Kieran Donaghy.

Donaghy had even stopped by at my final music session at Baily's Pub. It was the first time any of the players had heard me play; the Irish players were accepting of my playing music and would ask about it to be polite. But they'd never showed up at a session. Donaghy preferred the ballad singers and the "rebel songs" (he disliked the British), but he sat patiently that night like a mature gentleman.

And boy, would I miss those music sessions. With the end of the basketball season I was even playing the entire session on Saturdays.

I stood in the doorway to the Women's Resource Center when Colette drove up. It was misty and drizzling, typical soft Irish weather. My belongings were separated into two piles. One pile was my two overstuffed gym bags, my fiddle, and my computer. The other was seven boxes of things I could leave packed up during the summer—sweaters, corduroys, scarves, blankets, my raincoat—but would need if I did return to Tralee.

Even through the wet glass I could see someone else in the car. It was Ciaran. Evidently he'd taken a rare day off from his postman duties to say his goodbye. He climbed out, waving an old-time Doc Watson CD he'd brought along for the ride.

"Don't you have the sense not to stand in the rain?" he asked.

I hadn't realized I *was* standing in the rain. "It feels good," I said. I looked up at the moving clouds. It was my first day in Ireland without my raincoat, and I didn't mind.

Ciaran said, "Off to the post office first, is it?"

I said no.

Instead I asked if they could store the boxes for me over the summer. Just in case the Tigers got a sponsor and I returned to Ireland.

PART THREE

BANISHED TO AMERICA

Life was different in Las Cruces, New Mexico: sunny mornings, seeing old friends, loads of green chile on everything I ate. The stress of the season was a world away. Each evening I'd listen to my Paddy Jones tapes and try to recall his tunes. Hearing his voice made me sad.

Connie and I were getting married in August. She was supportive of two of my passions—fiddling and writing. But she didn't get the basketball part. One June morning I told her I wanted to return to Tralee.

"How could you even think about going back, the way things ended?" she demanded. We were on one of our walks over the backroads near the Rio Grande. It was another gorgeous morning in New Mexico. She let go of my hand and turned to face me. "You've told me yourself. Every time you get involved in basketball, it ends in heartbreak."

What could I say? That *was* how things seemed to conclude. I tried to explain my position, appealing to her literary background. "You know," I said, "the Hero goes on a Journey. Like in the Odyssey." This was a smart idea. Connie loved Homer. "Like in all those Joseph Campbell books about myth, too," I said.

"Aren't you getting a little old for this?" Connie asked.

I was—approaching forty-five and at a loss to explain most of my career decisions. Like how I assumed, with my basketball pedigree, that I would mop up the competition in Ireland.

"So what if you came in last place?" Connie continued. "Nobody cares about that but you and the Tigers."

Coming in last place *was* humiliating, and I had grown to care about my Tigers. Connie admitted that she liked the Tigers, too. She was charmed by Kieran Donaghy and even annoyed me by insisting that I should listen to John Teahan more. It's true that last place was bad for the ego, but it was disastrous for the resume if I ever decided to coach again.

I wasn't able to explain things to Connie very well—my wish to return was nearly as mysterious as the allure of Irish music. I only knew that I had to go back to Tralee for another season.

Cheer Up Old Hag

In July of 2003, the Tralee Tigers secured a new sponsor: Horan's Health Stores. They had three or four little shops around County Kerry, with one in Tralee. The deal was cut by John O'Riordan, a Garda, or police, lieutenant. He'd worked the door at Tigers' games, taking tickets, and had begun leading our committee behind the scenes. William Main made a formal request for O'Riordan to join the Tigers; O'Riordan did, spearheading the club's financial comeback. O'Riordan was a no-nonsense guy who would provide a much stronger hand in running the club. William Main had decided to pass on much of the chairman's role, while still being involved from a distance. William's aunt had died in Dublin that summer—they had been close—and that would keep him home more.

Horan's Health Stores would give us only thirty thousand euros, half the amount Kellogg's had been paying. Salaries would have to be cut for the imported players and the coach—who I was hoping would be me.

It was a start. We were alive, with a chance for some kind of atonement. We'd have to raise money through church-gate collections, sidewalk collections, greyhound race nights, basketball clinics, and Table Quizzes—the pub-based Irish version of game shows.

O'Riordan phoned me every two weeks concerning the solidifying of the sponsorship. I reminded him of a player whom I'd seen the year before on the Garda basketball team. During one of these calls he invited me to return to Tralee.

By late July I was able to get Connie to agree: I'd be going back to Tralee. Alone. We tried to figure ways in which she could come with me—maybe just the first semester, or take a leave of absence for a year—but in the end it would have been too costly. We'd get married in August, in a civil ceremony officiated by the man who built my fiddle, Bill Bussmann. (Bill had gotten his certificate by mailing in a coupon to *Rolling Stone* magazine in the 1970s).

Connie would come over again for a month-long visit at Christmas to break up our time apart.

I rang Junior Collins and told him to find an apartment for me. I'd call him later with my flight times.

"The conquering hero returns, like," Junior said.

"Not exactly," I said.

I got busy, spending most mornings on the phone in a quest to find two new Americans and a Bosman. John Teahan still considered it his captainly duty to assist me in the search. That was awkward. For one thing, John only knew American players who had played in Ireland.

Teahan phoned Kenny Gamble, the American star from Neptune, and actually offered him a contract. This seemed to me a terrible move: a player offering another player a job. Gamble was the Super League's MVP, but he wanted nearly twice what we'd be able to pay. Gamble decided to return to Neptune and I let it pass without comment.

Naturally, Teahan also set his sights on Jermaine Turner. So did I.

I rang Jermaine each week at his home in New York City. He was also being wooed by Dublin's Tolka Rovers. I was wary of his using us merely to squeeze more money out of Tolka. One August morning I asked Jermaine for an e-mail address so I could send him a sample contract and he could compare offers.

"Sure," he said. "It's JermaineTurner@TolkaRovers.com."

At that point, I figured he was already gone.

In my best recruiting days at UTEP and New Mexico State I relied heavily on Chicago players. For my new imports to Ireland I went back to my roots.

A friend who coaches in the NBA's minor league, the CBA, told me about Chris Bracey, a 6'5" African-American from Chicago who had Irish grandparents and thus a chance at an Irish passport and Bosman status. Bracey's West Texas A&M team had finished 25–9. I watched two films on him—he was tough, active, and loved to play defense. Although he'd averaged only 5 points per game, I saw a vast upside in him. He had played only one year of high school ball, and he'd been hurt his entire junior year of college. The Tigers signed him for half of what our previous Bosman, Barnaby Craddock, had been getting.

"I need to improve," Bracey kept saying. I knew then we'd get along fine. Bracey didn't even ask for a toaster.

I still had to find two players with U.S. passports.

Brandon Mason was a 6'4" guard that I'd helped recruit and coach at New Mexico State before resigning to get my MFA degree. I sat in row twenty-three for most of his home games after I stopped coaching. We became friends, chatting between classes and in the weight room. He excelled at what I came to believe was most important for an American to do in Ireland: he could create his own shot off the dribble. Brandon averaged 13 points per game at NMSU, but personal trouble meant he didn't attract a big money job in Europe. His problems—driving without a license, then missing the ensuing court date—seemed minor. But both resulted in arrests in Las Cruces, and bad publicity, which reduced his marketability. Ireland was his only option. Also, Brandon was enthusiastic and boisterous. He gave out chest-bumps at every opportunity.

One day in late July, Connie stomped past me on the couch. "You've been on the phone for two solid weeks," she said.

Damond Williams had come to New Mexico State a year before Brandon Mason. Damond had been a seventeen-year-old freshman, too raw to help us. When he had a problem—"borrowing" a teammate's telephone credit card—we decided not to renew his scholarship.

Damond had transferred to a junior college, then surfaced at McNeese State University in Louisiana, where he blossomed as a 6'5" leaper. Getting canned at NMSU forced him to redshirt a year and grow up. He even graduated on time from McNeese State. Luckily, Damond didn't hold a grudge over our not renewing his full ride at NMSU. He'd been immature, he said, made some mistakes, but it all wound up positive. Damond had known Brandon Mason during his high school days and was excited about being his teammate.

Incidentally, the Tigers never used contracts for their imported Yanks, preferring the old-fashioned verbal assurance. We were the only club left that conducted business that way. That summer I insisted on Tralee joining the modern era, and whipped up my idea of contracts for Chris Bracey, Brandon Mason, and Damond Williams.

Ricardo Leonard rang me every few weeks over the summer. He would talk for an hour without saying much, but I knew what he wanted—a contract, or at least an estimate on what he'd be paid.

But the Tigers were no longer the Kellogg's Frosties Tigers, who could afford to make Ricardo Ireland's best-paid player.

Our financial plan was to get everyone else signed up, then let Ricardo practice with the Tigers for two weeks, so I could assess the damaged Achilles. We'd see how far his game had slipped and how much the scales had tipped. Then we'd figure what we had left in the budget. This seemed fair to me; I volunteered for a pay cut myself, down to 250 euros a week. Essentially, Ricardo would be trying out. I wanted Ricardo to play because even at half-speed he was better than most of the Irish guys. But I wanted to pay him what he was worth.

"It's not the money," Ricardo assured me over the phone. Not yet it wasn't.

The Wild Irishman

As my flight was landing at Shannon Airport, the lady from County Kerry I'd been chatting with leaned toward me and asked if I needed a lift to Tralee. "It's certainly no bother for me," she said. "Is someone picking you up?"

"A good friend," I said.

I'd hardly gotten through baggage claim and customs when I saw him.

"Junior," I sputtered. "You've got to burn that jacket."

He grumbled and grabbed my heaviest bag.

"How's Connie?" he asked. "She'll be back at Christmas, will she?"

"Connie's fine, but Kellogg's is gone," I said. "What do you think the Horan's Health Store folks will say if they see you wearing a Frosties jacket?"

"I'm just the manager, like," he said, backing the car up.

"Not anymore you're not," I said. "You're the Horan's Health Store Tigers' Director of Basketball Operations. I just promoted you."

Junior and I had a lot of business to catch up on. The Irish Super League decided over the summer to change the structure of the league, dividing the twelve teams into Southern and Northern Conferences.

The North would feature the five Dublin teams plus Belfast. For Tralee that meant less travel; we'd play Southern Conference teams three times, Northern squads just once.

The South would be tougher: Neptune (regular season champs), as well as the Demons (Cup champs) from Cork would be in our half. Two years earlier, Waterford and Limerick had won those titles, and they'd be in the South, as well as our arch rival Killarney.

Because of the new format—and perhaps also to have less emphasis on the Cup—the Super League decided to give plenty of attention to the end-of-season champions.

The league would be, for the first time, promoting a Final Four. There would be no regular season champ like Neptune the year before. Instead it would be two conference champions, then the new Final Four, where some lucky team would be crowned the Super League's National Champs.

"It'll be exactly like the Final Four in the States, like," Junior said.

I didn't want to nap that first morning back, as I was determined again to stay awake and fight the fatigue. My first impulse after Junior had deposited me was to go see Kieran Donaghy and begin getting him emotionally ready to play on an improved team. But it was 9:30 A.M., and I didn't want to wake him. So I unpacked, got my closet organized, went shopping for some essentials, and at noon I walked the mile to the Donaghy home. I figured I could have a cup of tea with his Nan until Kieran awoke to us chatting downstairs, then got showered and dressed. Maybe I'd treat him to lunch at the Greyhound Pub.

Nan and I shared a pot of tea and scones. Finally she caught me looking at my watch. "Oh, you're probably busy. But it's grand to see you."

I told her it was good to see her, too. "Would you mind if I went upstairs and woke up Kieran?"

"You'd be five hours too late," Nan said.

"What?"

"Kieran's working," she said proudly. "He found his own job."

Donaghy had secured work at the new SuperMac's franchise in Tralee, an Irish-owned-and-operated fast-food place in the heart of Tralee. He was flipping burgers full-time, starting at 8 A.M.

There was a long line for lunch when I got there. Sometimes those fast-food outfits—matching hat, shirt, and pants—make a guy look foolish. But Donaghy looked impressive, sweating from the face, his big right hand around the spatula. He'd eye the deep fryer, splash a little ketchup, seal a box, call out the order, then whirl back to the grill. When he finally noticed me, he gave me the signal: fifteen minutes and he'd be on break. I got an order of chips and waited.

"Fucking hot at the grill, Coach," he said when he came out.

That first night back in Ireland, I jumped in a taxi to Kate Brown's Pub.

"Kate Brown's is mostly older folks," the taxi driver said. "There'll be more single women at one of the discos."

"I'm married," I said.

"Visiting from America, is it?" he asked.

"No," I said. "I live here in Tralee."

Ciaran Dalton was hosting the session at the usual table, mandolin on his knee, banjo on one side and his wife Colette on the other; a turf fire roared on the other side of the room. I got a big grin from Ciaran and a crushing handshake, as well as a cold pint. We exchanged tunes all evening, both Irish and American, as was his preference. He must have figured we could talk and catch up after we'd played all night.

"We decided to sell your boxes of books and clothes," he finally said at the end of the evening. "I hope that's no bother."

Nothing could have bothered me that evening. I felt great, like I was home. When I was packing up, Ciaran took my arm with one hand and stuffed twenty euros in my pocket with the other.

I was shocked. I tried to give it back to him, but he insisted that I keep it for taxicab fare. It was my first time being paid to play music in Ireland. Of course the message meant much more than the money.

Junior Collins, despite his new job title, had mostly the same duties—getting the uniforms washed, driving the Americans around, slapping up our new game posters around town, helping with the many fund-raisers we had to do without our old multinational corporate sponsor. He even got a spiffy haircut at the start of the season.

But the big question was—What would Junior do about his old Frosties Tigers jacket?

"You can't continue to wear that thing, Junior," I insisted again over breakfast that September. "You're jeopardizing our sponsorship."

Junior guffawed, but I was serious. I even asked William Main to call him and demand that he honor our new sponsor. Then I called John O'Riordan to enlist his help on my dress code demands.

A week later, Junior stopped by for a cup of tea. He didn't say anything about it, but I noticed he'd pulled on our new navy-blue Horan's Health Store jacket, over his frazzled Frosties Tigers one.

There was another problem with our beloved Sports Complex. Besides putting in another state-of-the-art pool to replace the last fully modern one, the Complex's director had decided it was finally time to upgrade the locker rooms. During the construction, the Tigers would have to go *outside* each game, through the drizzle, to a crude brick building that had rustic showers. The floors were muddy, the toilets rank, and the walls wet. The room wasn't fit for sheep. The showers stayed hot for only the first couple players. There was no heat, so each home game I'd pack up my beloved space heater, then crank it up an hour before the Tigers were to arrive. Still, we'd shiver our way through pregame and halftime talks all season.

Here was how our Irish roster was shaping up that September:

Kieran Donaghy earned a spot on the Kerry Gaelic Football squad for under-twenty-ones. That was a worry. But in August they lost in the playoffs so he seemed eager to have a winning team in hoops. The plumbing apprenticeship was on hold because of SuperMac's. Donaghy had also taken his first steady girlfriend, a smart and ambitious university student. He seemed overly concerned about his playing time, but I knew there'd be plenty for him.

Donaghy would be with us from the first practice this time, and I expected a great season from him. By November the gym's caretaker, Buddy O'Grady, would have to chase Donaghy away to lock up after practice. Also, it had gotten back to me from a few sources that Donaghy had completely stopped drinking to prepare for the season. He'd really been off the drink— and it would be more than six weeks.

Giant scholar **Micheal Quirke** would be with us full-time. His Gaelic Football club had a poor season a year after its stunning record-setting one. Although he was chosen as a sub on the Kerry Senior squad, it lost in the August semifinals. He informed me that he'd be with us all season, after having played in just one-third of our games the previous year. Also, he'd finished nearly all of his college degree requirements. But Junior Collins put this in the back of my mind: "Don't depend on Quirke—he'll dump us for Gaelic Football."

Alan Keane had hardly played basketball all summer. Instead he toured Europe with a backpack. I hoped his three-point shooting wouldn't suffer as he became more cultured.

John Teahan found time to get his lower back healthy in addition to helping with the player search. He still worried openly that his back would give out. His son Sean had made a full recovery. Despite having only one kidney, he was vibrant and happy. I hoped Teahan would bounce back as quickly as Sean had. Teahan reminded me that I hadn't ever seen him play his best, and I wondered if I ever would. His courage and output in big games were part of Irish basketball lore, but we hadn't even *played* a big game my first year, so I had no idea what the fuss was about.

I'd met a player named **Rob Lynch** at a February tournament my first season. He was playing for the police, or Garda, team. He was 6'5", dropped in most every shot from fifteen feet, and was square-shouldered and bouncy. He'd scored 20 points in the Cup championship game two years before as a forward for Limerick. But he'd quarreled with the Limerick coach and quit; now he was waiting to hear where he'd be stationed as a cop. I informed John O'Riordan about Lynch twice, but he quickly changed the subject. Yet that summer Rob Lynch was, perhaps coincidentally, assigned to be a Garda in Tralee.

Kevin O'Donoghue was still 5'6", but he kept his great mindset and even helped the committee with fund-raising over the summer. He told me he didn't care if he had a reduced role—he wanted the Tigers out of last place. John Teahan insisted that Kevin O'Donoghue remain our official captain, although Teahan was clearly our spiritual leader. I'd already planned on showing my appreciation by starting O'Donoghue in our first and last home games.

Liam Culloty and **Super Dave Cronin** both signed on again, realizing they wouldn't play as much with our improved roster. They had both started games for us the year before, but seemed happy to be part of what could be a much-improved squad. Also, Liam had fallen in love with Kieran Donaghy's sister, and that would keep him upbeat all season.

Roscoe Patterson waited patiently—again—for his Irish passport to come through. "Like the immigrants in the movie *Casablanca*," Junior suggested. Roscoe had done everything necessary. But even our new chairman,

John O'Riordan, said that it was impossible to predict when he'd have his papers. I hoped it would be before our October 11 debut. It wouldn't be, and Roscoe and the Tigers would wait. And wait. And wait.

Ricardo Leonard was still heavy, yet his Achilles was healthy and ready to be tested. But there was more to Ricardo's story.

A built-in Irish music session schedule awaited me: Saturdays at Kate Brown's Pub with Ciaran Dalton. Sundays again with Ciaran at Betty's Pub. Tuesdays at Baily's Corner with the thoughtful and dignified guitar wizard, Paul DeGrae. Twice that year Paul DeGrae and his wife Dee invited me to their old home overlooking Tralee Bay to play more tunes until sunrise. Thursdays out to Ardfert's Abbey Pub, which had the most raucous session. Fridays it was back to Betty's Pub, where eighty-year-old Sean Bradley, a national treasure, held court with his archaic County Donegal–style fiddling.

Junior Collins switched practice days for me—basketball practice—to Monday-Wednesday-Friday to accommodate my music schedule. Kieran Donaghy and Micheal Quirke no longer had to miss half the Tigers' practice, as they did the previous year when they walked in with bloody knees and mud-splattered shorts.

I went back to the Christian Brothers School to start a free basketball program for kids when I heard that Brother O'Connell had retired as headmaster. His replacement, Brother Coleman, was 6'4" and loved basketball. All winter I'd take our imported Americans to CBS for a weekly basketball practice. And all season their young kids would come to our matches and holler for the Tigers, often now at appropriate times, and not when someone from the *other* team dunked.

The Christian Brothers boys sometimes stopped me on the street to ask me basketball questions. My new apartment was a block from CBS, and I'd often walk by while they were on lunch break in the playground. Once again it would be December before I got my new apartment's heat working properly.

We didn't unite with St. Brendan's after all. They were nervous about our financial problems. Any young player who aspired to be in the Super League would eventually have to jump ship to join the Tigers. That was disappointing, but I was weary of trying to force a merger, and wanted to focus on getting the Tigers out of last place.

Cap the Barrel

I'd rather have had nothing to do with contract stuff, but after a year of watching us bungle the club's business, it was time to get involved.

Ricardo went ballistic when I told him the club's money situation over tea in downtown Tralee. You learn a lot about a person when things don't go right. Ricardo squawked, cursed, ranted, and threatened. Then he quit. Again. Just like he had when I told him he was fat and lazy during our first phone conversation a year and a half earlier.

The next day he called our rival clubs, offering his services. Ricardo was working a new job, four days per week in Limerick—sixty miles away—as a counselor at a juvenile home. So he called Limerick's coach. Also, Cork was less than two hours, so he gave Neptune a ring. Killarney was only twenty miles away, so they got a call.

I didn't want to play against Ricardo, but William Main and John O'Riordan were determined to pay him as little as possible. Ricardo had bullied William financially in the past and had been a bust. William didn't see the point in paying him any salary.

Ricardo continued to stress "It's not about the money" enough that I was certain it was becoming about one thing: the money.

Not having negotiating power was quite a shock for Ricardo. I understood that. He'd been pudgy and complacent for so long while still getting paid that his injury, age, and the extra hundred pounds he was bellying around didn't register. Also, he had his wife in his ear. I'm sure the extra 350 euros a week he'd been making seven months a year was a very big deal to her as well. "She won't sleep with me if I take a pay cut with Tralee," he confided during the only quiet part of one phone call.

Finally he announced he was finished with the Tigers if we didn't meet his demands, pronto.

Five days and three ultimatums later, Ricardo phoned me again.

"Rus, I think you know I really want to play for the Tigers." He was calm, contrite even.

I knew this meant that no other club had offered to pay him. Ricardo agreed to come to practice without a contract and train while we worked out his contractual specifics off the court. This was what I'd insisted all along.

"But," he reminded me, "this isn't a tryout. I'm definitely not trying out. And I'm not playing at practice to impress you."

I told him I wouldn't be coaching to impress him either.

One of our new Americans, Damond Williams, worried me. During his first week in Tralee, over lunch at the Greyhound Pub, I told him what was expected from him on the court. His defense especially had to be up to scratch. He had to do more than score points; he'd have to shut down the opponent's American and also do a great job helping out the Irish guys.

"What you do on the weak side will be just as important as what you do when your man has the ball," I said. I had a napkin and pen ready.

Damond said, "So you want me to be discreet."

"*Discreet?*" I said.

"Yeah. You know. Be discreet."

"I'm trying to tell you that you have to lock your man up, but be ready to help the Irish players, too," I said. "Don't forget your help-side responsibilities."

"So, be discreet," he said.

"I'll show you tonight in practice," I said.

After a few training sessions—and numerous calls between Ricardo, William Main, John O'Riordan, and myself—we were still at an impasse concerning Ricardo's salary.

At practice Ricardo was looking a bit better than I anticipated. His calves were like hams. His fingers were thick sausages. But speedy sausages. He looked as though he had a barrel of pork hidden in his jersey. He was at least a hundred pounds overweight, yet he was still a force, with his soft touch and deft passing ability. Not only was he hustling as best he could, he was keeping his infamous mouth shut.

The most serious hurdle in our negotiations was that Ricardo's work at the juvenile home in Limerick forced him to stay there overnight. That meant he would miss plenty of training sessions. Because of our new financial constraints, his salary had to be cut in half, and I insisted on paychecks being contingent on his attendance at practice. If he made all three training sessions per week and we won the game, he'd make 140 euros. If he didn't practice, he wouldn't play, and he'd get nothing for the week.

A few days went by. Ricardo came to me with another proposal, but it was more than our two imported American imports were making. He wanted 265 a week, in addition to a 50-euro win bonus. In effect, he was demanding to be our highest-paid player. Again. Of course William Main and John O'Riordan would say "no way."

PRESEASON WIND SPRINTS AT THE END OF TRAINING

He finally took our offer—less than half what he'd made the previous year. The season was three weeks away. And the Tralee Tigers had a ten-game losing streak and last-place finish hanging over us.

Paddy Go Easy

My lessons with Paddy Jones went a bit longer. I'd signed up for a solid hour this time, and not all of the time was spent fiddling. I continued to be Paddy's first student of the day, which was fortunate for me—he wasn't worn down by children scratching through "Twinkle, Twinkle, Little Star." We focused on the tunes and style of two Kerry legends, Denis Murphy and the late Padraic O'Keeffe.

Padraic O'Keeffe remained a mythic figure in Irish music; although he made a couple of recordings, neither was a commercial release. Originally a schoolteacher, O'Keeffe was completely undependable and was asked to retire at age thirty. He never worked again at a formal job. As O'Keeffe's fiddling legend grew, so did his love of the drink. In fact, he couldn't keep a fiddle for long without trading it for whiskey. O'Keeffe didn't even own a fiddle in his last years. If you wanted him to play, you had to supply one, along with a bottle. Paddy Jones was O'Keeffe's last student, something that was always mentioned in print whenever Paddy played in public. I was anxious to hear Paddy's stories of learning from the master. Where, I first wanted to know, did those lessons occur?

"Lessons?" Paddy asked. "You have to understand about O'Keeffe. He traveled all over the county with his fiddle in a burlap sack, playing songs and teaching tunes. There wouldn't be a fiddler around that wasn't influenced by him."

"But where did he actually teach you?" I asked.

"When I turned twelve, every Sunday I would walk to O'Keeffe's home. But he was a rough man. He didn't always make it home from Saturday night."

O'Keeffe didn't always return home?

"That was at least half the time," Paddy said. "I'd get up Sunday morning and walk to O'Keeffe's home in the hills and wait for a few hours. If it got dark, I'd turn around and go home with no lesson, often in the rain." It was very trying, he said, but he badly wanted to learn.

"How long a walk was it, to get from your home to Padraic O'Keeffe's place?"

"Four miles," Paddy said.

The Frost Is All Over

The roster for the Horan's Health Store Tigers listed quite a few players in the 6'5" range: the three imported Yanks, plus Kieran Donaghy, Micheal Quirke, and Rob Lynch. We'd have no true center unless Ricardo got in shape.

We'd have to play a faster pace that complemented our quickness. Over the summer I'd visited with Lou Henson and my own college coach, Dan McCarrell. The Tigers needed an attack that made use of our speed. I combined what they'd suggested and implemented a slashing-and-cutting offense that left Micheal Quirke in the high post, where his passing and solid three-point shooting would be most effective. Quirke wasn't a low-post scorer—we had no low-post scorer—but we had our Chicago quicksters diving into that area and clearing out again. We also incorporated a high-pressure defensive system, including a match-up zone and a trapping man-to-man that would be unique. Playing ten players—also unheard of in Ireland—became our cornerstone. I insisted on more intensity in fewer minutes.

When John Teahan cornered me after training in September, I had no inkling that anything was bothering him.

"Rus," he said, "don't you think that our imports are a bit small?"

They were, but I didn't care. The Tigers were going to gamble on playing differently from anyone in Ireland. Teahan's question was typical of the Irish indirectness that was usually endearing. This time I had no patience for it and I asked Teahan what he was getting at.

"I'm worried that Brandon Mason won't be good enough," Teahan said. "We'd better change him for a bigger American while we still can."

I was mad, but I laughed it off, pretending that his meddling didn't concern me. Once again we hadn't played a game, but our Americans were under the microscope.

My hope was that it would be difficult for our opponents to prepare for our quickness and unique style, especially early in the season. I wanted to get off to a fast start so that morale would be healthy. Still, I thought we had far too many new faces to jell right away.

Also, I didn't tell the Tigers that Connie and I had gotten married because I didn't want them to know it would be my last year.

Minutes before our season opener against the Waterford Crystals, Ricardo Leonard pulled me aside. This would be his first game playing for me, and I had reminded him several times that if I wanted coaching advice

I would ask for it. No coach wants to be distracted before games. That's why most college coaches stay hidden until minutes before a contest. I would have tried that, but our locker room was even colder than our court. Was Ricardo going to start making suggestions now before the match even began?

"I can't play in these shorts, man," Ricardo said. "They're too tight."

"Those are triple X," I said. "You'll have to make do."

He pulled and bent and yanked every which way. Then he lumbered back into the Tigers' layup line.

We beat the Waterford Crystals anyway.

Despite Ricardo's style and comfort issues, we shocked the Super League—and me—during the first eight weeks. After Waterford, a first-time-ever win at Neptune sparked us, and the Tigers even knocked off the Cup champion Blue Demons. Then we beat Neptune yet again. Before we knew it we were 8–0.

All of the Irish lads were contributing, but the biggest difference was the commitment of Micheal Quirke. Although he was dedicated to the Kerry football team, he had sat on their bench every minute. The football training, however, had done him good. He'd lost much of his puffiness and showed a toughness that I hadn't seen the year before, his year of excuses. He was clearly our top Irish player, and he was playing like one of the best in the Super League. Halfway through the season he was shooting a blazing 70 percent from the floor and was the only Irishman among the top rebounders. And this was his first season as a starter. Quirke had lost most of his baby fat and a stubbly beard made him look mean. He had always been Ricardo Leonard's backup in the past. After a win in November, I cornered Quirke and told him, "You're *better* than Ricardo Leonard."

Quirke thought I was joking. I wasn't. Still, Ricardo was helping us a bit by coming off the bench. That is, the weeks Ricardo came to practice. He wasn't scoring much, but if Quirke tired or got in foul trouble, Ricardo did a solid job of plugging up the middle. I didn't play Ricardo in both our surprising wins against Neptune, because he'd missed training all week.

MICHEAL QUIRKE TAKES A RARE BREAK

The Rights of Man

One October weekend I went with Marc, a banjo-playing pal from the States, to O'Connell's Pub in a village called Knocknagree, a well-known haven for Irish music. As we were passing through Castleisland, about half-way there, I spied Paddy Jones walking the streets.

Paddy was, well, duded up. He had on a stylish fedora and a leather sport coat, ready for a night on the town in little Castleisland. I told him we were off for Knocknagree and suggested he come along. Of course he'd been there countless times, but he hadn't been back "in donkey's years," he said. It was a Sunday, which meant "set-dancing" was in progress, the Irish equivalent of an American square dance.

Paddy whispered to me about the origins of tunes that the accordion player chose or the meaning of the dances. He seemed to know most of the dancers by name. Several of the women came and asked him to dance—a sur-prising role reversal in this village—but Paddy graciously declined. I thought it was because he wanted to keep talking with me. It was as though we'd landed in another decade, a simpler, romantic time when community dances dominated Ireland. Paddy told me there were likely less than five pubs in all of Ireland that were as authentic as O'Connell's in Knocknagree, where the traditional music was played for the locals regardless of tourists or trends.

On the way home, Paddy said, "Would you like to see Padraic O'Keeffe's home?" Of course we wanted to. The house had been derelict since O'Keeffe died in 1963.

We got there after several turns on narrow country roads. I knew I could never retrace our journey; it was completely dark, and the cloud cover obscured the stars and the moon. When Paddy told me to stop, we struggled out of the rental car and stared. I could hardly see Marc's car, let alone the house in the distance. It began raining, but we stood there anyway and listened to Paddy Jones tell O'Keeffe stories. Finally, Paddy invited us to his home, which was a ten-minute drive. He said he had a good bottle of Irish whiskey.

Although I'd seen Paddy at least once a week, I'd never been to his remote home because my lessons were at the Kerry School of Music in Tralee.

His home was a surprise.

He had very little. A table made of plywood. Stacks of records and books. Three fiddles. One of Ireland's fiddling masters was living a Spartan lifestyle with few comforts.

"What's the story with this stove?" I asked Paddy. A crude black cast-iron box hissed and thumped as it radiated heat.

Paddy had designed a way to incorporate used cooking oil from the town of Castleisland's "chipper" (or burger and fries joint) to actually heat his entire home.

His living situation made me sad, but Paddy seemed buoyant showing us around. All he had were CDs and records, his fiddle. A desk. Basic pots and pans. No television. Rustic furniture. But then . . . Paddy's home, on the inside at least, seemed quite a bit like my place in Tralee, although his was certainly warmer. It was as though *he* was on a journey thousands of miles from home and was learning the Irish fiddle in the meantime.

Marc said, "Paddy, do you have a CD for sale as a souvenir?"

I knew Paddy had never made his own CD, although he'd been a guest artist on a handful of other folks' recordings.

"I'm not an entrepreneur, you see," Paddy said. "No true artist should sell his art. There's a loss of purity as money gets involved."

Even, I supposed, the 250 I was making each week with the Tralee Tigers.

The more we talked to Paddy—and the more whiskey we had—the more I realized that Paddy was at peace with himself. He'd always be a spiritual seeker, he said. Nobody had all the answers. He talked about other jobs he'd had in England, some of which paid very well. Paddy lived the way he did—fiddles, desk, books, and bed—because it made him happy.

The Super League's random Cup draw stuck us with Neptune for a third time on December 6. Despite the fact that we'd beaten them twice without Ricardo, I elected to use him for the big Cup match, hoping our added size would be too much.

I'd second-guess myself for that move the rest of the year.

Neptune came out with a vengeance and drilled us by 10 points. The Tigers were out of the glamour tournament. Kieran Donaghy gave me a look after that match, and he didn't have to say a word. I knew what he thought. Why play Ricardo at all when we'd beaten Neptune twice already?

We'd have to set our sights on having the best record in Ireland. That night, going from last place to first place—and becoming National Champs at the first-ever Final Four—became our mission.

I didn't see John Folan much that second year. It must have been tough, being a newly married assistant coach and living an hour away. When his wife had a baby in October, I saw him even less. He never came to training, but found time to appear on the bench for the high-profile games. Still, I was glad to have him around.

One of the things Folan had told me at our initial meetings was that John Teahan, because of ambulance duties, wouldn't be at every practice.

"But you don't have any worries," Folan said. "Teahan has the keys to the local high school gym in his town, and he trains on his own like mad."

That's fair, I thought. But the second year, with his back better, Teahan still seemed a bit heavy, slower, and sluggish on defense. He had slipped to being the Tigers' third-best Irish player. When I asked him about his training habits he confessed: he *never* trained on his own, and hadn't for a couple years, since his second child was born. Teahan only practiced with the Tigers one day a week, usually Monday, then played the Saturday games. That wasn't enough. And I'd been wondering for a year when we would see the guy who had been voted Irish-born Player of the Year before I took over. Trying not to feel hurt by what might be called misinformation, I told Teahan that he had to find time to train on his own two other days a week, and to be sure to run wind-sprints at the conclusion. He assured me he would from that day on.

Early in November, Junior Collins stopped by to give me this news: "Jermaine Turner's team, the Tolka Rovers, folded for financial reasons."

"You're not expecting us to try and sign Jermaine Turner again, are you?" I asked. Jermaine was good, but this year we had better.

Junior was not. "But it's a blow to the Super League," he said. "Just like that, no Tolka Rovers, and now the Northern Conference has just five teams. It will screw up everyone's schedule, like." St. Vincent's quickly picked up Jermaine when one of its imports got hurt.

In December our new de facto chairman, John O'Riordan, told me the Tigers were financially in the black for the first time ever. Still, I was concerned about our budget. I knew that without William Main's generosity we would have never completed the previous season. Now we were having fund-raisers for the first time. The church-gate collections and street collections both involved players sitting with buckets, shaking them while begging for change. Later in the year, we'd have a Dog Night at the local greyhound racetrack.

The Tigers also sponsored Table Quiz nights, a unique part of Irish pub culture. The Table Quiz was like a quiz show, each foursome buying a table for twenty euros and a chance to win prizes donated from businesses around Tralee.

At the first Table Quiz I sat near Dan Horan, the owner of Horan's Health Stores. O'Riordan had convinced him that the Tralee Tigers would be a good investment, although Horan admitted to knowing little about sports and less about hoops. Midway through the quiz, one of the questions was this:

"What is the nickname of the NBA's Boston franchise?"

Dan Horan said, "What's the NBA?"

A few months later, I heard him ask Chris Bracey, "Is there professional basketball in the United States?"

Yes, Bracey assured him.

Horan's next question was, "And would they pay more than Ireland?"

Turns out that a lack of understanding of the sporting world was a family trait for the Horans. At the 2004 Olympics in Athens, Neil Horan, a defrocked priest and Dan Horan's brother, stunned a worldwide television audience. During the conclusion of the marathon, he tackled the leader, likely costing the unsuspecting runner a gold medal. Father Horan did it to illustrate that the end of the world was near.

Cheer Up Old Hag

Losing at Limerick right before the holiday break left us at 8–1. We were still in first place in the Southern Conference and had the best record in Ireland. I couldn't walk in downtown Tralee on the weekends without bumping into kids we did clinics for. When was the next game? Could I get them Kieran Donaghy's autograph?

First place at Christmas was a vast improvement from last season's 4–7 start. I was satisfied and I assumed the Americans would be too. So it was disappointing when I heard—through his agent, a week later—that Damond Williams wasn't going to come back to Tralee after the holidays. Whether it was a "discreet" way to handle his business, I didn't know. He did seem to pack a lot of luggage to take with him for the week over Christmas, but Damond never said goodbye, or thanks, or find someone else. I found out later that one of our basketballs was in his bags.

The Horan's Health Store Tigers were left scrambling to secure a good player just a week before our December 28 game against Notre Dame. I called a dozen agents and coaches, finally finding an available forward named Travarus Bennett. He'd broken an ankle in Germany the previous season and was just now recovering. Before that he played at the University of Minnesota. At 6'7", Travarus gave us the height that Damond Williams lacked. Travarus was a monster defender; in fact, he had been Defensive Player of the Year in his prestigious league.

We beat Notre Dame with Travarus still jet-lagged, but alert enough to grab 21 rebounds, and we were pointed back toward our goal: Super League champs.

I knew what Christmas gifts to get for Junior Collins's freckled eleven-year-old son Tomas. The fiddle I'd given him the previous Christmas was buried in his closet at home. He'd hardly taken it out of the case after the initial excitement wore off. I figured the holidays would be a good time to take the next logical step: lessons. And who else to seek out but Paddy Jones? Fiddle lessons were my way of saying thank you to Junior and his family for all of their volunteer work.

"Tomas is a wonderful boy," I told Paddy at my next lesson. "You'll like him."

"What's his surname?" Paddy asked.

"Collins," I said. "They live outside Castleisland."

"I think I know that family," Paddy said. "Who is the boy's grandfather?"

He had me there. I didn't have a clue.

I told Paddy my recollection of how to get to Junior's home in the hills of the Stack's Mountains, outside Tralee. Paddy said he thought he might know exactly where the Collins family lived. Anyway, Tomas was set for lessons with Paddy in January.

The Hag's Purse

John Teahan was slowly coming around, and he had a big game in our crucial win on the Cork Blue Demons' court—10 points, a half-dozen rebounds, and he seemed to come up with every loose ball.

The next week, Teahan cornered me after practice. He had a stack of physio and doctors bills from last year, and also wanted to get gas money for his long drives to Tralee.

"Give them to William Main," I said. That had always been the Tigers' policy: William handled the financial stuff. I was surprised Teahan even mentioned it to me.

Teahan said, "William said to give them to you."

"Me?" I asked.

William Main told me on several occasions that Teahan never asked for a nickel, in fact refused money, and was the unselfish road warrior whose attitude held the club together.

"Give them to me," I told Teahan. "Let me show them to the committee."

Unbeknownst to me, William Main and our new acting president, John O'Riordan, had made an agreement: William would pay any *past* debts that the former Frosties Tigers owed. But the current club structure would be responsible for expenses after September 1. In other words, the Horan's Health Store Tigers would try to stand alone, without the longtime financial support of William Main.

But all of Teahan's physio bills were from our disastrous previous season. Four hundred euros worth. John O'Riordan told me, "Those are William's responsibility."

The request for gas money complicated things further. Teahan wanted five hundred for *after* September 1. (Gas in Ireland cost more than in the States, nearly four dollars a gallon.) No one else on the committee—including the coach—was aware that John Teahan had been getting gas money, ever. We'd only heard the same stories from William about John Teahan's unselfish commitment. But it appeared William had been paying him expense money without anyone's knowledge for quite some time.

Why didn't William continue to do so? Perhaps he wanted to distance himself financially. Still, why didn't he warn me, or the committee, that he'd been quietly taking care of Teahan, and suggest that the club do the same?

Even then William was building twenty-five homes along the Ring of Kerry that would be worth millions. Certainly nobody within the Tigers organization, including players, would have objected to Teahan getting gas money.

Connie and I remained in Tralee for the holidays. My pay cut and her flight had depleted our funds, and with the Tigers doing so much better, I didn't feel an urgency to get out of town. Instead we loaded the freezer up with fresh fish, stocked up on turf and coal for the fireplace, and had a romantic Christmas at home. Also, Kieran Donaghy's mother made us two porter cakes.

The Sword in the Hand

By the end of January the Horan's Health Store Tigers were 11–2, and sailing. We were so far ahead of the second-place Demons of Cork, who were 7–5, that only a major disaster in the final seven games could keep us from being crowned Southern Conference champions of the Irish Super League. That meant an automatic bid to the Final Four. It was hard to believe, dizzying even. People I'd never met in town were calling, "Well done, Coach!" We were getting color photos in the three local papers. The crowd of youngsters at games continued to grow.

Paddy Jones picked out a difficult tune for me to learn that week called "Tom Billy's Reel." It was a tune that was characteristic of Kerry fiddlers—from the playing of a long-gone blind fiddler named Tom Billy Murphy—but more subtle than much of what I'd been learning.

"Can you slow it down for me?" I asked, as we were, rather, I was struggling through.

"Certainly," Paddy said, and we started in again, but slower. Fiddling together with Paddy was the best part of the lesson, and getting entrained with him was becoming less elusive. But that afternoon, trying to slow down "Tom Billy's Reel," Paddy was screwing it up too. We ground to a halt. Could entrainment work both ways? Were my problems and limitations now rubbing off on Paddy?

Paddy set his fiddle on his lap. He knew what the trouble was. "Sometimes playing is like going across an icy pond," Paddy said. "We don't get much ice around here anymore. Ireland has gotten warmer. When I was a boy, the ponds would freeze once or twice a winter. And if you walked across the pond, the ice would collapse and you'd fall in. Up to your waist, or you might even drown.

"But if you ran across the ice, it would crack slightly where you had stepped. You could get momentum and move on in a lighter sort of way, before things cracked under your feet. Sometimes learning reels on the fiddle is like that. You have to keep up the pace and not look down at your feet."

A year and a half after I'd met Paddy, it was time to speed up without the fear of mangling a tune.

"You have to trust in what you've learned," Paddy said. "Go ahead and let the tune come out."

Before the holidays I was playing Ricardo Leonard just fifteen minutes per game. Sometimes he would miss an entire week of practice, then seemed miffed when I informed him he couldn't dress for the game. After a convincing win in early February over the struggling Waterford Crystals, Ricardo told John O'Riordan he was retiring from basketball. It was too much of a struggle, with his aching joints and work commitments. Ricardo hadn't practiced or played in a game since before Christmas. He mentioned to O'Riordan that he wasn't "getting on" with the coach. His career appeared over, and not one person, media or fan, mentioned it. He'd scored a grand total of 30 points all season.

Meanwhile, Micheal Quirke had emerged from being a weakly committed caddy for Ricardo Leonard to being the best Irish-born player in the Super League. He was still racking up great stats. Since we had imported a relatively small American player in Brandon Mason, Quirke was needed to guard one of the opponent's big imports, and he usually outplayed them. Most of the Irish teams insisted on hiring American low-post players in the 6'8" range. But all three of ours—Brandon Mason, Chris Bracey, and Travarus Bennett—were skillful perimeter players, and were small, even by Irish standards.

Quirke was still practicing with the Kerry football team on Tuesdays and Thursdays, so he had six days a week of intense training. Often I'd excuse him from the sprints that the others groaned about at the end of practice.

Although Quirke was a star for us, at that time he'd never seen a single minute of action in the top league for Gaelic Football, so I was astonished to learn he was going to miss our game at Neptune for football. The new coach had actually promised him he'd get plenty of action and the Kerry team was counting on him.

For the first time all season I felt the sense of collapse and dread that had clouded my mind much of the previous season. Kieran Donaghy, who knew the inner workings of Gaelic Football, told me we'd better prepare to play the rest of the schedule without Quirke. I thought we could still be competitive and perhaps still finish with the best record in Ireland. But we wouldn't capture the Final Four title Quirke-less.

To my relief, the Tigers won at Neptune without him. On the bus ride back to Tralee, Junior Collins plopped down next to me, squeezing me into the window. He'd been on the phone with a Kerry sportswriter. "Quirke didn't played one single minute for the Kerry team," Junior said. Quirke had surrendered his spot as a basketball star to be a cheerleader for Gaelic Football.

When Quirke rang me the next morning, he insisted he wouldn't miss the Super League's Final Four on March 20–21 for which the Tigers had already qualified. Final Four weekend was the only conflicting date on the rest of our schedule, and it was good to hear that we could count on him the rest of the way. For the first time I sensed that Quirke was frustrated with his benchwarmer role in football. But I recalled how he had blown us off in the past to sit on the bench for Kerry football or to study. I began teaching his high-post position to our cop, Rob Lynch, and American Travarus Bennett during practice, just in case. The pull of Gaelic Football in Kerry should never be underestimated.

By the end of February, the Irish Super League standings—table, they said— looked like this:

Northern Conference

Killester	10–6
Belfast-Star	9–6
UCD Marian	9–8
St Vincent's	7–9
Notre Dame	5–11
Tolka Rovers	0–5 (folded)

Horan's Health Store Tigers	15–2
Cork-UCC Demons	10–7
Cork-Neptune	9–9
Killarney Lakers	9–9
Burger King Limerick	7–11
Waterford Crystals	3–15

With only three games to go, we were so far in front that we could lose the remaining games and still finish with Ireland's best record.

In Dublin, during our game against Marian, Brandon Mason turned his ankle badly in the first quarter. We cut into the lead near the end, but lost. We wouldn't have him for the next game against rival Killarney, but he'd have twenty days to get ready for the Final Four in Cork. We lost at Killarney without Brandon, but he gamely limped through our season finale against the Blue Demons.

I started five Irish-born players in that contest, and our fans were ecstatic. The move represented a vote of confidence for my loyal, unpaid Irish guys. The Demons never seemed to get over the surprise—no team had started five Irish players since the early 1970s—and we won comfortably.

The Tigers finished the regular season with the best record in Ireland, 16–4. Still, under the new format, the Final Four would determine the national champion, not overall record as in the previous season.

One day in March, Junior Collins and his wife Jackie arrived at their home in the hills outside Tralee to find Paddy Jones waiting on their doorstep. They'd never met Paddy, so an awkward moment ensued. Paddy was to begin teaching young Tomas Collins the very next afternoon and he simply wanted to meet the boy and tell him he was looking forward to it.

"Jackie was touched, like," Junior said. "I've never heard of a teacher coming to meet a student before a lesson in anything."

Paddy was a pretty special guy, I said. The music was everything to him, a sacred tradition that he was honored to pass on. What did they talk about with Paddy?

"He seemed to think he knew my grandfather, but I don't know if it's the same Collins family or not," Junior said. "We invited him for tea and biscuits. We got out some old photographs to see if he recognized anyone in the family. Then he and Jackie talked on the porch for a good while. She tried to invite him back in for dinner, but he said no."

"Well," I told Junior, "I'm glad you got to meet Paddy Jones."

"But Jackie asked Paddy where his car was. She couldn't see one on the road and just ours was in the driveway."

And?

"He didn't come in a car, he'd walked. So Jackie said she'd drive him home."

"It's good that you live so close to him," I said. A nice coincidence.

"But that's what I'm saying," Junior said. "He actually does live close, but he'd taken a wrong turn and walked a circle before he found us. She measured on the odometer. He'd traveled a fair bit on foot to meet Tomas, like."

How far?

"Four miles."

Same Old Cup of Tea

Final Four weekend in Cork was getting closer. The Demons were hosting the games on the UCC campus. I didn't know if we could beat them again, especially on their own court.

Micheal Quirke continued his practices with Kerry's Gaelic Football team. The weekend before the Final Four, March 13, the Tigers had no game, a rare basketball holiday.

Surprisingly, the Kerry coach announced that Quirke would be a starter on that day's football game against County Westmeath. Quirke had instantly gone from not playing a single minute to starting for the prestigious team. If we were to lose Quirke to football, we would suddenly be in real danger of collapsing at the very time we needed to be hitting on all cylinders. The Kerry football team also had a big match the same weekend as our Final Four.

I went to scout in Belfast the weekend of March 13, watching Belfast's Star of the Sea beat the Demons in a close contest. That was a relief. Luckily, Neptune hadn't survived either, so no remaining team would have a home court advantage. Our first opponent would be the experienced and gritty Belfast boys.

Junior Collins was waiting for me when I got off the train. I pulled open the door of his muddy car.

"Junior," I said, "will you please not wear that Frosties jacket in public? They're not our sponsor anymore."

Junior wasn't laughing this time. Maybe my badgering him about his clothes had gone too far.

Then I noticed. On his front seat—my seat—was a stack of Irish newspapers.

Quirke's picture was on the front page of the *Irish Times*. "It's the biggest national paper, like," Junior pointed out. He smiled, finally, but it was forced.

I skimmed the article. Turns out our Quirke had been the hero of the football match by using his size to grab a couple high kicks and dish the ball off for crucial goals.

Junior handed me another couple of newspapers. I felt sick. Quirke was on the front of the *Irish Independent*, too. Desperately scrambling through the other newspapers, I found Quirke's photo on the front of every sports page.

"Listen to this one," Junior said, as I sunk lower into my seat. "It says Quirke is *a basketball star of some renown*." He pointed to the newspaper column. When I refused to look, Junior read it. "Quirke used basketball-style passes that resulted in the game-breaking goals."

"What's going to happen?" I asked Junior. We had only a week before our Final Four, and suddenly the Tigers might lose Quirke. "Is Quirke as good as gone?"

"He is and he isn't," Junior offered. "The Kerry team has another big match next weekend."

"But that's *our* weekend," I said.

"I'd say you'd better be ready to lose him."

I braced myself for the bad news from Quirke, and even decided to leave Travarus Bennett in the high-post spot every minute during practice. We had been lucky to win once at Neptune without Quirke. Now Gaelic Football was about to ruin our dream season, crushing the Tigers' hopes of being Irish National Champions. Ours were the smallest imports in Ireland by far, and finally we'd pay for it. I felt the same sense of dread as when Ricardo had torn his Achilles.

The best part about working his rural postal route, Ciaran Dalton said, was being invited in for cups of tea and sandwiches. When he first began working in Kerry, the postman was often the only visitor who'd stop by.

Ciaran had been telling me for weeks that he had a special place to take me.

On March 16, he took me to the Weather's Well, an ancient site not far from Tralee. This sacred well was behind a home on that route, and the owners didn't mind Ciaran going back there.

I ran into the mist when he tooted his horn outside my apartment. I enjoyed showing visitors around in New Mexico because it breathed life into the place for me. Ciaran would enjoy this journey too, as well as my reaction, I figured. He popped in a cassette tape I handed him; it was an Uilleann pipes player named Mick O'Brien. The pipes are uniquely Irish; they're not powered by human breath like the Scottish bagpipes, but rather by a flapping elbow that pumps air into the bellows, a small bladder. (Uilleann means elbow in Irish.) A drone that continues behind the melody makes the sound absolutely haunting.

After a few minutes he turned down the tape and said the Weather's Well was a thousand years old, or more. "The world was so much different then," Ciaran said as he sped out of Tralee. "Cruel but simple. A man might only have one set of clothes."

"Laundry day would be easy," I said.

Ciaran said, "Laundry day? I reckon a man mightn't wash his clothes for years. In those days people all over the world probably wore the same wool outfit until it fell off. Or animal skins."

Instantly I thought of Junior Collins, his black Frosties Tigers jacket tugged over his Horan's Health Store Tigers top. I explained to Ciaran about Junior and his black jacket, and how he'd been wearing it for two consecutive years. And about Junior's son Tomas, who was learning traditional fiddling from Paddy Jones. It was Ciaran who had taught me that some lost ships from the Spanish Armada had landed in Ireland hundreds of years ago. I told Ciaran my theory about Junior being the Irish version of Sancho Panza. Could it be that Junior Collins was a descendant of the Spanish? Or could Junior be a mythical man living in the wrong time, a mysterious ancient Irishman stuck in the wrong century? Fighting demons and Viking invaders? And not changing his woolen outfit until it fell off?

"Yeah, well, I doubt it," Ciaran sniffed. He cranked the Uilleann piper music back up.

Ten minutes later we stopped at the side of a narrow road. "Most of the Christians simply took over pagan sites and claimed them as their own," he said as we backed into the gravel drive of a small stone house. "You've never seen anything like this." He grinned mischievously, as if I were in for a treat.

"Scholars claim this place has religious significance, and that it was a place of worship for Catholics," Ciaran said as we trekked up a small hill behind the house. He said it was not a typical well—maybe fifteen feet across and rectangular in shape. "It's more like a rustic jacuzzi," he said as we approached.

Except it was dry.

Was that why he brought me? Did he know it would be dry?

No. Ciaran said he'd been to this sacred site dozens of times and it *always* had water. He appeared frightened and kept looking around, as if Viking invaders might storm over the hill at any moment.

"I had no idea," he said. "The old folks would say that this is definitely some kind of sign. Something highly unusual is going to happen. Or maybe already has happened." He looked up at the sky, and then around at the hills again. It was getting ready to pour rain, he said. He paced back toward the entrance, leaving me in front of the dry well. Then he motioned me over to the tiny stone church oratory next to the well, hardly big enough for a bed. As though we'd better take shelter.

Follow Me Down

I couldn't shake the strange sense of doom in the air before the Final Four. We'd astounded the Super League with our worst-to-first season, but that was with Quirke in the middle.

Belfast had the same three players who had been on Ireland's national team for years, including former Seton Hall star John Leahy, the deadly 6'6" shooter, a pesky Bosman, and its two big Americans. It was nearly the identical team that had finished second in both the Cup and league standings just a year ago.

If we could somehow beat Belfast in the semifinals *without* Quirke, maybe he'd join us for the championship game on Sunday.

I came home from celebrating St. Patrick's Day to a phone message: Quirke wanted me to ring him no matter how late. My heart sank. It was one o'clock in the morning, and I badly needed a good night's sleep, which was about to be dashed.

"I've talked things over with my coach for football," Quirke said.

And? I had my forehead in my left hand.

"I told him I'd prefer to play basketball this weekend. The coach said it's fine. He even said I should skip football training this week to keep my basketball legs fresh."

I let out a whoop. Quirke's decision was the rough equivalent of Coach Dean Smith telling a player at North Carolina to go ahead and play tennis over the weekend, the Tar Heels could do without him in the NCAA tournament. It was astounding.

It wasn't all good news, though. Four days before the Final Four, John Teahan was grabbing at his lower back, rolling on the floor. It had gone out again for the first time all season. Although he wasn't always a starter, he was our most experienced player and had been scoring more since Christmas. We were already making our run with the youngest team in the Irish Super League. I'd heard the Americans asking Teahan what to expect during the playoffs. If Teahan couldn't play we'd be even younger. Belfast was exactly the kind of team that Teahan usually played well against.

Rather than spending an expensive Friday night in a hotel, I decided that the Tigers should drive to Cork Saturday morning and check into a hotel after a team meal. We were better off sleeping the night before in our own beds. The two-hour drive to Cork would be easy to stretch off before our 3 P.M. semifinal start. We could stay over in a hotel on Saturday night. Of course, if we lost, that would be money wasted, as we'd have nothing to do on Sunday.

I should have protested when Junior said that the committee had decided the players should also carpool to save the club even more money. We crammed in and caravanned to Cork. Late Saturday morning, the car with our three imports got lost on the way to the hotel. Their two-hour car ride became three hours, and it was looking like I'd made my first blunder even before the opening tip. When Brandon Mason, Chris Bracey, and Travarus Bennett struggled out of the cramped car, they were in a foul mood.

John Teahan had spent every afternoon in physiotherapy and his back had loosened up slightly. He said he'd try to play. In the hotel lobby he asked me, "Can I talk to the team?"

Last minute instructions — John Teahan intense and focused

A year earlier I would have asked Teahan, "Talk about what?" and then told him to forget about it. I generally didn't allow players to make speeches—for one thing, Ricardo would have kept us for hours—but Teahan had gone nearly a decade without winning a national championship. I gave him my blessing. Ten minutes later, when I walked by his room, I could hear him hollering at our guys about something.

Before we left the hotel for the arena, Kieran Donaghy grabbed me by the sportcoat sleeve.

"How's John Teahan's back?" he wanted to know.

"Better," I said. "He says he can play." Then I reminded Donaghy not to get in early foul trouble. Donaghy could still be excitable, and that sometimes meant a cheap foul in the first quarter.

"You should start John Teahan," he said.

Teahan had been getting as much playing time as the starters, but he'd been our sixth man since Christmas.

"Start Teahan? Instead of who?" I asked.

Donaghy was offering up *his* starting spot to Teahan. "He hasn't played for a championship in ages," he said. Since 1996 to be exact. The last thing a coach wants before a championship series is a disruption. But I took it as a good sign. Last year as a rookie, Donaghy would have sulked about not starting. Now he was offering his spot to the team's elder statesman.

Despite neither Cork team being in the Final Four, the Mardyke Arena was jammed. The Irish Super League office had sworn it would make a big event out of its first Final Four. Music blared, TV cameras were posted around the arena, signs and banners supporting the teams hung in every corner, and security personnel were at each door. Before our game, a women's semifinal came down to the last shot. The crowd grew louder as that one progressed.

When it was over, Junior Collins and I followed the Tigers out for warm-ups.

"Pretty impressive, huh Junior?" I asked, looking around.

He just grunted. Was he jealous of the Cork facility? Did he prefer our decrepit Sports Complex? Did he consider this just business as usual, the Tigers in the Final Four where he knew we belonged? Then I noticed: Junior was wearing his Horan's Health Stores jacket still, but the old Kellogg's Frosties jacket was not underneath.

"I'll write the starters' names in the scorebook, like," he said. "Did you see who's sitting behind my family?"

It was Ricardo Leonard, slumped down so that he looked almost small.

The Tigers started off against Belfast with what we'd been doing all season: our matchup zone after made baskets and straight man-to-man defense after we missed. Travarus Bennett, who had begun to dominate games with his defense, was assigned to Leahy in the first quarter, and his manic long arms kept Leahy from attempting a single shot.

Kieran Donaghy, whom I elected to start despite his offer, was able to sneak behind the Belfast defense for slashing layups over its more experienced but smaller guards. Quirke once again outplayed Belfast's big American, beating him to the ball repeatedly.

In the second quarter, we went to the special defense that we'd adopted after Travarus's holiday arrival. He guarded Belfast's poorest shooter and ran off and trapped the ball whenever he saw fit. Sometimes he'd only bluff, which added to Belfast's confusion. Brandon Mason would have to guard Leahy the rest of the contest. With the twenty-four-second clock seemingly on high speed, Belfast was visibly frustrated. It was a game plan I feared they were too seasoned to fall for, but Travarus repeatedly stole the ball or tipped passes that his teammates grabbed. We roared to a 13-point halftime lead.

Kieran Donaghy was our leading scorer at the break with 13 points. Micheal Quirke topped both squads with an impressive 12 rebounds.

In the second half, Quirke continued to wear down their Americans with his physical inside play. Twice John Teahan went into a trio of Belfast players to miraculously emerge with the loose ball. Minutes later Teahan broke Belfast's back with a succession of his simple-but-devastating medium-range shots. In the fourth quarter Brandon Mason reeled off seven buckets in a row without a miss—many after Travarus's steals or deflections—to bust the game wide open.

I cleared the bench with a few minutes to go, and Kevin O'Donoghue, Alan Keane, and Liam Culloty all got points on the board for the Tigers. I made all the lads eat one banana each the instant the final horn blew. One of my superstitions, but based in fact: replace calories quickly when you have a match the next day.

KIERAN DONAGHY STOPS BY FOR FREE ADVICE

William Main gave me two hundred euros to feed the Tigers after the game. My mind wasn't on our budget, so I thanked him. But with our party of twelve players, stat man, Junior and his wife and myself, our allowance meant we'd be eating in downtown Cork for thirteen euros a person. And we had the championship game the next afternoon, less than twenty-four hours away. The meal was skimpy, but the Tigers didn't complain; several of them even bought their own desserts. We resolved to order pizzas out of our own pockets after watching Killester take on Killarney in the other semifinal.

Killester won easily. That meant a showdown: the winners of the North and South would meet for the national championship. We'd beaten Killester in a hotly contested double-overtime game in November, and they'd be looking for revenge.

A Night at the Fair

Killester had its own three-point bomber in former University of Virginia star Keith Friel. It also had a player from the Irish National Team named Damien Sealy, whom the Tigers hated. He'd irritated us in the past with obvious cheapshots, usually directed at the back of our smallest player's head. Their Bosman was a 6'9" Aussie named Blair Smith. Finally, Killester had the intimidating New Yorker Clyde Ellis in the middle. Clyde Ellis had sent shock waves through the Super League when he stormed into Notre Dame's locker room and got in a fistfight with the *entire team*. And that was after a Killester victory. He had the demeanor of Sonny Liston, and I was worried he'd intimidate our young squad.

We started the game with Travarus Bennett guarding Friel, as the strategy had worked so well against Belfast. But Friel got loose in the first quarter for 8 points, including two deep bombs.

With six minutes left in the second quarter, Damien Sealy bashed John Teahan across the jaw. Teahan wobbled, then crumpled. Teahan was constantly getting knocked to the floor in games, but I'd never seen him on the deck for more than an instant. He always bounced up. This time he lay flat. Quirke hoisted Teahan to his feet, and I signaled for a timeout.

"John, are you all right?" I asked. His eyes were glassy, even as I waved a hand in front of them and slapped his cheek.

Kieran Donaghy splashed some water in Teahan's face. "Come on, John Teahan boy!" Donaghy shouted.

Teahan rolled from side to side in his seat. I was certain he had suffered a concussion. Donaghy threw a whole cup of water in his face this time. Suddenly Teahan appeared lucid, as if he'd awoken from a dream. Maybe a dream where his back was crippled, or the Tralee Tigers had come in last place. The entire team was crouched around us in a semicircle, me on my knees in front of Teahan. A precious timeout was ticking away and I hadn't given the Tigers a single word of strategy.

Raising his arms, Teahan pushed his teammates away. They stood back and looked at him in wonder. I got my notepad and pen ready. "Look now. Here's what I want to do on defense. Let's try—" But nobody was paying the least bit of attention to me.

Then Teahan let out a roar. Soon the Tigers were roaring with him, and the noise lasted the final fifteen seconds of the timeout. It was a strange moment. Not a bit of guidance had been spoken, yet the huddle ended with a bestial bellow that grew louder and louder. The message was clear: Killester had inflamed the Tigers, and John Teahan wouldn't be intimidated. The horn sounded, and they swaggered back onto the court, Donaghy hollering expletives in Teahan's ear as he went to the free throw line. Teahan sunk them both.

I grabbed Travarus Bennett by the back of the jersey as Teahan was dropping in the second free throw. "Change our defense to one hot," I said, our trapping man-to-man. Brandon Mason switched onto Killester's best shooter, Friel—just as we had done against Belfast—and Travarus went to work, disrupting its offense with traps that resulted in deflections and steals. We took a small lead. Brandon Mason seemed content to distribute the ball, likely because he was spending most of his energy frustrating Friel with his manic defense.

We took a second timeout with two seconds left in the half.

It was Tigers' ball on the baseline. I wanted to set up a dramatic ninety-foot pass, a play we'd practiced every week. We even had a simple name for it—"last-second play"—but we'd never gotten a chance to use it in games.

Now we could.

Quirke was supposed to heave the ball the length of the floor to a leaping Chris Bracey, our Bosman, the only Tiger near our basket. Then Bracey would drop a pass off—mid-air, before coming down—to either wing, both of whom should be streaking up the sidelines from half court for a short jumpshot.

But Quirke must have decided Bracey was not open—he wouldn't throw the long pass—and Rob Lynch, one of the jump-shooters, recognized the problem from half court and ran toward Quirke, who zinged it to Lynch. Lynch turned and heaved the ball from seventy feet at the basket, where Bracey was still all alone with his defender, a guy named Quigley. While Quigley waited flatfooted for Lynch's desperate shot (or was it a pass?) to hit the rim, Bracey timed his jump perfectly and soared over his lone defender. He caught the ball and, without coming down, dropped it softly in the basket right before the horn sounded.

What transpired wasn't at all the way we'd practiced, but the play worked perfectly—an ingenious alley-oop pass. Junior Collins yelled, "Brilliant play, Coach," as we trotted past the delirious fans to our dressing room. The Tigers led by 13 points at the half.

In the locker room I warned Travarus Bennett to be careful. Killester had planned for his wandering traps and was constantly cutting its poor-shooting point guard, Travarus's man, to the basket, where he surely wouldn't miss if Killester could get the ball to him. The Irish players would have to cover for him. I praised Quirke for his relentless defense and tenacious board work, and Teahan for his guts. When Junior Collins said it was time to take the court, Teahan shouted, "This is our time, lads."

Donaghy, who had done a fine job of guarding Sealy, was spewing expletives like a broken spigot—"fuck Sealy" and "fuck Killester"—but everyone agreed with him, so I let it pass. His mother was in the stands, but not within earshot.

With five minutes left in the third quarter, Killester had whittled our lead to 6 points. We were having trouble controlling the brutal Clyde Ellis, even with Travarus trapping him. You could feel the momentum shifting, and I felt my gut tighten.

Then, with 3:40 left in the third quarter, Brandon Mason drove into the teeth of Killester's defense and found John Teahan open for his dangerous mid-range jumper. As Teahan swished the shot, Quigley—whom we'd caught napping just before the half—hammered him. When the referee signaled a foul and that the basket counted, Quigley looked disdainfully at Teahan lying on the ground. Whether it was out of frustration or malice, Quigley stomped on Teahan hard, right in the gut. And in clear view of the referee.

A technical foul was assessed. Teahan rolled on the floor in the fetal position, the wind knocked out of him. Quirke and Donaghy—it took two Tigers this time—lifted Teahan to his feet and led him to the free throw line. I thought Teahan might go take a swing at Quigley, or talk a little trash. Instead he hunched patiently at the foul line, as though he was used to long waits, staring at the rim until the ref gave him the ball. Teahan swished both free throws, then Quirke scored on the ensuing possession. Our 6-point lead was suddenly 11. Twice Killester had tried to intimidate John Teahan, and twice he'd responded heroically, scraping himself up off the floor with the help of the Tigers.

Chris Bracey opened up the game with his sweet shooting, tallying 20 points for the second contest in a row. He frantically harassed Killester's bully, Clyde Ellis, until, with five minutes on the clock, Ellis—who had assaulted an entire team in its own locker room—checked himself out of the game and collapsed on the sideline with cramps. An ambulance took him to the hospital to treat him for exhaustion and dehydration. The only photo in one of the national newspapers the next day would be a prostrate Ellis hooked up to oxygen and an IV.

With four minutes remaining in the game, and me still very much worried about the outcome, Kieran Donaghy cut out to the wing, caught a pass from Teahan, and set his feet for a three-pointer. When his defender approached, Donaghy popped his eyes up in a shot fake, then drove hard to his left. As the defender scrambled to stop the drive, Donaghy skidded to a stop and rose over the stumbling Killester player for a jumpshot. It was the move that Antoine Gillespie drilled him on the year before, and Donaghy swished it. The shot put us up 12 points, and the Killester players bickered with each other on the way back down the floor.

We never looked back.

The Tralee Tigers were Irish National Champions, from worst place to first place in a single history-making season. The postgame celebration included dozens of photos, TV and newspaper interviews, and an official, but modest, award ceremony. The Super League commissioner called the players out one by one and presented each with a wristwatch.

KEVIN O'DONOGHUE ACCEPTS THE TROPHY IN PLACE OF JOHN TEAHAN

William Main was beaming like a proud father. He and John O'Riordan stomped and hollered for each Tiger. When they ultimately called for our team captain, John Teahan insisted tiny Kevin O'Donoghue—who once again hadn't missed a practice all season, which made him an Irish oddity—go accept the trophy. O'Donoghue held it over his head with both hands, although it likely weighed more than he did. It wobbled from side to side, but he still held it high.

Instead of going for the trophy, Teahan grabbed me in a brutal bear hug and hoisted me off my feet. I could feel his frustration from the previous year and the joy of this season all in the same embrace as I gasped for air.

We took more photos, jumping around and pounding each other on the back. I finally cancelled my "Irish-only" policy and allowed the Americans to talk to the press, so they were engaged on one sideline while I gathered my Irish Tigers under the basket and told them we'd earned the right to cut down the net, as was the American custom.

The Irish players were horrified. They'd never heard of such a thing. Cut down the net?

"I don't think the gym's caretaker would appreciate it," said Kevin O'Donoghue. I could see it on his face—I might as well have suggested a human sacrifice.

"We'll get arrested," Quirke said. Suddenly our enforcer was our peacemaker. He tried to ease me toward the locker room.

"Fuck the caretaker," said Kieran Donaghy.

So the Tigers did it anyway. By then the Americans had joined us, and they knew the ritual. Things went quickly until the net hung stubbornly onto the rim with one final loop.

"One more, guys," I said. "Finish it up."

Someone was grabbing my shin—what the—Junior!

"Up you go, like," Junior said, and I was indeed going up, but wobbling like a drunkard at closing time. Just before I toppled, John Teahan grabbed my other leg to steady me, then Donaghy tossed me the scissors all in one instant, as though they'd been practicing the move. I got the last snip.

CHEER, BOYS, CHEER

Walking past the Christian Brothers School on Monday, I saw the third-grade class I had been teaching basketball to each week. They abandoned their lunchtime soccer match and raced over, swarming me on the sidewalk.

"Hey, Rus! When's the Tigers next game?" one asked.

I told them the season was over, no more games and no more practices. I'd be going back home to America soon.

"When did the season end?"

"Yesterday."

They nodded solemnly.

"We won the championship," I added.

"Oh. But when do you play again?"

"Can you coach us in soccer?" asked another.

On Tuesday, Tralee's Lord Mayor, Terry O'Brien, and his city council honored the Tigers. They hosted a special presentation, drew up a certificate, and even gave me an engraved crystal bowl that I'd never be able to fit in a suitcase.

Later that evening we gathered to watch the delayed-telecast Irish National Basketball Championship. Every player was there, along with Junior Collins and some of our committee members. Junior and I sat side by side, eager to relive our finest hour.

The TV crew had an irritating pattern. It would replay made baskets while play was still in motion on the other end of the court. So we missed nearly a third of the game while common plays often not worth repeating ran again in slow motion. Still, it was a wonderful time. We cheered each Tiger shot, jeered at Sealy's cheapshot on John Teahan, and made catcalls as I paced the sideline. The incredible ninety-feet-in-two-seconds play that ended the first half brought nearly the same roar from the Tigers that John Teahan had summoned in the huddle. No one mentioned that the play was a broken one that accidentally emerged as perfection. We jumped up at the half to use the toilet, grab a beer and sandwich, or just stretch our legs.

Then a funny thing happened.

We sat and waited for the second half to start, but the TV station cut to a different program, a sitcom. The second half never materialized.

Only in Ireland.

Before leaving Ireland I gathered the Irish players for our final meeting. I told them I wasn't coming back to Tralee the next season. I'd stayed eight years at UTEP and six at New Mexico State. Both terms were far too long for the ephemeral world of coaching. I had made up my mind to go out a winner and wanted to hold on to my happy ending.

I told them about getting married the previous summer, and how Connie had agreed to let me return for one more season. Despite knowing this would be my last season, I hadn't wanted that to be a distraction. My job in Tralee could never support a family, and we needed health insurance and stability.

The Irish lads took this news well and thanked me for coming to Tralee. It got quiet for a moment as they fidgeted. They all looked at little Kevin O'Donaghue. Our captain had something to say. I figured that maybe they'd all chipped in for a going-away gift. They didn't need to do that, but I was honored. I looked around on the floor for the present.

"Say, Rus," O'Donaghue said. "Do you think you could help us find another coach and two more Americans?"

I'd likely miss the Tralee Tigers more than they were going to miss me.

Journey's end

Contentment is Wealth

I'd been back from Ireland for a month when I got a call from the Memphis Grizzlies of the NBA. Their general manager, an old friend named Dick Versace, was one of the only basketball people I'd met with as much an interest in literature as I had. His mother had been a poet and short story writer of some renown—the television show *The Flying Nun* had been based on her writing. Versace had an interesting job offer. The Grizzlies wanted me to come to Memphis for a week in June. I was to teach my old dribbling drills—the ones that had fueled my own improvement, the same drills I'd taught to Antoine Gillespie during his redshirt year—to one of Memphis's forwards, Shane Battier.

I wasn't awfully busy. I told Versace yes without even asking what it would pay. (In fact the job paid half of what I'd made my entire second season in Ireland.)

"There's a local high school kid that wants to work out with you and Shane Battier," Versace said. "If you don't mind him."

No problem, I said. Who was the kid?

"Jonnie West," Versace said.

A country and western singer, I joked.

"It's Jerry West's son."

Versace didn't have to explain the rest. Jerry West, a perennial All-Star with the Los Angeles Lakers, was maybe the greatest shooting guard in basketball history. West was an All-American at West Virginia University, then an Olympic hero. The NBA's very logo—on every poster, program, advertisement, and uniform—was an image of Jerry West, who starred in the 1960s and 70s. He'd retired recently as Lakers president after several championships, but the Memphis Grizzlies had convinced him to forgo his retirement.

I'd taught my dribbling drills to some well-known players and coaches before, but this would be the ultimate honor.

I'd have to do a lot of demonstrating, so for the next month I struggled to get back in dribbling shape. Strained hamstrings—from trying to run sprints too soon after a winter spent fiddling and typing—hampered me. But I practiced with a purpose for the first time in years.

Jerry West arrived while we were in the midst of a difficult two-ball dribbling drill. I pretended not to notice. Both Shane Battier and Jonnie West had botched the exercise and balls were ricocheting in all directions. One of Jonnie's hit me right in the nose. But I was feeling good—my timing was back—and handled both my basketballs deftly, yo-yoing them between and around my legs.

Yet I sensed that Jerry West, a no-nonsense guy, desired something different. I aborted the two-ball series and went right into a basic walking drill that I use to teach the "in-and-out" move, what amounts to a fake crossover. It's a simple move, but one that doesn't often get taught step-by-step.

When Battier and Jonnie walked to the other end using my four-count rhythm, Jerry West approached me. He introduced himself—as though he needed to—then pointed and said, "I've always thought this was the most important dribbling move to teach a fellow. Hell, this was all I could ever do."

"And shoot the ball a little," I could have added.

I didn't see Jerry West again until five days later. Amazingly, his son Jonnie had nearly mastered even the most intricate two-ball drills. I knew Jonnie's improvement likely had more to do with his genetic makeup and quiet determination than my teaching, but I felt proud. Jerry West even offered me a ride back to my hotel when we finished. He asked me where I'd been coaching this last year.

"Tralee," I said.

He nodded.

Then I added, "That's in Ireland."

Two weeks later Dick Versace called a second time.

Now Jerry West wanted me to come to Los Angeles in July, where the Wests still kept a home. Evidently he thought I did good work. The Grizzlies wanted me to teach the same dribbling drills to one of their guards, Earl Watson, and to Jonnie West again. There would be some trouble finding a quiet gym in LA, so they'd reserved a court at one of the Wests' neighbors' home in Bel-Air.

"One of his neighbors has a outdoor court?" I asked.

No. It was an indoor, regulation court. Versace said he'd e-mail me directions to Jerry West's home.

As I passed the gated security to the Wests' Bel-Air home, I rehearsed in my mind what would be best to include and best to leave out about my time in Ireland. We hadn't talked much in Memphis, but this would be different, more personal. I'd see Jerry West each morning at our workouts.

Jerry West didn't need to know that Ireland was likely the lowest level of pro basketball in Europe. Or that the Tralee Tigers had had to overcome the loss of the Kellogg's sponsorship. He wouldn't care about Gaelic Football. It would be enough to tell him about going from last place to first place. I knew that much of our success was due to good fortune, but Jerry West didn't need to know that either. I wanted to tell him that I'd been going to West Virginia each summer to learn old-time music. He was from a tiny town called Cabin Creek, and he certainly must have heard old-time fiddling growing up.

A Filipino butler led me into the kitchen, where Jerry West was in his pajamas reading the paper. (He wore pajamas!) He was eating cereal and reading the sports section.

"Hello, Rus," he said. (He remembered my name!) "Jonnie! Hurry up." The *Los Angeles Times* detailed the breakup of the Lakers team that Jerry West had put together as their president. Kobe Bryant didn't get along with Phil Jackson anymore; Jackson had resigned as coach. Shaquille O'Neal was about to be traded. The Gary Payton deal, which West said he had nothing to do with, hadn't worked out. Karl Malone was likely going to retire.

Crafting a team was an art, and nobody knew that better than Jerry West. I wanted to tell him how Ricardo Leonard again hadn't worked out for us, but fortunately Micheal Quirke had actually been an improvement. West would have loved a healthy John Teahan and also Kieran Donaghy's aggressiveness.

"Where were you coaching this past season?" Jerry West asked.

"I just came back from Ireland," I reminded him. I asked him if he'd ever been there.

"No," he said, then returned to his sports section where the Lakers were collapsing. At least they didn't have to worry about losing sponsorship.

Soon after Jonnie West came downstairs, Earl Watson appeared. We drove a block—there aren't city blocks in Bel-Air, but it was about a block—in Earl's silver Mercedes to the home of the man who owned LA Gear and the company that made the gym shoe Shaquille O'Neal wore. The man was a friend of Jerry West's and had agreed to allow us the use of his gym.

The new court served as the private playground for the owner's family, as well as a spot where NBA players had already begun meeting occasionally after paying homage to Jerry West. The owner had built this full-court gymnasium behind his home. It had six glass backboards and mercury-vapor lighting. A refrigerator stocked with bottled spring water was on one sideline, as well as a ballrack stacked with a dozen official NBA leather basketballs. The court was trimmed with Laker purple and gold. A half-dozen matching championship banners hung from the walls, representing teams Jerry West had played for and administered. I dragged my finger across the shiny floor. It was spotless.

I'd come from winning the Irish national title with a team that could only manage to secure a court for the Tigers a measly five hours a week. Our home court had a crummy tile floor, dark green walls, disgusting locker rooms, and wooden backboards. This state-of-the-art court was in somebody's backyard.

After a few minutes of drills, we heard the door open across the glistening hardwood. Jerry West had arrived to watch our workout.

I never would get the chance to describe the Tralee Tigers' dramatic season to Jerry West. And I'd never get up the nerve to ask him if he liked old-time West Virginia mountain music as much as I did.

Instead, on that pretentious private court, with the most powerful man in basketball watching me teach his son and an NBA guard—basketball's past, present, and future—I thought about our tiled tundra of a gym in Tralee. I thought about Paddy Jones, who had chosen a life of poverty—material poverty—to pursue his craft. And I thought about Micheal Quirke and John Teahan, who'd grown up playing twice a week because of limited gym space. And Kieran Donaghy, who had Jerry West's rawboned athleticism and long arms, but not his shot. No one had his shot. And I wondered what Ciaran Dalton would think about me dribbling two basketballs between my legs in the midst of these riches. What would Junior Collins say if he could see this swanky gym that we could use any time, without considering indoor soccer or badminton's schedule?

In Dublin there's an old pub called the Cobblestone. It's well-known among Irish musicians for its elite sessions, but off the tourist-beaten path a bit. The Cobblestone featured live Irish music, and the crowd huddled around and roared its approval.

My first journey to Ireland, on vacation in 2001, I'd stopped there for a pint on my final evening there. I lugged my fiddle along on that holiday but didn't take it out of the case that evening. I'd been in the country ten days and made a point of hearing traditional music nearly every night, often trying to play along quietly until I was too overwhelmed to continue. The music at the Cobblestone had just started and I was lucky to find a rare open stool, next to a glass trophy case, where I could watch the fiddler.

I'd met Bill Dooley that evening and was hanging my modest hopes of finding a basketball job in Ireland on the fact that the Irish National Coach had said he'd notify me about openings in the Super League. With the last of my vacation money dwindling in the pocket where I'd put Dooley's business card, I nursed my pint slowly. Returning to Ireland to learn traditional Irish music was a great idea, I thought. Maybe I could use basketball to make money and not have the sport pull at me emotionally.

Dooley's final words, spoken in his New Jersey accent, echoed in my head: "Forget everything you think you've learned about basketball."

Everything I thought I'd learned about basketball—did he mean from a tactical standpoint? Or did he mean the way the business world of basketball operates? I'd learned plenty in my years coaching Division I ball and as a player, if only as a small college walk-on. Was it best to forget about that? I'd learned a barrel full of negatives, too. Did he mean to forget those? The burnout, the hypocrisy, the twisting of a great game into a business?

During a break in the music, I swiveled in my stool to look at the memorabilia in the glass case: antiquated and worn sports gear, what I would later learn was equipment for hurling and Gaelic Football. Plaques and trophies. Also some musical instruments. And in the corner, a ten-by-sixteen framed photograph.

The photo was black and white, or rather black and off-yellow. I couldn't be sure how old it was, maybe from the 1950s. It showed a row of men standing in dark suits, pressed white shirts, and neckties. Naturally, linear perspective dictated that the closest person to the camera was the largest in the photo, and the size of the men—the ones closest to the front were young—diminished with distance. There was a total of maybe ten. The line bent in an "L" shape until it ended with a small man, the only one seated, at the opposite end at the right of the photo. The athletic gear in the glass case hinted that perhaps this was a sports team.

The first young man's head was turned over his left shoulder, to the back of the line. The next young man's head was turned also, and the one after him and so on. They were all looking back toward the end of the line. I wondered why the sharp-dressed lads in dark suits were in a row until I realized what was at their feet: a coffin.

Next to the coffin was the grave. They were ready to lower someone—a teammate?—into that grave, but they were looking back, as if waiting respectfully for someone. Perhaps a priest. And in the midst of the Cobblestone, this crowded Dublin pub, with a session blasting away just a few feet across the room, a strange quiet fell, but of course it must have fallen only on me. Who were these young men, and who was in the coffin? What were they looking back at?

I slid closer to the photo then leaned to the side, so that the small amount of light from a Guinness sign behind the bar would aid me. I realized then that the photo's seated man, at the end of the "L"-shaped line, was playing the Uilleann pipes. It was as though the music from the pipes had pulled a string attached to the chins of the young men.

And time—which of course stands still in any photo for the observer— was frozen for all these young men, frozen by the piper in that moment. The piper was likely playing an ancient march, or perhaps a slow air.

And I thought then, as I do now, that there must be an extraordinary power in that music, a music at the same time sorrowful and joyous, angry and passionate, disconsolate and hopeful. A music that could stop time at a funeral and turn the head of the very optimism of youth. In that moment—frozen for me, as it was in the old photo—I vowed silently to return to Ireland and find work, in order to write and learn the music that had an irresistible power. I instinctively believed I would finish writing my book in Ireland, although it wasn't supposed to be this book. It would be a move contrary to the Irish pattern of the last two hundred years, coming to America for a better life.

What I didn't know was that I would find peace with the broken romance that was my relationship with basketball. How could I have known that I'd find solace in the rainbow of emotions alive in the music, and reconciliation on a forlorn and drafty tile basketball court with wooden backboards?

Who would believe it, like?

Acknowledgments

The first time I met the journalist John Conroy, he punched me in the nose. We were taking boxing lessons in Chicago—I was a struggling young high school basketball coach, he was completing *Belfast Diary*, the classic book about the troubles in Northern Ireland. Conroy's stories about the old country piqued my interest in Irish culture. More than a good writer, Conroy is a courageous journalist who attacks corruption and injustice the way John Teahan went after a loose ball.

Twenty years later, I went to Ireland for the first time with a writer friend from Chicago named Barry Pearce. He'd been over before, and had Kerry roots. We had a rollicking time on our bicycles; in fact we had such an adventure that I didn't understand that "vacation fun" didn't translate into "ideal job location." Barry Pearce is the best writer you've never heard of. But you will.

It's fitting that both John Conroy and Barry Pearce struggled through my manuscript with sound, if exasperated, editing advice—they were the two who got me over to Ireland in the first place.

My literary grandparents, Lee and Bobby Byrd, were the first people I ever met whom I hoped I'd turn out like.

My literary parents, Robert Boswell and Antonya Nelson, are cherished friends.

There are many others to thank, so here goes:

My musical parents in New Mexico, Ken Keppeler and Jeannie McLerie.

Super-agent, Jordan Hyman.

Brian Faison at NMSU Athletics; Chris Burnham and Harriet Linkin in the NMSU English Department.

Beth Hadas, editor extraordinaire at UNM Press.

Few writers have needed the support system that I've had access to.

First, Dagoberto Gilb didn't let me lose faith. Also Kevin McIlvoy, Don Kurtz, Tony Hoagland, Brian Kirby, Tripp Hartigan, Franklin Tate, Jeff Vance, Joe Somoza, Albert Martinez, Jon Billman, Jon Ferguson, Bill Gildea, Alexander Wolff, Ladette Randolph, David McCormick, Jill Stukenberg, Rob Wilder, Henry Shukman, Carol Houck Smith, and Wendy Strothman.

Genuine American sports heroes Mike James, David Meggyesy, Doug Harris, and David Zirin.

I was lucky to have played or worked for three of the greatest coaches of all time: Lou Henson, Don Haskins, and Dan McCarrell.

Other coaches have been great teachers: Rocky Galarza, Ron Hecklinski, Dick Hunsaker, Dick Versace, Tony Barone, Greg Lackey, Larry Gipson, Tom Bennett, Tim Floyd, Mike Peterson, Jeff Reep, Thomas Trotter, Charles Redmond, Mark Pytel, Casey Owens, Bob Oceipka, Bosko Djurickovic, Harvey Braus, Glen Heffernan, Bob Hallberg, Will Rey, Fred Degerberg, Mark Scully, Tony Stubblefield, Norm Ellenberger, Steve Papas, Lance Lavetter, and Debbie and Dee Weinreis.

Thanks to the classy Irish Super League coaches: Pat Price, Martin Ahern, Gerry Fitzpatrick, Danny Fulton, Mark Ingles, Anthony Jenkins, Bride Saunders, Mark Scannell, Tommy Hehir, Joey Boylan, Darren O'Neill, Mick Evans, and Martin McKittrick.

I had plenty of visitors who came to Ireland and kept my spirits up: Eddie Holland, Bill Bussmann, Mike and Paige James, Marc Robert, Jeff Vance, Steve and Tracey Yellen.

The families of Roy Brandys, Tom Speiczny, Miguel Flores, Joe Gomez, Brendan Sugrue, and Spira Sports Shoe.

Thanks to the Deming Fusiliers, who kept a seat for me in our old-time string band at the High Desert Brewery. Also, the American musicians who encouraged me in the beginning: Rhys Jones, Paul Tyler, Steve Rosen, Steve Smith, Claudia Kauffman, Dave Parman, M. Mueller, and Bob Herring.

For help with my lessons in Irish basketball history: Jim Dineen, Karl Donnelly, Jerome Howe, Dave Collins, Brendan Mooney, Pat Price, Paul Brennan, Botty Callahan, and especially basketball writer par excellence John Coughlin of the *Cork Evening Echo*.

For help with the history of Ireland and the Republican movement in Tralee, thanks to Jerry Riordan and Martin Ferris at the Sinn Fein office.

The Irish Anti-War Movement.

The Tralee Tigers committee and friends: William Main, a true gentleman who took a chance and kept basketball alive for Tralee and me. Junior Collins, his wonderful wife and family, who never doubted, even when I did.

Also John O'Riordan, Bernie Reidy, Timmy Sheehan, Terry O'Brien, Liam O'Regan, Aidan O'Connor (and Ireland's best lunch at the Greyhound Pub), John and Tara Folan, Brendan McCarthy, Vinnie Murphy, Boty O'Callahan, Joe O'Mahoney at Radio Kerry, Padraig Locke, Digger, Moggs, Pop, Shaq, and Murt Murphy. Also taxi driver Michael O'Sullivan for loaning me his late brother's bicycle.

The Tralee Tigers players.

The great traditional music pubs of County Kerry: Baily's Corner Pub, Betty's Pub, Kate Brown's Pub, and Jo's Abbey Tavern. Also, O'Connell's Pub in Knocknagree, Dublin's Cobblestone Pub, and the Kerry School of Music.

The Irish musicians who were quick to slide over and offer me a pint: Colette Dalton, Phillip Crickert, Sean Abeyta, Sean Bradley (RIP), Dave Heggarty, Brendan McCarthy, Eugene McGrath, Paudie and Delores Stack, Mick Dooley, Johnny O'Leary (RIP), Johnny Fadgin, Sile Boylan, Sean Ryan and Clodagh Boylan, Maeve Boylan, Mick O'Brien, Fidelma O'Brien, Maurice O'Keefe, Paul DeGrae and Dee O'Sullivan, Kevin Ryan, Kerry Barrett, Ruari Costello, Mary Lawless, Barry Pearce, Mike Rice, Bernadette Nic'Gabbhan, Ana Nic'Gabbhan, Andy Dixon, "Fiddle Gerry" O'Connor, Ann Lawler, Danny O'Mahony, Patrick Fleming, Garoid Dineen, Eamon O'Sullivan, Johnny Moynahan, Johnny "Ringo" McDonough, Diana Boulier, Davey Graham, Fleming Christoferson, Matt Mooney, John Brown, Mike and Sean McLaren, Bob and May Scott, Frank Hall, Mick Culloty, John Hurley, and Tim Kiley.

And most especially, Irish music legends Paddy Jones and Ciaran Dalton. They're legends to me, anyway.

My own parents, Arnold and Julia Bradburd, and my family that encouraged me in everything, especially music. My grandfather was a violin player and a journalist, so he may be to blame for this whole mess.

Finally, my Lady Dulcinea, Connie Voisine.